NIGHT FEVER 4

Hospitality Design

Frame Publishers

CONTENTS

Drink

Eat

Sleep

12 featured venues are in a nightclub

3 have a minimum age requirement of 21 years

62% cater for more than 100 guests

DRINK

76%
**are suitable for
late night revellers**

5
**bars serve
craft beers**

1NUL8
Heineken Interior Design

CNC-cut metalwork and a combination of leather and vibrantly-patterned upholstery make for a rich, textured feel.

When Floris van der Sluis acquired the premises of the future 1NUL8, he commissioned Ferry Tabeling of Heineken Interior Design to restyle the dark and gloomy venue into an open and accessible modern wine bar (ground floor), with a beer and cocktail bar in the basement. Design Electro Products (DEP) was then asked to take care of the lighting design for the entire project, including construction and assembly.

The briefing contained the keywords: no-nonsense, open atmosphere and daylight experience. To go along with this, the interior makes use of unfussy materials – a semi-industrial feel is softened with vintage furniture with contemporary furnishings, fabrics and upholstery. Walls are left as bare brick, with screed concrete on the floor and exposed concrete columns, as well as different wood finishes in the furniture.

DEP's Robert Burgstad advised using real daylight as much as possible. During the hours of darkness, the lighting concept gives the illusion of daylight, thanks to the use the warmest light bulbs. Spots are placed in a wooden frame to integrate the lighting elements with the interior, which is a mix of seemingly random materials and furniture – a calculated effect that gives a homely feel.

The materials of the interior – concrete, steel and wood – may look rough, but they are 'softened' by well chosen fabrics, selected and applied by the interior construction partner, Inris. In the basement bar, LED-lighting placed behind CNC-lasered steelwork gives way to an attractive feature whilst having a functional form. The overall effect transforms a formerly dark location into a bright and vivid environment.

WHERE **Meent 108, Rotterdam, the Netherlands**
OPENING **March 2012**
CLIENT **Floris van der Sluis**
DESIGNER **Heineken Interior Design (p.545)**
FLOOR AREA **360 m²**
WEBSITE **1NUL8.nl**

MINIMUM AGE **21**
SIGNATURE DRINK **Beers**
PRICE OF A GLASS OF HOUSE WINE **EUR 5**
OPENING HOURS **Sun–Thu 10.00–01.00, Fri–Sat 10.00–02.00**
CAPACITY **400 guests**

A lighting concept gives the illusion of daylight

DEP created a highlighted Heineken Starbottle feature on the back wall with an infinity effect, partly to compensate for the lack of natural light.

ABE CLUB & LOUNGE

Lotz Interior Design & Styling

The bank vault doors make an impressive entrance into the lounge.

A historic Amsterdam bank has become a high-end new club, thanks to a collaboration between designer Charlotte Emmerig (Lotz) and artist Peter Korver. The building dates from the economic boom of the late 19th century, a time known as the Gilded Age in Holland. It was commissioned by finance supremo Abraham Wertheim – so the new club was named after him.

The design team set out to bring Wertheim's story to life, revisiting the *belle époque* era, which was famous for its eclecticism – a reflection of today's cosmopolitanism. Certain elements of the old bank remain: antique safe-deposit lockers hover high over the stairs in the lobby, and an original bank-counter features in the cloakroom.

Thorough acoustic reconstruction means much of the interior is new, however. Featuring one of the longest bars in Europe at 8.5 m in length, the space is decorated in a bright but soft palette, while murals in the dusty green of printed money are gilded to mimic a *fin-de-siècle* banker's boudoir.

Abe's Peacock Room is the VIP lounge, with the work of Korver adorning the walls (a reference to the room James Whistler painted for London shipping tycoon Frederick Leyland in the 1870s). However, Abe's peacocks – two monumental statues in gold leaf behind brass vault bars – see their space invaded by magpies. In the lounge bar, Korver has painted four more of these birds, now blown up to almost man-sized proportions. Magpies of course love glittering objects, so a former bank is a perfect place for them – as it is for the glamorous clientele of the club.

WHERE **Amstelstraat 30, Amsterdam, the Netherlands**
OPENING **September 2013**
CLIENT **Alon Levy, Allon Kijl and Marcel Norbart**
DESIGNER **Lotz Interior Design & Styling (p.546)**
FLOOR AREA **375 m²**
WEBSITE **clubabe.com**

MINIMUM AGE **23**
SIGNATURE DRINK **Black Diamond**
PRICE OF A GLASS OF HOUSE WINE **EUR 5**
OPENING HOURS **Mon-Thu 22.00-04.00, Fri-Sat 22.00-05.00, Sun 20.00-03.00**
CAPACITY **200 guests**

The elongated bar has an eye-catching illuminated display wall at the far end.

A rich material palette of velvets and shimmery metallics decorate the space in the hues of peacock feathers.

Original features are turned into attractive details, like this cluster of safe-deposit boxes in the lobby.

Illumination is key throughout the space, including in the rest rooms.

A former bank makes a glittering nightclub venue

The interior is inspired by an age notorious for its eclecticism, an unabashed melting pot of styles.

FLOOR PLAN

1 Entrance foyer
2 Cloakroom
3 Lounge
4 Bar
5 Dancefloor
6 Peacock Room (VIP area)
7 VIP dancefloor
8 Smoking room
9 Back-of-house
10 Lavatories

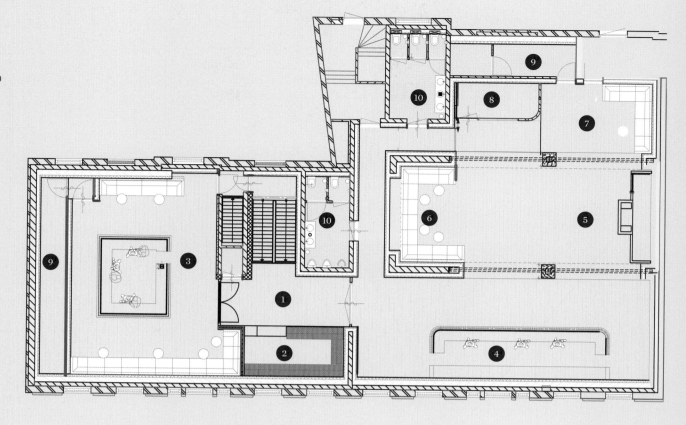

The bar, which is long and elegant, has large golden lamps at either end with equally graceful proportions.

Peter Korver's hand-painted magpies flutter across the walls

The monumental interior forms a perfect canvas for the artist's paintbrush.

The fine artist Peter Korver is a masterful storyteller, conjuring images that bridge art and natural history (peterkorver.com).

AIX AROME CAFE
One Plus Partnership

The interior is inspired by an ocean theme thriving with sea life, such as octopi and coral reef.

Given Aix Arome Cafe's location, in Shenzhen Bay OCT Harbor Theme Park, an oceanic theme was an obvious choice for One Plus Partnership, the design office charged with creating the interior for this coffee bar. After all, you can't make coffee without water – or for that matter without coffee beans.

Underlying this point, a huge egg-shaped structure placed in the middle of the space contains the dual functions of cashier and coffee supply. It was clearly inspired in shape and form by the dark, matte, oval coffee bean. On the other hand, the egg-like booth could easily also represent the earth, sandwiched between sea (the grey floor) and sky (the off-white ceiling), or it could perhaps be a pebble or a shell on the sea bed – or even, maybe, a submarine.

By placing this enigmatic structure in a fairly neutral setting, the designers have left it somewhat open to interpretation. They have further envisaged the blue-toned furnishings of the coffee bar as a coral reef, attracting customers to graze here like fishes. The chairs and tables in turquoise and sea-green have organic, rounded forms. Meanwhile a long, multi-legged and curvy table suggests both bubbles and octopi, and overhead there are clusters of blue lighting tubes which resemble branching coral – or the surface of the ocean, with its shimmering ripples, as seen by the fishes beneath. A palette of blues, greens and greys underlies the ocean theme, which is subtly abstract, and never literal or laboured.

WHERE **Baishi Road East, Shenzhen, China**
OPENING **May 2012**
CLIENT **Aix Arome Cafe**
CLIENT **Alon Levy, Allon Kijl and Marcel Norbart**
DESIGNER **One Plus Partnership (p.547)**
FLOOR AREA **150 m²**
WEBSITE **aixcoffee.com**

MINIMUM AGE **n/a**
SIGNATURE DRINK **Coconut Coffee Frappuccino**
PRICE OF A REGULAR COFFEE **JPY 500**
OPENING HOURS **9.30–23.30**
CAPACITY **80 guests**

The service point of the
coffee bar is located in the
shiny, elongated structure.

Bespoke blue, linear lights accommodate custom-made tungsten bulbs

A palette of blues, greens and greys underlies the ocean theme

Tumbling tube lights create a dynamic effect.

The underwater effect is subtle, and never forced.

APPLE DAILY
Projects of Imagination

Strong signage, in the form of an eye-catching light box, marks the entrance to the venue.

Named after Hong Kong's popular daily newspaper, Apple Daily is a first floor bar and eating house located in a heritage building in Perth – formerly the home of one of the city's daily newspapers. This has recently been refurbished as Print Hall, a multi-level hospitality destination which houses a number of bar and restaurant options.

Apple Daily, with its Asian-style cuisine, occupies the first level space flanking the atrium and features a large bar area and two dining zones and a mezzanine. As with the name, the decor also pays homage to the newspaper past of the building, with whole areas swathed in bespoke vintage wallpaper: Hong Kong newsprint. This is combined with elements that recall the heritage surroundings, but also evoke the colonial era of Hong Kong and Shanghai – plenty of polished wood and timber louvres, highlighted with brass. Colours are deep and rich, and furniture and lighting have a vintage, almost deco atmosphere about them. Lighting is low-key, and red neon signage in Chinese characters helps to set the scene.

Despite the Hong Kong theme, the bar has a patriotic side: the drinks served here are exclusively confined to Western Australian craft beer and wines. The food is another matter: served as shared plates, it draws its inspiration from Asian street food. Drinking clientele and diners can choose where to sit, with tall stools near the bar and booths along one wall for small groups. Small tables and a large communal table increase the options. The mezzanine level, with views of the main bar below, ensures that the space maintains its social buzz.

WHERE **Print Hall, St Georges Terrace, Perth, Australia**
OPENING **October 2012**
CLIENT **Colonial Group**
DESIGNER **Projects of Imagination (p.548)**
FLOOR AREA **100 m²**
WEBSITE **appledailyperth.com**

MINIMUM AGE **n/a**
SIGNATURE DRINK **Western Australian craft beer and wines**
PRICE OF A GLASS OF HOUSE WINE **AUD 8**
OPENING HOURS **Mon–Fri 11.30–00.00, Sat 16.00–00.00**
CAPACITY **80 guests**

PHOTOS **Earl Carter**

Neon messaging illuminates the communal dining corner.

Heritage parquet flooring is the base for custom tables and Peg chairs by Tom Dixon.

Custom period lighting creates a vintage, art deco atmosphere.

Verdigris green is a recurring colour accent.

Carpentry evokes traditional Chinese woodwork.

Newspaper print and polished wood recall Hong Kong's colonial era

Leather banquettes and bentwood stools conjure up a period feel.

Lining the alcove with the waiters' station is a bespoke wallpaper consisting of old Hong Kong newsprint.

AURIGA
Sanjay Puri Architects

To create this bar and nightclub, with adjoining restaurant, an old factory warehouse was stripped of its external walls. Replacing the solid walls, the entire exterior was then wrapped in a web of aluminum fins that are folded into angular planes.

Inside this intriguing shell, the lower level, opening into an outdoor patio, houses the nightclub whilst upstairs is the restaurant space. The exterior metal geometry is carried through into the interior of the ground-floor bar, where it creates a spectacular surface for the walls, ceiling, staircase, bar and columns.

Thanks to the angular forms executed in strips of galvanized metal sheeting that glow thanks to backlighting, the entire space is rendered sculptural and gives the unworldly impression of an abstractly woven web. A black palette forms the backdrop for this metal web, with a flamed dark-grey granite floor, black walls and black sound-insulating fibreboards constituting the ceiling.

A single flight of stairs leads from the metal-dominated bar to the wood-lined restaurant above. Here, all the elements are sheathed in undulating angular planes of thin wood strip, creating a softer and more fluid volume for the restaurant. The two levels are thus in complete contrast, with one dominated by steel and the other by wood to create different experiences within the same space. Both levels create the feeling of being within a sculpture, redefining the way internal spaces can be perceived.

Angular planes of galvanized metal sheeting shape the cave-like geometric interior of the bar on the ground floor.

WHERE **Famous Studio Lane, Mumbai, India**
OPENING **September 2013**
CLIENT **Alliance Restaurants and Bars**
DESIGNER **Sanjay Puri Architects (p.549)**
FLOOR AREA **335 m²**
WEBSITE **auriga.net.in**

MINIMUM AGE **18**
SIGNATURE DRINK **Auriga Cocktail**
PRICE OF A GLASS OF HOUSE WINE **INR 600**
OPENING HOURS **19.00–01.00**
CAPACITY **110 guests**

PHOTOS Vinesh Gandhi

Backlighting gives the impression of a metallic structure glowing eerily from within.

The entire space is rendered sculptural

Upstairs, the restaurant interior repeats the slatted, angular envelope – in a softer way – with wood.

BAR BROUW
DesignPact

A simple material palette of copper and wood is complemented by a blue spot colour.

Bar Brouw is a new destination in Amsterdam for an American-style concept of serving up craft beers matched with the organic, slow-cooked and smoked meats. Floortje Donia of studio DesignPact, was tasked with fitting out the interior within an incredibly short timeframe.

In just 6 weeks, from first drawings to opening night, the designer needed to portray the American concept in Dutch fashion, and on a limited budget. 'The small budget demanded smart solutions, so we reworked and repurposed a lot of materials,' she says. Besides invariably reusing some of the interior's existing features, DesignPact built tables and the bar out of wood from vintage French wagons, and turned old workshop stools into bar seating.

Blue is used as a spot colour, both in a feature wall behind the serving counter and in the chequered tablecloths on the 'tables for two'. One another wall, white penny tile walls flirt with the feel of old butcheries and factory canteens. On this wall also, focus goes immediately to the lighting. The neon 'meat' sign makes it clear what Bar Brouw serves up on the food menu. This eye-catching feature combines well with the custom-designed, handmade copper tube lighting that lends the space the industrial touch that the brief called for – a challenging feat given the complete lack of rawness in the original space.

The neighbourhood is being tipped as the next hotspot area of Amsterdam-West, and the adjacent market has an important social value to it, so the goal was to connect with outside by placing long tables facing the window and making the light tubes visible from outside.

WHERE **Ten Katestraat 16, Amsterdam, the Netherlands**
OPENING **October 2013**
CLIENT **Tim van Dijk and Sjoerd Brinkman**
DESIGNER **DesignPact (p.543)**
FLOOR AREA **85 m²**
WEBSITE **barbrouw.nl**

MINIMUM AGE **18**
SIGNATURE DRINK **Craft beers**
PRICE OF A GLASS OF HOUSE WINE **EUR 5**
OPENING HOURS **Sun–Thu 12.00–00.00, Fri–Sat 12.00–01.00**
CAPACITY **42 guests**

Furnishings include old workshop stools and a countertop made from reclaimed wood.

BAR SAINT JEAN

Thilo Reich

The anteroom of the toilet has a **rusted-metal side** table — made with pieces found on scrap heaps.

For a young Frenchman who had just moved from Paris to Berlin to start his own business, Thilo Reich created a little bar with a Gallic – and very personal – touch. The brief called for a comfortable space with a cosy, welcoming atmosphere and a simple clarity of design, with 'no chi-chi'.

The location for this new bar was the basement of an old building, and the budget was tight – which made using recycled materials essential. 'Another very important point was the owner's strong charisma, appearance and personality,' says Thilo Reich. In other words, the aim was 'to design an atmosphere that suits him' and create a bar tailored like a suit for its proprietor.

A palette of muted greys, greens and browns was chosen to create a conspiratorial air. Dark green walls and anthracite oak floorboards make for a secluded, snug space, which is dominated by a generously-proportioned bar that allows most of the guests to gather around the host/barman. This was constructed out of piled-up old ship timbers – ancient pieces of wood that had formerly been tarred and used as a fence on a farm in France; their artistic assemblage here lends the space a feeling of rustic charm.

Industrial black bar stools and French lamps with rusted lampshades generate contrasts that are taken up by further with reused rust-hued objects hanging like artworks, indirectly illuminated on the walls. They provide a pleasing lighting feature and pick up on the looks of the owner, with his reddish hair and beard.

WHERE **Steinstrasse 21, Berlin, Germany**
OPENING **January 2013**
CLIENT **Johann Courgibet**
DESIGNER **Thilo Reich (p.551)**
FLOOR AREA **85 m²**
WEBSITE **barsaintjean.com**

MINIMUM AGE **18**
SIGNATURE DRINK **Le Saint Jean**
PRICE OF A GLASS OF HOUSE WINE **EUR 4**
OPENING HOURS **Tue-Thu, Sun 19.00-02.00, Fri-Sat 21.00-03.00**
CAPACITY **50 guests**

PHOTOS **Stefan Wolf Lucks**

The piled-up timbers travelled from ship to shore, from a farm in France to a bar in Berlin.

Dark walls and floorboards make for a secluded, snug space

A rusted object, hung as an artwork behind the bar, has a contorted shape akin to the layout of the old building.

The tarred wooden planks have a rustic, textured arrangement.

CARLOFT BAR & LOUNGE

Dittel Architekten

In Berlin's cool Kreuzberg neighbourhood, Dittel Architekten has designed an exclusive showroom to satisfy even the most devoted car-lover. Carloft allows you to park your wheels within clear view, in the 'CarLoggia' behind a glass frontage: the car virtually becomes part of the interior, which includes a bar with a lounge for guests and a show area with an adjoining patio.

Getting the car up here is part of the fun – the driver remains seated in the car while it is elevated safely to the loft. It's a formula ideal for parties, photo shoots, city stays (there's a sleeping area) and other events.

An open interior design was implemented in the 230-m² space, allowing the rooms to merge and so form a coherent unity. Walls were removed where possible in order to create a generous and extensive feeling of space. The focal point of the loft is the large bar and kitchen area. The kitchen island is completely clad with anthracite tiles which are combined with attractive brass details to form the heart of the space. This element is an eye-catcher the minute you enter the loft. The bar flows into a spacious lounge area, harmoniously styled with brass again featuring in several details. Adjoining the lounge there is a library and a working area, with a continuous and harmonious flow in the colour palette.

The furniture in the loft space is a mix of classic interior design, built-in aspects and new design elements. Reconditioned antique furniture adds that certain something to the overall view.

The tile-clad bar, with its sleek style and attractive brass details, is a central feature acting as a linking unit to the rest of the loft.

WHERE **Liegnitzer Strasse 30, Berlin, Germany**
OPENING **August 2013**
CLIENT **Hook & Eye**
DESIGNER **Dittel Architekten (p.544)**
FLOOR AREA **230 m²**
WEBSITE **n/a**

MINIMUM AGE **n/a**
SIGNATURE DRINK **n/a**
PRICE OF A GLASS OF HOUSE WINE **Complimentary**
OPENING HOURS **By arrangement**
CAPACITY **50 guests**

A rich palette of materials is made up of smoky mirrored glass, oak wood flooring and dusty green velour panels on one wall.

The open, glass-fronted architecture of the building is fully appreciated from the meeting room and patio areas.

The loft is used for commercial purposes, and has a luxurious private wing that contains a sleeping area comprising a high-class dressing room and spa.

A formula ideal for parties, photo shoots and city stays

Carefully-placed lighting gives the impression that the bar's counter is floating.

Refreshments are provided as compliments of the host in the loft.

Walls were removed where possible in order to create a generous feeling of space.

Refined vintage furniture pieces are placed alongside contemporary decorations.

CLUB DISCO
Estudio Guto Requena and Maurício Arruda
arquitetos + designers

Ebonised wood boards were used to clad the bar area, with a brushed steel countertop and rows of spotlights adding a touch of glamour.

The project to renovate Club Disco was guided by a range of concepts: 'Brazility' was one, 'Daft Punk spends holiday in the countryside' was another. The designers set out to combine a high-tech, industrial vibe with a certain organic naturalness featuring lots of wood and leather.

But first things first: the layout was changed to resize the dance floor, emphasising circulation and creating varied atmospheres in the fully-renovated venue. The ceiling over the three bars and the three VIP areas was lowered to create a more intimate mood; conversely, the ceiling was raised above the dance floor, exposing beams and infrastructure to create an electro-underground atmosphere together with the lighting.

New furniture was designed for the space inspired by 1970s Brazilian design, mixing black fabrics and PVC. The masculine atmosphere is complemented in the more exclusive, secluded seating areas around the edge of the dance floor, with a selection of vintage armchairs in black leather and wood. The side tables for glasses and bottles also feature a new design which mixes the rawness of concrete and the sophistication of shiny, black acrylic.

A new sound system by English brand Funktion One is in use, installed in two towers which flank the DJ. A new acoustic system was designed, which makes use of a special rockwool cloth, wood, fabrics and cellulose foam. Finally, the famous 'tunnel' – an iconic part of the club's identity – retells the 12 years of its history through an intervention by Brazilian artist Kleber Mateus.

WHERE **Prof. Atílio Inocennti 160, São Paulo, Brazil**
OPENING **August 2012**
CLIENT **Michel Saad, Marcos Mion, Marcos Maria and Marcos Campos**
DESIGNERS **Estudio Guto Requena (p.544), Maurício Arruda arquitetos + designers (p.547)**
FLOOR AREA **490 m²**
WEBSITE **clubdisco.com.br**

MINIMUM AGE **18**
SIGNATURE DRINK **n/a**
PRICE OF A GLASS OF HOUSE WINE **BRL 90**
OPENING HOURS **From 12.00 until late**
CAPACITY **510 guests**

Dynamic lighting frames the space, highlighting and amplifying the interior architecture with some 250 m of metallic rail containing LEDs used to create the changing effects.

The bathrooms also benefit from changing mood lighting.

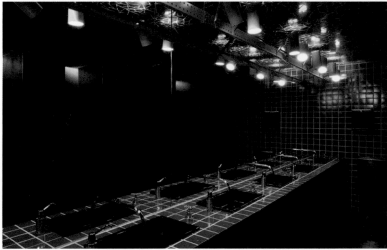

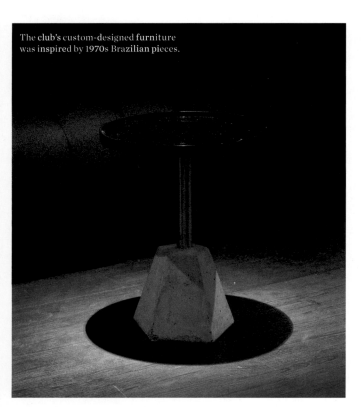

The club's custom-designed furniture was inspired by 1970s Brazilian pieces.

Lighting contributes hugely to the electro-underground atmosphere

SEATING DRAWINGS

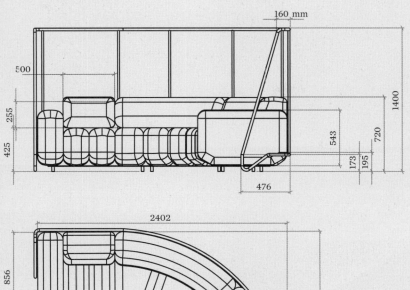
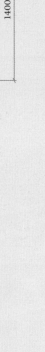
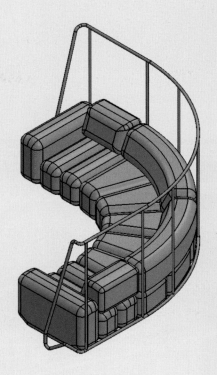

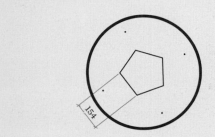

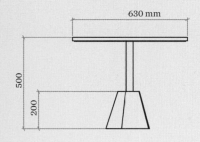

TABLE DRAWINGS

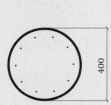

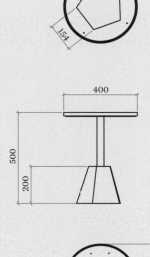
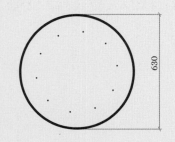

One of the raised VIP areas around
the circumference of the space can be
converted into a stage for shows.

The entrance to the club was treated to a spectacular, tunnel-like intervention by Brazilian artist Kleber Mateus.

DISCO

FLOOR PLAN

1 Cash desk
2 Tunnel
3 Box
4 Bar
5 Dance floor
6 DJ booth
7 Lavatories (men)
8 Lavatories (women)

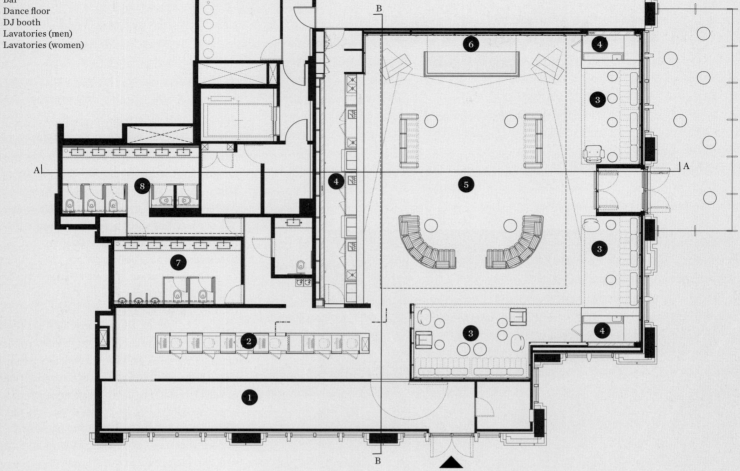

The 'tunnel' is an iconic part of the club's identity

SECTION A

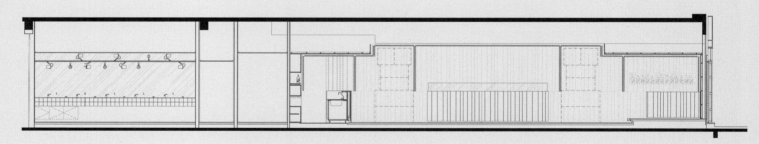

SECTION B

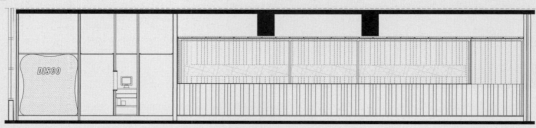

CLUB NYX
Design Electro Products

In total, more than 452 m of digi-LED was integrated into the walls and portals throughout the space.

The owner of Club NYX, Rob de Jong, wanted his venue to be 'a melting pot of like-minded people, who are out to have a good time in an extravagant, outrageous and mind-blowing atmosphere'. To create this space, Sam Anders Jr of Design Electro Products was given 'carte blanche' to realise an amazing interior, with a lighting design to match, based on ultimate contrasts.

In the location, a decayed four-storey warehouse, the newest light and sound technologies were integrated in four different bars on the various levels. Artists from the art collective Venour then bombed every corner of the place with graffiti. On the dance floor, the artists painted layer-over-layer on a wall of wooden slats, to produce an artwork with a 'years old' feel. After completion, half of the slats were torn down, revealing parts of a 142-m² digi-LED pixel wall. Videomapping was used to create a prominent yet surreptitious branding zone behind the main DJ booth to highlight the club's favourite spirit and signature drink.

The restrooms also got the star treatment – better known as The Toilletterette, even here the clubbers can drink a cocktail and dance around while another DJ spins his records. Anders let two sniper marksmen loose in this space, shooting paint from aerosol cans, covering the doors, floor and ceiling – in fact, the entire space – in an exploding rainbow. As they say, nothing succeeds like excess.

WHERE **Reguliersdwarsstraat 42, Amsterdam, the Netherlands**
OPENING **October 2012**
CLIENT **The Crossing Factory**
DESIGNER **Design Electro Products (p.543)**
FLOOR AREA **600 m²**
WEBSITE **clubnyx.nl**

MINIMUM AGE **18**
SIGNATURE DRINK **Absolut Vodka**
PRICE OF A GLASS OF HOUSE WINE **EUR 4**
OPENING HOURS **Thu 23.00–04.00, Fri–Sat 23.00–05.00, Sun 18.00–00.00**
CAPACITY **600 guests**

The ambient lighting in the club was all custom-made so as to heighten the visual experience.

The design team presented the club as a canvas for artistic discharge resulting in a vibrant, graffiti-clad space.

An art collective bombed every corner of the place with graffiti

The branding behind the DJ booth is kept nicely in tune with the club aesthetic thanks to video mapping.

CUMULUS UP
Pascale Gomes-McNabb Design

Classic Thonet chairs were customised
to add a twist to the bar's traditional
bistro aesthetic.

Cumulus Up is a late-night wine bar with food
located on the first floor of an old factory in
Melbourne, a new sister establishment to the
downstairs restaurant Cumulus Inc. Designed
and owned by Pascale Gomes-McNabb, the
space is warm and woody, with the upstairs
venue offering top-notch bottles of vino to
accompany its 'food for sharing' menu –
everything from nibbles to steaks – and an
interior having a convivial, comfortable feel
that supports the concept.

The new design sits harmoniously
within the existing shell. The lofty ceilings,
enormous metal-framed windows, layers of
old peeling paint and old exposed brick were
left in situ and now sit side-by-side with new
herringbone patterned walls, matt-blackened-
steel bartops, and shimmering metallic
leather accents. The result is a warm, cocoon-
like, almost reclusive, clubby feel, and a space
which feels as though it's been here for an
indefinite amount of time.

The use of classic materials – metal,
marble, timber and fluted glass – borders on
the traditional, but this is offset with some
quirkiness of form. An example is the oak
floor in heavily patterned, two-tone parquet,
which provides an interesting counterpoint
to the industrial shell. Similarly, the bevelled
mirrors are in abstracted cloud shapes. Angled
and backlit, they reflect and open up the room
and make a stunning and unexpected feature.
The furniture includes a banquette modelled
on an overgrown armchair, customised
versions of Le Corbusier's favourite Thonet
chair, and tables of rough-cut timber and
arabescato marble that tip a nostalgic wink
to bygone eras. With abstracted classic ideas,
it all adds up to a welcoming interior that's
casually chic and a bit cheeky with it.

WHERE **45 Flinders Lane, Melbourne, Australia**
OPENING **February 2013**
CLIENT **Pascale Gomes-McNabb, Andrew McConnell
and Jayden Ong**
DESIGNER **Pascale Gomes-McNabb Design (p.548)**
FLOOR AREA **153 m²**
WEBSITE **cumulusinc.com.au/up**

MINIMUM AGE **18**
SIGNATURE DRINK **International wine selection**
PRICE OF A GLASS OF HOUSE WINE **n/a**
OPENING HOURS **Sun-Thu 17.00-24.00, Fri-Sat
16.00-01.00**
CAPACITY **70 guests**

The seating area is illuminated with backlit custom-designed mirrors and Tolomeo micro-clamp wall lights from Artemide.

Two-tone coloured glass pendant lights (Cleo Incalmo by Mark Douglass) make an interesting feature above the diners.

The glints of metallic sheen can be seen in the banquette's upholstery and feet.

The design team made the most of existing elements in the former industrial building.

FLOOR PLAN

1   Bar
2   Seating area
3   Kitchen
4   Dish wash area
5   Cool room
6   Storage
7   Lavatories

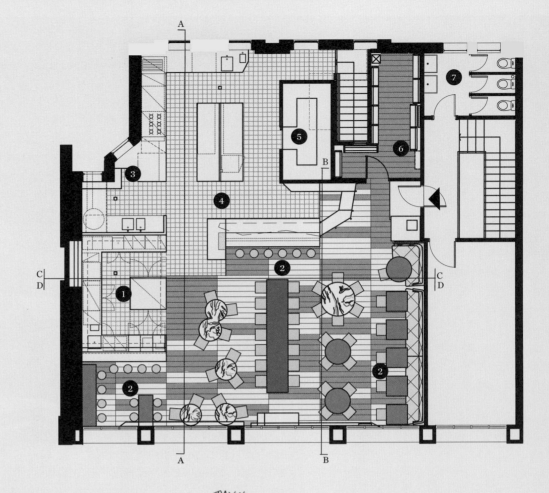

CONCEPT SKETCHES

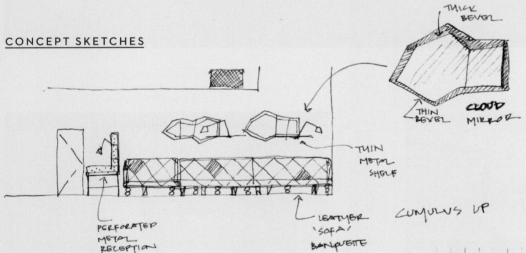

Concept sketches for the bespoke furniture detailing the materials to be used: glass, timber, steel, perforated metal, mirror, leather and marble.

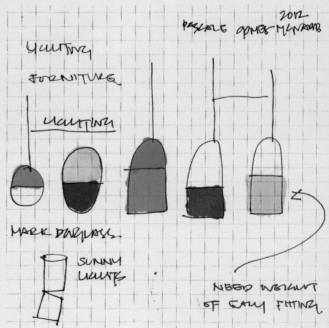

Classic materials offset with a quirkiness of form

SECTION A

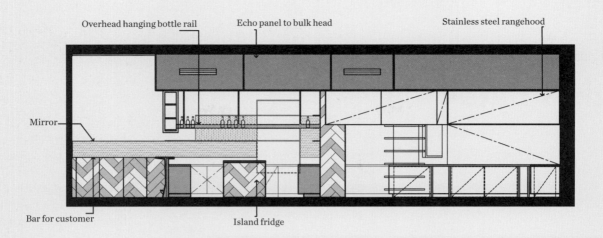

Overhead hanging bottle rail

Echo panel to bulk head

Stainless steel rangehood

Mirror

Bar for customer

Island fridge

SECTION B

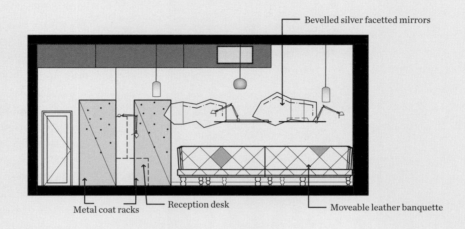

Bevelled silver facetted mirrors

Metal coat racks

Reception desk

Moveable leather banquette

SECTION C

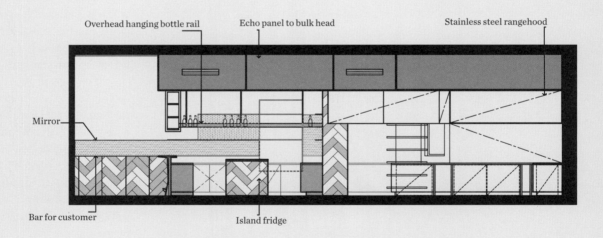

Overhead hanging bottle rail

Echo panel to bulk head

Stainless steel rangehood

Mirror

Bar for customer

Island fridge

SECTION D

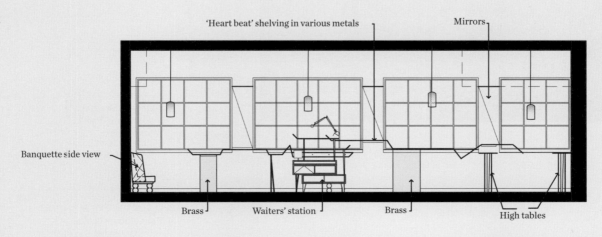

'Heart beat' shelving in various metals

Mirrors

Banquette side view

Brass

Waiters' station

Brass

High tables

DEAN
Bruzkus Batek

Smokey, mirrored surfaces play a big role in expanding the space in this city centre club.

Glamour and glitz have not, hitherto, been part of Berlin's 'poor but sexy' image, but the owners of Dean were determined to change all that with the launch of their club. They asked the designers at Bruzkus Batek to add some sophisticated bling to the nightspot. The club – nestled in a long, narrow space in the formerly, grungy city centre – features a long bar for seeing and being seen, a dance floor and comfortable lounge areas for sipping cocktails.

The first thing guests see once past the dark, mysterious-looking and marble-clad entrance area is the bar, shimmering under a golden ceiling. As though on a catwalk, guests are guided along the massive bar and past the lounge niches with their dark-grey velvet upholstery towards the elevated dance floor. Lights above the dance floor move to the beat of the music, giving a hypnotic effect.

Materials were chosen to look luxurious, expensive and chic: golden panels for the ceilings, polished mastic asphalt, black and white marble. Plush velvet seating adds a comfortable touch. Lighting is kept low but warm, bathing the club in a golden glow.

The biggest challenge the designers faced on the project was how to organise the long and narrow space while giving the relatively compact club a generous and glamorous atmosphere. This was achieved by moving the entrance – which had been centrally placed and so divided the space – to the far end of the building. Reflective materials and lighting effects help to create the illusion of a bigger place.

WHERE **Rosenthaler Str. 9, Berlin, Germany**
OPENING **October 2013**
CLIENT **Amano Group**
DESIGNER **Bruzkus Batek (p.542)**
FLOOR AREA **255 m²**
WEBSITE **amanogroup.de/eat-drink/dean**

MINIMUM AGE **21**
SIGNATURE DRINK **Dean Diamond Fizz**
PRICE OF A GLASS OF HOUSE WINE **EUR 5**
OPENING HOURS **Thu 21.00 until late, Fri–Sat 22.00 until late**
CAPACITY **150 guests**

Reinventing Berlin nightlife with glamour and glitz

The lights above the dancefloor oscillate in time with the music.

DONNY'S BAR

Luchetti Krelle

Merbau timber, with its natural lustre, was used for the directional woodworking above the bar.

Conjuring up images of a back alley in Chinatown, Donny's Bar is an unexpected find in Sydney's coastal suburb of Manly. The interior features a careful balancing of the rustic versus the refined – where urban meets with an Asian-Australian flavour.

The existing space was a stark, white plasterboard box with a commercial look and feel. The brief was to create a warm, friendly New York style loft bar – which would serve Asian style tapas and dumplings – on a tight budget. Avoiding overt Asian theming, designers Stuart Krelle and Rachel Luchetti instead opted for a pared-back approach to the design.

The space is barn-like, with raw lighting a key element in the decor. The intriguingly illuminated bar front is made from railway sleepers casually bundled together with adjustable ratchet straps, more usually used to tie down a load on a truck. The rustic quality of the timber contrasts with a shiny copper top and perfectly joined lining boards weaving diagonally across the lower ceiling and walls. Canvas lorry tarps are casually tied off to walls and chain-link fencing stretches across the upper ceiling, screening the acoustic treatment from the eye. Recycled materials play a big role – from the brickwork painstakingly cladding the walls to the old toilet cisterns.

Given the tight budget, the designers report that they had to work hard to edit the concept down to its bare bones. Money was saved by their creative and clever use of features that might be found lying around the yard, like chain-link fencing used as a decorative tool, and the recycled timber and brick that forms the basis of the material palette.

WHERE **7 Market Place, Manly, Australia**
OPENING **December 2013**
CLIENT **MNT Investments**
DESIGNER **Luchetti Krelle (p.546)**
FLOOR AREA **154 m²**
WEBSITE **donnys.com.au**

MINIMUM AGE **18**
SIGNATURE DRINK **Blueberry n Rose Bramble**
PRICE OF A GLASS OF HOUSE WINE **AUD 9**
OPENING HOURS **Tue-Fri 16.00 until late, Sat-Sun 12.00 until late**
CAPACITY **100 guests**

Shiny copper radiates amidst a raw material palette of wood, concrete and recycled bricks.

Recycled and everyday materials play a big role

Naked bulbs harmonise with the recycled and unfinished surfaces.

An eye-catching light installation hangs at one end of the bar.

Sound proofing was placed within the
exposed joists with chain-link fencing laid
over the top to complete the look.

GAMSEI

Buero Wagner, Fabian A Wagner with Andreas Kreft

The bar serves cocktails made from fresh ingredients that are either wildly foraged or grown by local farmers.

In opening Gamsei in Munich's trendy Glockenbach neighbourhood, owner Matthew Bax had an unusual mission in mind: to create an antidote to the globalised cocktail bar. Why, he reasoned, should you drink the same cocktail in every bar all over the world? Bax's own imaginative cocktails use local ingredients – grown by artisan farmers or foraged from the wild. This 'hyper-localism' as designer Fabian Wagner calls it, spills over into the space itself. Buero Wagner's bar interior, executed together with Andreas Kreft, pays tribute to local Bavarian culture and craftsmanship.

Amphitheatre-style benches are set against opposite walls, thus eliminating the common separation of bartender and guest. Here, interaction is key and everybody has a front-row seat, in keeping with Bavarian beer-drinking tradition. Guests enjoy a view of the two centrally placed bars and can watch Bax and his team mix the cocktails.

The more unusual ingredients – dried flowers, herbs and leaves – are stored and displayed in a wooden built-in cabinet that stretches the full length of the back wall. Seating, bars and cupboards are executed in solid oak with a natural oil finish. White ceramic bottles, containing homemade liqueurs, syrups and essences, are suspended from a black steel mesh attached to the ceiling. In-between, bare light bulbs make for a reduced lighting scheme by night.

As with Bax's cocktail ingredients, the architects procured all the materials including wood and ceramics locally, working with local carpenters and manufacturers to produce custom-made solutions.

WHERE **Buttermelcherstrasse 9, Munich, Germany**
OPENING **April 2013**
CLIENT **Matthew Bax**
DESIGNER **Buero Wagner/Andreas Kreft (p.542)**
FLOOR AREA **40 m²**
WEBSITE **gamsei.com**

MINIMUM AGE **18**
SIGNATURE DRINK *Lavender Drunk Bee*
PRICE OF A GLASS OF HOUSE BEER **EUR 5**
OPENING HOURS **20.00–02.00**
CAPACITY **25 guests**

Ceramic bottles – containing various
home-brewed concoctions – provide the
main decorative detailing in the space.

A restricted palette of materials used for, and on, the shelving makes for a restful, rhythmic effect.

Interaction is key – everyone has a front-row seat

Detailing adds to the artisanal atmosphere.

Bottles become a ceiling installation when suspended in between the lighting elements.

Stepped seating on two sides evokes a mini-amphitheatre.

The coffee machine is seamlessly integrated and can be flexibly displayed or disguised behind lattices.

Preparing the unusual drinks becomes a kind of entertainment.

GESSLER 1862

atelier 522

The interior is designed
to have a homely feel.

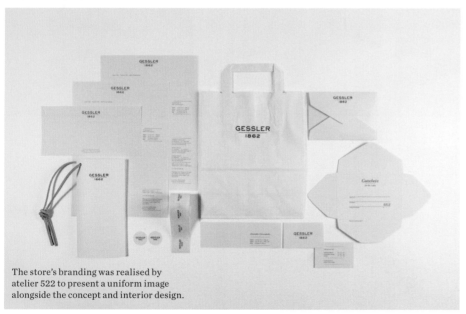

The store's branding was realised by
atelier 522 to present a uniform image
alongside the concept and interior design.

Like many bookstores today, Gessler 1862, at Lake Constance in Friedrichshafen, set out to reinvent itself by additionally offering a coffee and wine bar, as well as beautiful design items and accessories. The designers and architects at atelier 522 developed a holistic concept that turned Gessler 1862 into a place that goes beyond a bookstore and feels like home. The cafe is located in the middle of the store, while customers sit surrounded by luxurious books and other beautiful things, that the world doesn't really need but everyone wants, lining the LED-lit bookshelves.

It's all about sensation, according to the designers. Therefore, the new bookstore is designed to appeal to all the senses. Customers are invited to look, listen, smell, taste and feel. The team at atelier 522 has created themed areas of smooth transitions, rather than a series of niches. So next to a miniature Porsche you will find a lavish coffee-table book with wonderful photos of Route 66, giving patrons the feeling that experiencing the world starts on one of Gessler 1862's sofas.

Before heading for the check-out with your purchases, you can have an espresso at the bar, which is open daily after the closing hours of the store. The space is also a venue for readings, concerts and theme nights – a place where people can come together to enjoy performances of various kinds. Bottles of different-coloured contents complement the sea-coloured mosaic floor and counter of the bar. Every view, according to the designers, is intended as a further rotation in the kaleidoscope of impressions.

WHERE **Friedrichstrasse 53, Friedrichshafen, Germany**
OPENING **September 2012**
CLIENT **Andreas Gessler**
DESIGNER **atelier 522 (p.541)**
FLOOR AREA: **222 m²**
WEBSITE **gessler1862.de**

MINIMUM AGE **n/a**
SIGNATURE DRINK **Borgmann Ginger**
PRICE OF A GLASS OF HOUSE WINE **EUR 4**
OPENING HOURS **Mon–Sat 9.00–01.00, Sun 10.00–18.00**
CAPACITY **65 guests**

Customers are invited to look, listen, smell, taste and feel

In the bar area, tables of stained oak team up with Vitra Hal chairs and Tabouret stools.

HONEY B CLUB

Teo Cavallo Architects

Cocooned spaces are furnished
with custom-designed seats, carpets,
lighting and 3D ceiling panels.

Designing the Honey B Club involved reusing an abandoned basement space that had little or no architectural merit. It was characterised by low ceiling heights and a clear span between the external walls, only interrupted by a few concrete columns.

The client's brief was to create a cocktail bar and cabaret venue, a space with an interior environment that was insular and private, while also having its own unique character. The space had to create a sense of escape from the environment of the street. The designers therefore came up with a concept that relied on referencing the honeycomb as one of the most insulated spaces found in nature, both isolated and protected from its surroundings. The geometric and structured nature of hives was used as an inspiration to create the space in both an abstract and a literal way. It also ties in neatly with the name, Honey B.

The geometric structure of the hexagon becomes the major theme of the space, appearing in a variety of scales and materials on many different surfaces. Hexagons unify the space, and its use on the textured and mirrored ceiling adds a subtle fluidity to the volume of the club, which is enhanced by the warmth of the colours and lighting used. Shiny materials – mirror, metal, glass and vinyl – add a certain brightness to the formerly dark basement despite the subdued lighting. It all adds up to a fanciful and theatrical atmosphere – just right for a space devoted to meeting, socialising and performance.

WHERE **2 Caxton Street, Brisbane, Australia**
OPENING **February 2012**
CLIENT **AGS**
DESIGNER **Teo Cavallo Architects (p.551)**
FLOOR AREA **480 m²**
WEBSITE **honeybs.tv**

MINIMUM AGE **18**
SIGNATURE DRINK **Summer Nectar**
PRICE OF A GLASS OF HOUSE WINE **AUD 8**
OPENING HOURS **Tue–Sat 19.00–03.00**
CAPACITY **300 guests**

The colours, materials, patterns and textures in this late-night venue all have a distinct 1970s vibe.

Patterned carpets provide directionality for patrons as they navigate through the club.

Backlit, hexagonal-shaped mirrors in the bathrooms are in keeping with the design.

Hexagons reference the honeycomb as one of the most insulated spaces found in nature

The design team wanted to instil a sense of escape from the outside world.

HOT HOT
Estudio Guto Requena

Clubbers had an out-of-this world experience as they stepped inside and entered the tunnel of light, like a futuristic portal to another dimension.

The inspirations for the nightclub Hot Hot were diverse: the Op Art works of the Scandinavian designer Verner Panton and the 1970s culture he helped create, plus the brutalist architecture of Berlin's underground nightclub and sex club scene. The design team of Guto Requena, together with Alexandre Nino, set out to combine and contemporise these styles in Hot Hot.

Located in downtown São Paulo, the two-storey building chosen for the club had been completely abandoned for nearly two decades. The exterior was left unchanged – and dilapidated – while a 20-m-long 'tunnel of light' connects the outside world and the interior.

The lounge, bar, cloakroom and restrooms are located on the upper floor and feature a 1970s-style optical graphic pattern specially designed for the space. The pattern strikingly displays the appropriately hot club colour palette: royal blue, cherry red, vibrant orange, golden yellow and olive green. It surreally sweeps over the walls, floors and some of the fixtures and fittings. Also inspired by Panton, three huge, shimmering mother of pearl light fixtures highlight the bar. No less impressive is the high-shine restroom (dubbed the 'golden shower').

On the lower level, the dance floor dominates, with its unique Funktion One sound system. The light is provided by a huge, technicolour LED installation, which dazzles across the entire ceiling before permeating the staircase area and the lounge upstairs, like a living organism. High technology meets peeling walls and brilliant LEDs meet concrete in this space – the contrasts providing an intense sensory environment that adds more dimensions than just music to the Hot Hot experience.

WHERE **Rua Santo Antônio 570, São Paulo, Brazil**
OPENING **January 2011**
CLIENT **Flávia Ceccato and Ricardo Gonzalez**
DESIGNER **Estudio Guto Requena (p.544)**
FLOOR AREA **630 m²**
WEBSITE **hothotsite.com.br**

MINIMUM AGE **18**
SIGNATURE DRINK **Hot Hot cocktail**
PRICE OF A GLASS OF HOUSE WINE **BRL 60**
OPENING HOURS **From 12.00 until late**
CAPACITY **500 guests**

The original staircase, with its exposed concrete balustrades and burnt cement floor, leads guests to the upper level patterned wallpaper, lush carpet and dynamic lighting awaits.

The dance floor is the ultimate
sensory explosion: technicolour
LED light panels create a
spectacular, ever-changing
show on the ceiling in time to
the beat of the music.

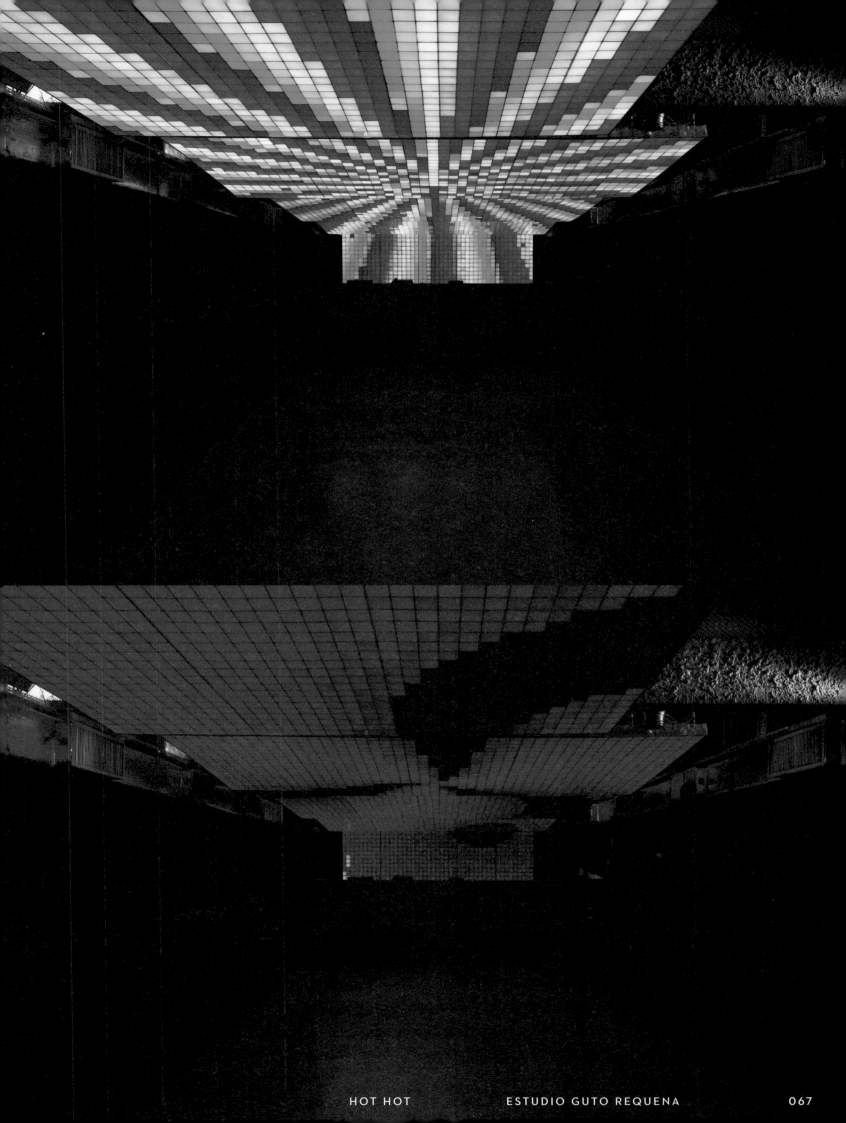

FIRST FLOOR

1 Cloakroom
2 Dressing room
3 Bar
4 Lounge
5 VIP lounge
6 Dance floor
7 DJ booth
8 Tunnel of light
9 Lavatories

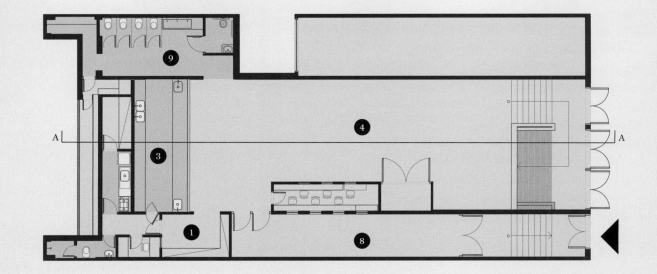

GROUND FLOOR

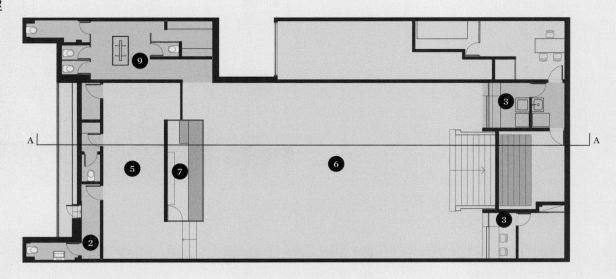

SECTION A

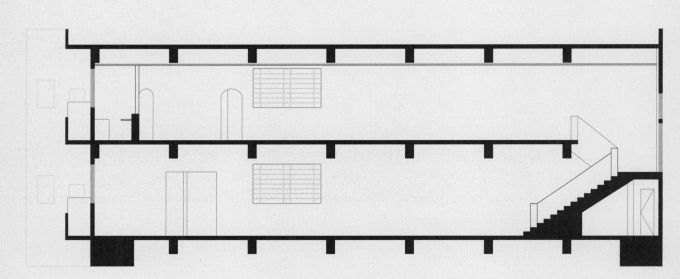

Upstairs, a trio of huge,
mother of pearl light fixtures
provide illumination over
the bar.

Verner Panton and Berlin's underground nightclubs inspired the design

The 1970s-style lounge space is quite the psychedelic experience.

The restrooms were given a futuristic, golden sheen.

HOWLER BAR
Splinter Society Architecture

The brief for Howler called for a venue with a 'hidden Melbourne' feel, incorporating a casual but stylish bar and beer garden that would appeal to individuals grabbing a relaxed midday coffee as much as the full-house audience attending the wide range of performances on offer.

The designers of Splinter Society, working closely with the client Brendan Brogan, worked their magic to transform an originally lifeless warehouse shell into a live entertainment space. The concept conjures up a theatrical fantasy world, based on an abstract urban forest. Part of the roof was removed to open the inside up to the elements and, with this intervention, the beer garden was created. What was once a large, single void turned into a layered and intimate space with a gradation between landscape and interior.

Layers of detail reveal themselves throughout, all working to enhance this fantasy forest idea. Tree trunks have been crafted in a contemporary manner to create big, communal benches with integrated tabletops positioned alongside rusted planters. By night, cube lights hover overhead like illuminated box kites.

Creating the required atmosphere, with a modest budget, required a unique approach. Several steel and timber workers with artistic interests were engaged to make the many custom elements on-site, including all the furniture and decorative light fittings. Simple, often recycled, low-cost materials and basic construction techniques give a handcrafted feeling with texture, tactility and warmth. Howler also expresses its warehouse roots, since the designers highlighted features of the original fabric and context, including the brick texture of the old shell, the windows and the trees outside the building.

The interior design for Howler is in keeping with its warehouse location.

WHERE **7–11 Dawson St, Melbourne, Australia**
OPENING **May 2013**
CLIENT **Brendan Brogan**
DESIGNER **Splinter Society Architecture (p.550)**
FLOOR AREA **1000 m²**
WEBSITE **h-w-l-r.com**

MINIMUM AGE **18**
SIGNATURE DRINK **Monkey of La Fee**
PRICE OF A GLASS OF HOUSE WINE **AUD 10**
OPENING HOURS **12.00–01.00**
CAPACITY **700 guests**

Howler's signature drink is Monkey 47 Gin, La Fee Absinthe, St Germain, cucumber slices and egg white.

Steel and timber artisans crafted the many custom elements on-site, like this light installation, resulting in a handmade look.

Tree trunks were used to make long communal benches with integrated tabletops.

Fantasy theatricals in an abstract urban forest

The glowing boxes were designed to be like hanging fruits (like grapes), enticing customers.

Removing part of the roof created an intriguingly layered, inside–outside space.

Abstract steel plant forms, snaking raised planter beds and natural finishes enhance the relaxed garden atmosphere.

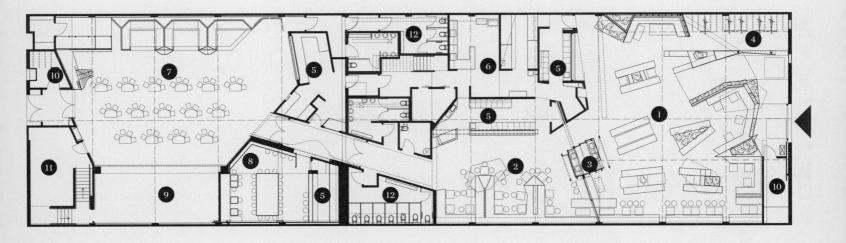

FLOOR PLAN

1 Beer garden
2 Interior bar seating area
3 DJ booth
4 Bike storage
5 Bar
6 Kitchen
7 Theatre area
8 Theatre bar seating area
9 Stage
10 Storage
11 Back-of-house
12 Lavatories

Howler expresses its warehouse roots, highlighting its original fabric and context

INTERNAL ELEVATION

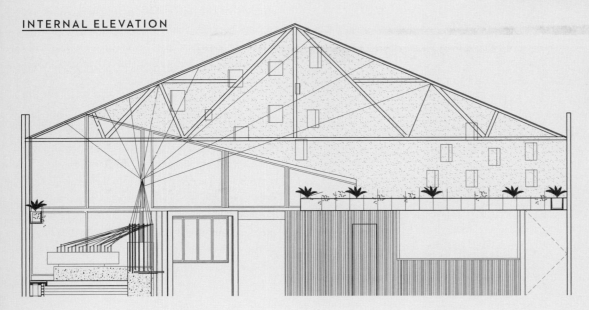

Early sketches show the concept developing like a theatrical forest.

ICEBAR BY ICEHOTEL JUKKASJÄRVI

Jens Thoms Ivarsson

Some 200 km north of the Arctic Circle, the Icebar – part of the famous Icehotel Jukkasjärvi – is a drinking spot with a difference. Every year, bar and hotel emerge from snow and ice in the winter, melting away as spring arrives. Nevertheless, the hotel's design team completes permanent projects too – ice bar interiors in Stockholm and London, ice installations at Milan Design Week, and many more.

Jens Thoms Ivarsson is director of design at the Icehotel. He worked with artists Tjåsa Gusfors from Sweden and Maurizio Perron from Italy for the 2013 edition of the bar. 'We wanted a design with a strong form that would work well with the room, which had big round arches made out of ice,' says Ivarsson. 'Therefore, we chose circular shapes for the bar, sofas, seating areas and lamps. We mixed both snow and ice to create contrast between the two 'colours': white and transparent. We planned the lighting to show the qualities of the materials.'

To add some extra fun to the project, the designers placed an 8-m-long fish-shaped ice sculpture across the bar, weighing in at 12 tonnes. The fish features in a local tale about the local Jukkasjärvi area, whilst in the bar, it works as a room divider and determines the flow through the space. It makes a spectacular sight when you enter the bar and see the three huge arcs made from ice, with the round bar in the centre. Drinks served in ice glasses complete the cool, polar atmosphere.

The 8-m-long ice fish is divided into slices, giving the scaly sculpture some air.

WHERE **Jukkasjärvi, Sweden**
OPENING **December 2013**
CLIENT **Icehotel**
DESIGNER **Jens Thoms Ivarsson (p.546)**
FLOOR AREA **150 m²**
WEBSITE **icehotel.com**

MINIMUM AGE **18**
SIGNATURE DRINK **Wolf Paw**
PRICE OF A GLASS OF HOUSE WINE **SEK 115**
OPENING HOURS **11.00–01.00**
CAPACITY **150 guests**

Loganberries and vodka make up the signature drink Wolf Paw, served in glasses which are themselves carved out of ice.

ICEBAR BY ICEHOTEL JUKKASJÄRVI   JENS THOMS IVARSSON

Everything in the bar is made from snow and ice ('snice') from the local Torne River, including the pendant lampshade which weighs 180 kg.

Illumination in the bar is mainly blue and white, staying true to the natural ice colours, with the bar exploding in pink hues once in a while like a mini Aurora Borealis.

At 200 km north of the Arctic Circle, this is a drinking spot with a difference

Hundreds of artists and designers create one-off pieces across the 5500-m² hotel, which closed in spring when the ice started to melt.

KAFE NORDIC
Nordic Bros Design Community

In the increasingly cool Itaewon district of Seoul, Kafe Nordic presents an unexpected corner of Sweden – in the shape of a yellow facade shaped like a typically Nordic house, complete with little square windows and a roof gable. For the designers, adding this cheery and unexpected intervention to an existing residential building creates maximum contrast with the 'quiet and peaceful mood of red bricks in the area' – and no doubt helps to lure customers inside.

When they enter via the glass doors and descend the stairs to the semi-basement space, guests encounter a tiny coffee bar in which contemporary design makes a big splash. It's all thanks to tiles by Mutina Azulej (in 27 patterns designed by Patricia Urquiola) on the walls and floor, and a colourful, eclectic mix of chairs and tables, by Emeco, Flototto, Hay, Ton and Nordic Bros' own Yong-hwan Shin, among others.

Nothing here specifically matches, yet the different shapes and colours work well to carve out a characterful space, with more than a touch of humour. Additional fantasy comes from the assorted animal figurines that are dotted throughout the cafe.

A strong contrast is provided by a sleek black-painted unit which frames the front of the serving counter, the kitchen and the drinks cabinet. This has dark mirror shapes – octagonal, hexagonal, quadrangle and circular – mounted onto its surface. This same jumbled geometric pattern continues on the back wall, where it forms the borders for the menu. At the back of the space, the bathroom a restful interlude, with pale surfaces and a plant climbing across its walls.

The bright-yellow exterior evokes a typical Swedish house, making a clear Nordic statement.

WHERE **B1, 683-46, Hannam-dong, Seoul, Korea**
OPENING **December 2013**
CLIENT **Kafe Nordic (Ha-jin Park)**
DESIGNER **Nordic Bros Design Community (p.547)**
FLOOR AREA **40 m²**
WEBSITE **n/a**

MINIMUM AGE **n/a**
SIGNATURE DRINK **Organic fruit teas**
PRICE OF A DRINK **KRW 7000**
OPENING HOURS **11.00–22.00**
CAPACITY **22 guests**

Bright splashes of colour stand out against the grey-and-white tiles.

Customers can choose between a vibrant mix of seating options.

KHOKOLAT BAR
Grant Amon Architects

A backlit bar references old jukeboxes, while Karim Rashid's Kant stools evoke melting chocolate fondant.

Located in the basement of an old building – a converted brick warehouse – in one of Melbourne's popular city laneways, Khokolat Bar nightclub was in need of some refreshment, so the owners called in Grant Amon Architects. A main aim was to create a new main 'attractor' bar – the designers obliged by referencing the allure of a backlit jukebox to create a glowing new centrepiece in what the designers call 'a chocolate box of desires'.

A lavishly layered look features a dark and light chocolate striped carpet like a wrapping, brown foil-like wallpaper, sweet cherry vinyl and rich brown curtains. The backlit bar is itself a giant confection, with a dark chocolate (Marblo) rim encasing a nougat centre with a minty bubbled core. The bar is framed by a cherry vinyl-clad wall with pod-like openings displaying the drinks. The bronze mirror and backlit cherry coloured acrylic panels add a vibrant emphasis to the variety of bottles presented.

Combined with its elevated position on a raised plinth, the bar ensemble is further enhanced by three overhead pink dot matrix light boxes which appear to pulsate. The dripping plastic forms of Rashid's Kant stools, in a chocolate shade of course, sit comfortably to the foreground as the venue flanks out to either side encompassing the dance floor and lounge and entry area. This part of the basement club, which is reached down a set of carpeted stairs, has also received a facelift, with a new desk, cloak room and signage completing the tempting tableau.

WHERE **43 Hardware Lane, Melbourne, Australia**
OPENING **December 2012**
CLIENT **Damion De Silva**
DESIGNER **Grant Amon Architects (p.545)**
FLOOR AREA **275 m²**
WEBSITE **khokolatbar.com.au**

MINIMUM AGE **18**
SIGNATURE DRINK **Sea Breeze**
PRICE OF A GLASS OF HOUSE WINE **AUD 10**
OPENING HOURS **21.00–03.00**
CAPACITY **200 guests**

The carpet, with its dark and light chocolate-coloured stripes, stands out in an interior of cocoa tones, with foil and cherry accents.

A club wrapped up as a chocolate box of desires

The warm chartreuse and cherry core of the glowing bar is enhanced by its raised position and the three pink dot-matrix light boxes overhead.

LOOF
Takenouchi Webb

The main bar is clad in veined green marble and has a trellis-like ceiling.

Loof was one of the first stand-alone rooftop bars in Singapore and, after 5 years it was in need of revival. Takenouchi Webb obliged by granting it a new look, with a design concept that introduces a garden feeling to the space.

Located on the top of a section of Odeon Towers with panoramic views of Raffles Hotel, the bar has a small lobby at the ground level with a lift to the rooftop. Guests enter to see four large circular planters recessed into the floor. Around the planter next to the lift, the designers added a 3.5-m-high green wall, creating what can be classed as an outdoor lobby space. Around the planter is a timber bench where guests can wait to be seated or shown to the bar.

For the quirky touch that is immediately evident to customers, there is a fun reception zone with a colourful 'mama-shop' (a typical corner shop in Singapore), made of painted corrugated metal. It is stocked with nostalgic snacks, traditional kids toys and bar merchandise.

The main 8.7-m-long bar sits under a glass canopy and the front is clad in a veined green marble. The back wall of the bar has alternating panels of overlapping timber shingles and glass windows. Opposite the bar is a 12-m-long lounge banquette, backed by a 3.5-m-high open timber trellis. The trellis pattern repeats the semi-circular pattern used for the shingles and ceramic tiles, a motif taken from the Loof logo. Greenery covers the trellis, creating an enclosure around the seating area. At the far end of the bar, opposite Raffles Hotel, is a solid timber ledge around the roof perimeter with high tables for drinkers to take in the amazing views.

WHERE **331 North Bridge Rd, Singapore**
OPENING **June 2012**
CLIENT **The Lo & Behold Group**
DESIGNER **Takenouchi Webb (p.550)**
FLOOR AREA **440 m²**
WEBSITE **loof.com.sg**

MINIMUM AGE **18**
SIGNATURE DRINK **Singapore Sour**
PRICE OF A GLASS OF HOUSE WINE **SGD 14**
OPENING HOURS **Mon–Thu 17.00–01.00,
Fri–Sat 17.00–03.00**
CAPACITY **168 guests**

A sky-high garden revives Singapore's first rooftop bar with flourishes of greenery

The same formula is also adapted to create snug spaces.

Once customers step out of the lift, they see greenery flourishing in the lush outdoor space.

Even the inside space incorporates greenery, giving it an outdoorsy feel.

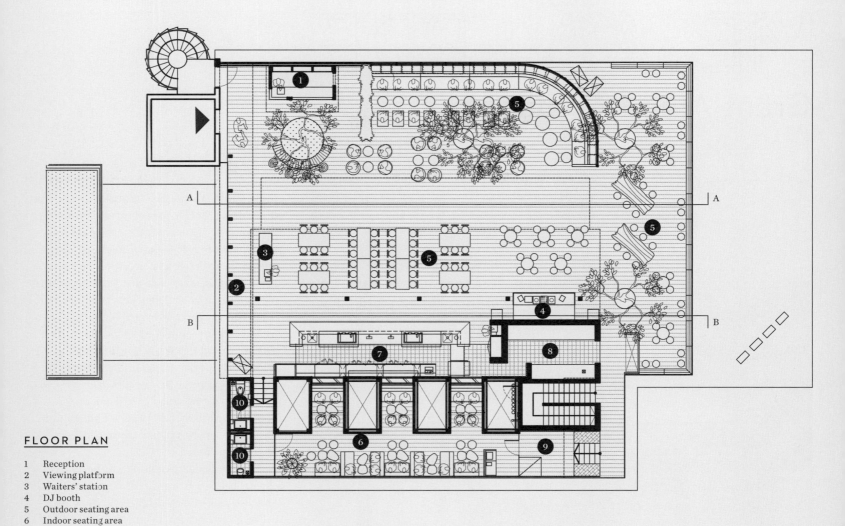

FLOOR PLAN

1 Reception
2 Viewing platform
3 Waiters' station
4 DJ booth
5 Outdoor seating area
6 Indoor seating area
7 Bar
8 Kitchen
9 Back-of-house
10 Lavatories

High tables for drinkers to take in the amazing views of Raffles Hotel

SECTION A

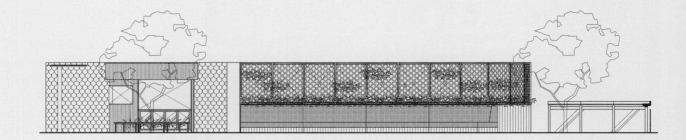

SECTION B

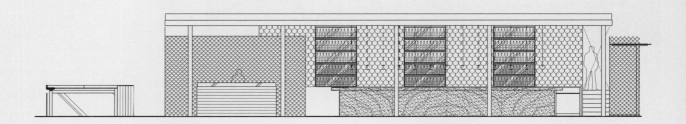

MESA VERDE

Grant Amon Architects

The Mesa Verde themed-painting, above
the orange banquette seating, is an original
artwork by musician and artist Jon Langford.

Mesa Verde is a bar that is located on the sixth floor of Curtin House in central downtown Melbourne. Christened after the name of a town in the Sergio Leone film, *A Fistful of Dynamite*, which is a favourite of the owner, naturally the venue also needed to serve up a mean margarita and delicious Mexican food.

The Spaghetti Western theme has been imaginatively applied to the interior, which unites several 1960s cowboy film motifs. A floor of American oak obliquely suggests the traditional spit 'n' sawdust saloon, illuminated cow skulls gaze down on diners, and the menus, posters and graphic identity of the restaurant evoke the style of Leone's classics.

The wooden panelling, similarly on theme, is made from oiled Tasmanian Myrtle and also reflects the original 1920s detailing found elsewhere in the building. A recycled Messmate Bar forms the main centrepiece and is enlivened by the backlit onyx panels to the bar front. Bevelled and aged mirrors combine with display shelves to the rear, which house a serious tequila bar. Built-in banquette seating is complemented by Thonet bentwood chairs, tall bar stools and tables, velvet curtains and an array of film posters (many featuring Clint Eastwood), flickering projected images and antique lanterns – all helping to evoke the spirit of the old, wild west.

The existing concrete ceiling, with its multitude of beams, was restored and discreetly up-lit with custom-designed strip LED lighting. In all, the bar creates a sophisticated take on a classic cinematic theme. Design notions of reinterpretation, humour, authenticity and memory are all evoked to great effect.

WHERE **252 Swanston Street, Melbourne, Australia**
OPENING **April 2013**
CLIENT **Tim Peach and Eric Firth**
DESIGNER **Grant Amon Architects (p.545)**
FLOOR AREA **280 m²**
WEBSITE **mesaverde.net.au**

MINIMUM AGE **18**
SIGNATURE DRINK *Margarita*
PRICE OF A GLASS OF HOUSE WINE **AUD 12**
OPENING HOURS **Tue–Sun 17.00 until late**
CAPACITY **175 guests**

Timber floor and wall panelling are an earthy base for the decor.

Lounge chairs give a modern feel to the wild-west saloon concept.

The stunning bar and its serious
tequila selection is watched
over by the Mesa Verde mascot.

Obliquely suggesting the traditional spit 'n' sawdust saloon

The backlit onyx of
the bar is effective
from all angles.

Scarlet drapes frame the walkway like a stage curtain, with classic posters and film stills all helping to make the Spaghetti Western allusions work.

MON BIJOU

Hachem

Extending from the geometric ceiling installation, mirrored-acrylic also decorates the side wall.

Situated atop the Adelphi Hotel, Mon Bijou – a cocktail bar and an upper-level function venue – sets out to dazzle with an intricate, deco-inspired interior that appears to be a continuation of the surrounding panorama of Melbourne's skyline: a glorious network of cathedral spires, rooftops and windowpanes. The brief for the venue, given to Hachem by The Collective Establishments, was to maximise the impact of the spectacular views and to create an atmosphere of rare decadence and charm.

The designers from Hachem positioned the venue's service areas (bar and bathrooms) discreetly, to allow for long, peripheral seating areas with a stunning proximity to the cityscape just beyond the windows. The furnishings chosen are timeless, elegant and subtly toned, while over the walls and ceiling an elaborate series of reflective three-dimensional geometric forms, inspired by French art deco jewellery, seems to shimmer and glide. Multi-facetted and variously aligned, they capture natural light and create a moiré effect as one moves through the space.

The intricacy and modularity of the concept meant that the feature interior elements could be built, taken apart, carried in – without the use of expensive cranes – and reconfigured on site. This was important, given the financial and time constraints of the project. Modelling techniques developed in planning were so precise that their actual installation took less than 3 weeks to complete. The result is an infinite play of jewel colours, shadows and intersecting shapes. Mon Bijou is a magical setting that makes an occasion of every visit.

WHERE **187 Flinders Lane, Melbourne, Australia**
OPENING **Early 2012**
CLIENT **The Collective Establishments**
DESIGNER **Hachem (p.545)**
FLOOR AREA **220 m²**
WEBSITE **monbijou.com.au**

MINIMUM AGE **18**
SIGNATURE DRINK **French champagne**
PRICE OF A GLASS OF HOUSE WINE **AUD 11**
OPENING HOURS **Private functions only**
CAPACITY **160 guests**

The dusty pink of the ceiling is picked up in the furnishings of the lounge area.

Guests can lounge in the Potocco 'Diva' and 'Eiles' armchairs whilst taking in the view.

From the cocktail bar, clad in lustrously-reflective Impala Black granite, guests can access the patio to gain views of the lower-level swimming pool.

ELEVENTH FLOOR

1   Function area
2   Booth
3   Lounge area
4   Bar and banquet table
5   Cocktail bar
6   Kitchen
7   Store
8   Service room

9   Lavatories
10 Patio
11 Poolside lounge (level 9)
12 Sun deck (level 9)
13 Adelphi pool (level 9)
14 Lift
15 Void
16 Mechanical room

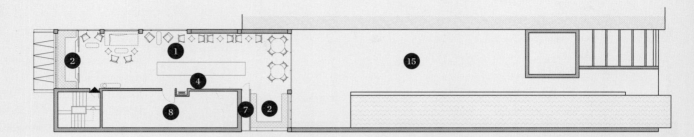

TENTH FLOOR

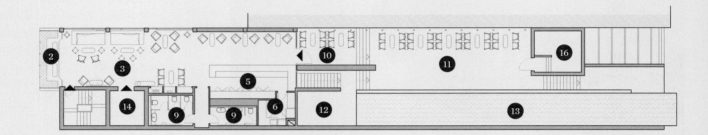

Mon Bijou sets out to dazzle with an intricate, deco-inspired interior

EAST ELEVATION

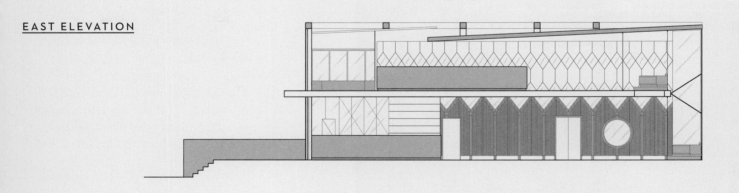

WEST ELEVATION

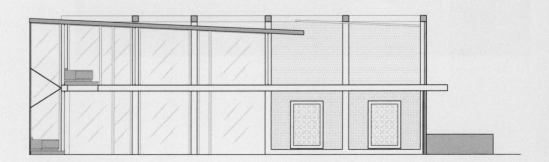

MONOPOLE
Pascale Gomes-McNabb Design

The grey ceiling panels, which were installed to aid acoustics in the small space, also form an important part of the design concept.

When opening Monopole in Sydney's busy and urbane Macleay Street, Brent Savage and Nick Hildebrandt approached Pascale Gomes-McNabb Design with a vision. They wanted a contemporary interpretation of an old-world European wine bar, a space that would match the considered, handcrafted and bespoke quality of the wine and cuisine on offer.

Working with a long and narrow existing interior, the designers stripped the tiled decor but left the layout intact. Darkly metallic finishes and materials transformed the space into a moodily lit, comfortable and intimate environment, where the theatre of food preparation and service is framed by an open-ended bar and kitchen.

The relatively compact space is enhanced by a wide range of finishes in sultry tones. There's a blackened, glossy timber bar with copper panels, and the gunmetal leather banquettes look extra lush when set against the burnt-wood tables. Shelves are made from recycled wooden wine boxes and a sound-absorbing 3D ceiling is made up of EchoPanels, made from recycled PET bottles. Up-lit bronze mirrors illuminate and extend the space, while making the most of the feature lighting by Mark Douglass, with his Kiki cluster chandelier made from hand-blown glass spheres, and Christopher Boots' pronged lights called Simple X and Simple Y. The handcrafted elements add to the sophisticated and contemporary effect.

The view from outside is guaranteed to intrigue passers-by, with rows of hanging grey strips (made from recycled plastic bottles) appearing like an art installation through the open windows.

WHERE **71a Macleay St, Sydney, Australia**
OPENING **December 2012**
CLIENT **Nick Hildebrandt and Brent Savage**
DESIGNER **Pascale Gomes-McNabb Design (p.548)**
FLOOR AREA **104 m²**
WEBSITE **monopolesydney.com.au**

MINIMUM AGE **18**
SIGNATURE DRINK **Organic wine selection**
PRICE OF A GLASS OF HOUSE WINE **AUD 10**
OPENING HOURS **12.00–00.00**
CAPACITY **50 guests**

FLOOR PLAN

1   Bar
2   Kitchen
3   Seating area
4   Waiters' station
5   Back-of-house

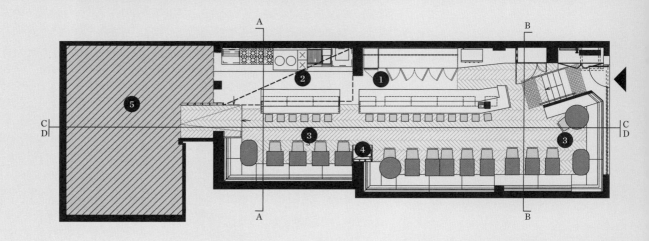

SECTION B

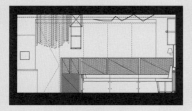

SECTION A

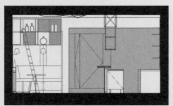

SECTION C

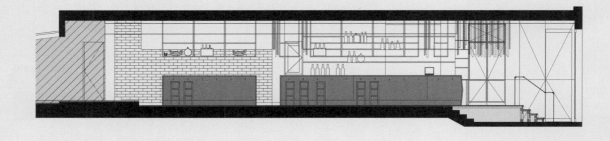

SECTION D

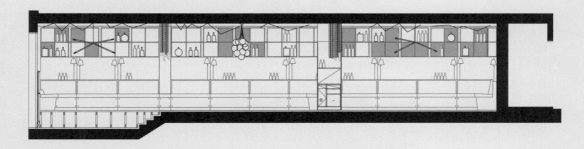

ENTRANCE ELEVATION

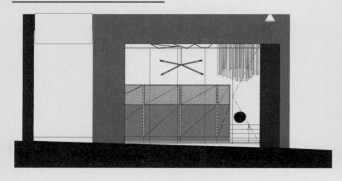

At the entrance, guests are greeted with perforated steel screens adorned with black anti-rust paint.

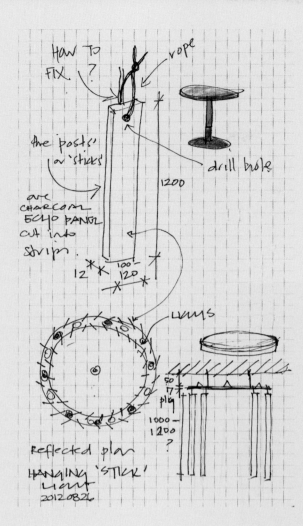

Contemporary interpretation matches handcrafted finishes

Initial ideas for the charcoal echo strips on the ceiling (above) and the counter detailing of the bar.

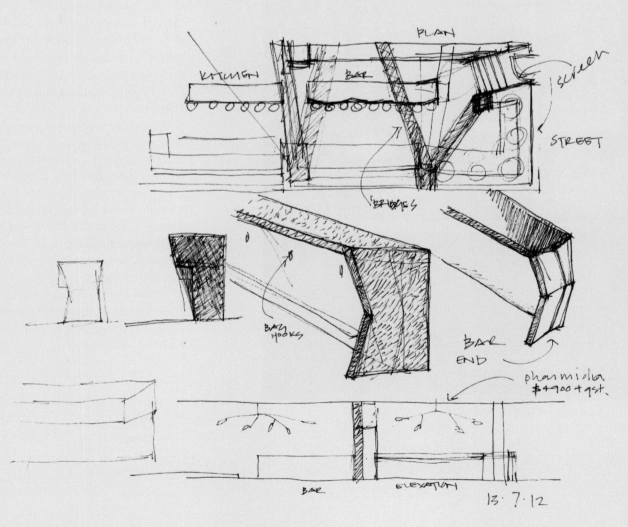

MR FOGG'S

d-raw

A bar with a copper top and oak-veneered front
hits the right period note – especially with
several penny farthings hanging overhead.

An immersive fusion of nightlife and theatre, Mr Fogg's bar attests to the evolution of the hospitality industry as a burgeoning sweet spot for fantastical experiential design: a new consumer appetite far beyond simple culinary excellence. Based around the life of Phileas Fogg – the fictional hero in Jules Verne's 19th century novel *Around the World in Eighty Days* – this venue trades wholeheartedly on its location in the depths of London's Mayfair, one of the city's most quintessentially English enclaves.

Part gentleman's club, part adventurer's den – the eccentrically styled interior is staged as much as it is designed, lavished in visual theatrics and overtly opulent design tics. Furnished with a brace of spoils supposedly belonging to the imaginary adventurer, including: a wall-mounted alligator and an elephant's foot; tables are littered with Victorian-era relics such a globe-turned-punchbowl; and the ceiling is festooned with gilded birdcages and penny-farthing bicycles.

The material and colour palettes are suitably rich, even bordering on the regal – pewter, etched brass, copper, mahogany and heavy sumptuous leathers dipped in burgundy and racing green – all combine to add weight to the novelty ambience. Chequered floor tiles, cosy banquettes and curved Chesterfield sofas underscore a very British heritage while hidden alcoves and a cloakroom featuring wallpaper embellished with the idiosyncratic prints of Italian designer Piero Fornesetti pump up the fantasy-factor.

Revelling in peculiarity, thespian staff delivers cocktails in full character – sealing a concept conceived as the ultimate cocktail-hour escape.

WHERE **15 Bruton Lane, London, United Kingdom**
OPENING **May 2013**
CLIENT **Inception Group**
DESIGNER **d-raw (p.543)**
FLOOR AREA **120 m²**
WEBSITE **mr-foggs.com**

MINIMUM AGE **21**
SIGNATURE DRINK **Tipsy Tea**
PRICE OF A GLASS OF HOUSE WINE **GBP 8**
OPENING HOURS **Mon–Sat 17.00–01.00**
CAPACITY **170 guests**

The entrance is refurbished with carriage lamps, grand walnut doors and a huge bay window – all evoking a Victorian town house.

Inside, the bar is furnished with a concoction of weird and wonderful items that the fictional Mr Fogg might have collected on his travels.

1   Bar
2   Seating area
3   Piano
4   Back-of-house
5   Lavatories

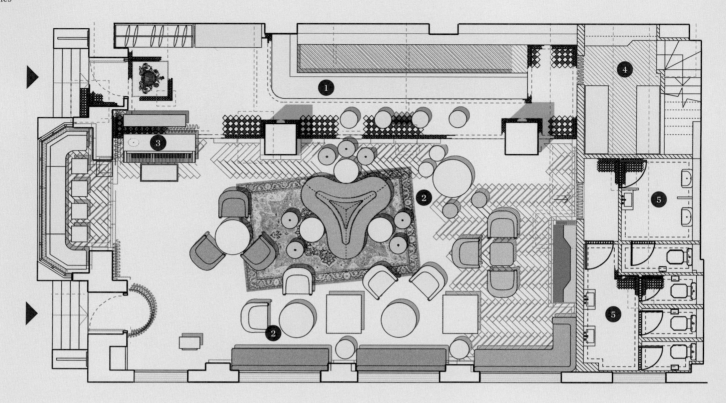

The eccentrically styled interior is lavished in visual theatrics

Traditional square Victorian tiles in black and white appear both outside and inside.

The venue has its own crest illustrating Mr Fogg's motto: 'Always Exploring'.

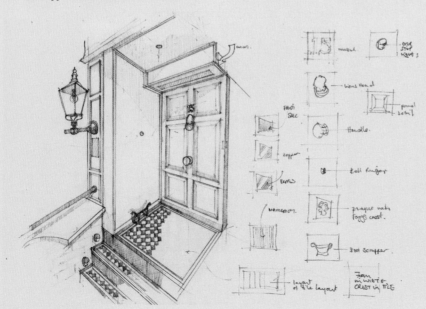

A drawing for the interior shows the
concept already fully formulated.

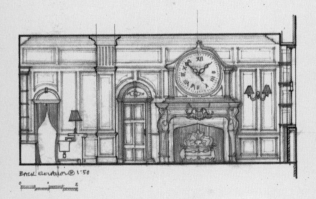

An initial sketch for the clock and fireplace area.

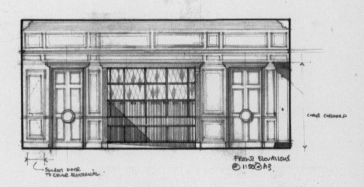

The facade, showing the two doors.

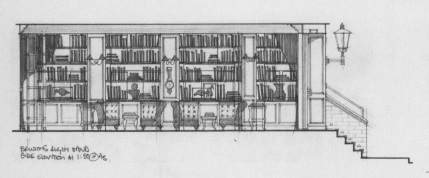

A library area was also part of the initial plan.

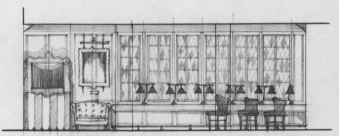

Initial sketch for the bar area.

The richly-layered space contains a staggering amount of 'souvenirs' from all corners of the globe, with animal parts decorating the walls and used as furniture.

NAZDROWJE
Design by Richard Lindvall

Raw concrete is teamed with contemporary copper detailing to create an appealing and subtly streamlined interior.

Commissioned to transform a dull concrete parking garage into a late-night bar and club, that also doubled-up as a zingy Polish restaurant during the daytime, designer Richard Lindvall set off to Poland in search of inspiration. Here, he found inspiration in the city's old factories – so not surprisingly, the concept he came up with for the new venue (called Nazdrowje, which is Polish for 'cheers') was resolutely industrial and true to the original raw concrete interior.

The rough-and-ready atmosphere of the original garage space is left intact but somewhat softened by concrete floors with a pleasant sheen and benches of a paler, cast concrete which are mounted directly onto the walls. Leather pads on these benches provide comfort and contrast.

Adding still more contrast, and a welcome touch of colour and warmth, are the copper pipes that snake their way through the space, forming a unique lighting installation. The radiators are also made of copper, as are the tops of the concrete tables and the facade of a large fireplace. Copper – 'which is guaranteed to age beautifully,' says Lindvall – also recurs in the utilitarian, white-tiled and concrete bathrooms.

The ambience is further enhanced in the dining area thanks to the vintage pendant lamps from a factory in the Czech Republic and some vintage metal Tolix stools. As an industrial finishing touch, Lindvall came up with the idea for some unique artworks – he commissioned a photographic portrait series of the construction workers who put together the project.

WHERE **Edövägen 2, Stockholm, Sweden**
OPENING **December 2011**
CLIENT **Nazdrowje KB**
DESIGNER **Design by Richard Lindval (p.543)**
FLOOR AREA **210 m²**
WEBSITE **n/a**

MINIMUM AGE **18**
SIGNATURE DRINK **Vodka Cocktail**
PRICE OF A GLASS OF HOUSE WINE **SEK 80**
OPENING HOURS **17.00–00.00**
CAPACITY **92 guests**

Vintage oversized lampshades and hunting trophies create quirky touches in the venue with a minimalistic, industrial air.

A specially-commissioned photo series by Mattias Lindbäck depicts the construction workers who took part in the renovation project.

Copper adds colour and warmth to the industrial interior

To break up the expanse of concrete, the walls in the bathroom (and behind the bar) had simple white tiles applied.

The designer chose copper as a feature since it ages well and its colour contrasts nicely with the concrete.

The exposed copper piping, as it snakes its way around the venue, was utilised as a decorative touch.

The concrete bartop was reclaimed from the
floor of the lower level of the building during
the renovation stage.

PHARMARIUM

Stylt Trampoli

The bar has an alchemical style with all the ingredients to create the house cocktail (vodka, lemon, powdered gold, 'herb elixir' and champagne).

Stortorget in Stockholm can be a tricky location for a bar. In summer, the beautiful Old Town is alive with tourists, but locals often stay away. When Stylt Trampoli was asked to create a bar here – in a small space that was part of a listed building – it was clear that in order to win over choosy locals, it would have to be something special.

Before heading for the drawing board, the design team took out the history books, and discovered that Sweden's first public apothecary had opened in this exact location, in 1575 – so that became the project concept for Pharmarium. In times past, the apothecary offered 'not just medicine, but poisons, perfumes and potions, with ingredients from the far corners of the world,' says Stylt Trampoli's Erik Nissen Johansen.

This exotic ambience is distilled in the interior, with the bar area furnished with dozens of wooden drawers, as in an apothecary's shop, with botanical prints and real plants enhancing the illusion. The lounge is totally enveloped in oriental carpets and furnished with plush velvet chairs and ornate cushions.

Pharmarium's cocktails are totally on theme, too, with magical concoctions calling for ingredients like powdered gold, cardamom, roses, seaweed and wild strawberries. 'Despite being a cocktail bar rather than a full-scale apothecary shop, Pharmarium is the latest incarnation of a tradition that reaches back over 400 years,' says Erik Nissen Johansen 'People still want to feel better, and they still search out pleasure, beauty – and magic.'

WHERE **Stortorget 7, Stockholm, Sweden**
OPENING **July 2013**
CLIENT **Stortorgskällaren**
DESIGNER **Stylt Trampoli (p.550)**
FLOOR AREA **60 m²**
WEBSITE **pharmarium.se**

MINIMUM AGE **18**
SIGNATURE DRINK **Roses of Gold**
PRICE OF A COCKTAIL **SEK 140**
OPENING HOURS **Mon-Tue 16.30-23.00,**
Wed-Sun 16.30-01.00
CAPACITY **60 guests**

The design concept has historical connotations: this was the location of Sweden's first apothecary.

The carpet-clad lounge has bespoke rugs with patterns made up of symbols from the pharmaceutical world.

FLOOR PLAN

1   Bar
2   Oriental lounge
3   Outdoor terrace
4   Lavatories

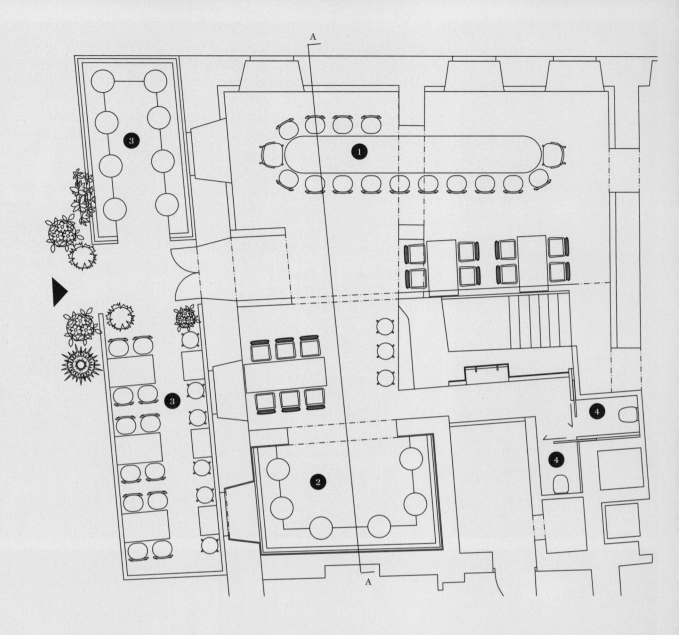

SECTION A

FRONT ELEVATION

An exotic ambience is distilled in the interior

Fossibly medicinal plants appear integrated into the wall of supplies.

PIED
Nordic Bros Design Community

A delicate pattern on one wall adds an additional layer to a minimal space.

A neutral palette contrasts with bold, black linear elements that emphasise the architectural structure.

'Attract attention without making a fuss,' was the client brief for a tea bar and cafe specialising in tasty desserts, established by musician Chan-hee Lee and pastry chef Hee-ju Song. A further request made to Nordic Bros Design Community for the interior was that it should be open and visible. Nordic Bros' Yong-hwan Shin started out by knocking down partition walls to create an open space, and replacing one facade wall with glass to give the formerly residential building an expansive shop-style front. 'I was fed up with using folding doors,' says Shin, 'so I designed a diametrically different style of shop window.' In his version, large pivoting panes rotate open and shut, and the entrance is recessed into the facade.

The interior itself is in a subtle palette of sepia, ivory, cream and soft grey colour tones. The designer calls this scheme 'achromatic colour' but nevertheless the neutral shades create a warm feel with a sophisticated ambience, aided by gentle and diffuse lighting. To add interest, an intricate graphic pattern by Lee Kwang-Moo occupies one wall.

Steel beams now replace supporting walls. Painted black, they add contrast to the pale palette and work well with the dark herringbone floor in ceramic tiles. Furnishings include items by Kartell, Ton and Ikea. Tables in marble and wood vary the materials palette.

At the back of the space, a dark grey counter stands before an almost invisible white partition wall. 'The cafe is very exposed,' says the designer, 'so I also needed to harmonise those parts you wouldn't want to show.'

WHERE **683-47, Hannam-dong, Seoul, Korea**
OPENING **November 2013**
CLIENT **Pied (Chan-hee Lee and Hee-ju Song)**
DESIGNER **Nordic Bros Design Community (p.547)**
FLOOR AREA **70 m²**
WEBSITE **n/a**

MINIMUM AGE **n/a**
SIGNATURE DRINK **Tea**
PRICE OF A DRINK **KRW 6000**
OPENING HOURS **11.00–22.00**
CAPACITY **30 guests**

There is an eclectic mix
of furniture and fittings,
which also includes
custom-designed pieces.

Achromatic decor adds sophistication with no loss of warmth

Grey herringbone flooring
helps to pull the monochrome
space together.

PRAHRAN HOTEL
Techne Architects

Stacked concrete pipes provided a bold solution
for the extension to this art deco bar.

The Prahran Hotel is a substantial two-storey corner pub with a striking streamlined art deco facade. The rear of the venue, however, had a badly executed extension – so Techne Architects was called in to replace it. The design office obliged by creating a dramatic, double-height space with a central courtyard.

The new addition connects the two levels of the existing buildings, while the courtyard creates an outdoorsy feel within the pub. The use of large, stacked concrete pipes for the street facade is unexpected and effective: the spherical forms have a dramatic, sculptural quality, referencing internal circular motifs and suggesting stacked kegs or barrels.

The steel-glazed courtyard cuts through the interior, allowing ample natural light to flood the space. A floating booth made of half pipes is supported on steel posts and accessed via a steel gantry that traverses the room. Much of the steel structure is exposed, and this, plus the concrete of the pipes, forms the base of the material palette. Adding warmth and contrast are the recycled spotted gum and leather upholstery and the fresh greenery that is woven throughout the interior.

Whilst the venue has gained some impressive spatial drama through the new intervention, the interior sets out to create a sociable ambience and sense of intimacy. Customers have various options: private spaces contrast with more open areas, there are nooks for couples and larger groups, and the circulation loops through both levels which encourages a voyeuristic procession through the old and new areas of the pub.

WHERE **82 High Street, Melbourne, Australia**
OPENING **May 2013**
CLIENT **Sand Hill Road**
DESIGNER **Techne Architects (p.550)**
FLOOR AREA **550 m²**
WEBSITE **prahranhotel.com**

MINIMUM AGE *18*
SIGNATURE DRINK *Carlton Draught*
PRICE OF A GLASS OF HOUSE WINE *AUD 8*
OPENING HOURS *From 12.00 until late*
CAPACITY *420 guests*

Lined with wood, individual sections of pipe offer pockets of privacy.

Spherical forms have a dramatic, sculptural quality

The contrast between old and new sections is stark yet harmonious, sharing a bold geometry.

A glazed atrium cuts
through the new building,
filling it with daylight.

Old pipes are upcycled to create a surprisingly beautiful and on-theme bar.

Irregular porthole windows puncture the solid walls.

Impressive spatial drama creates a sociable ambience

Oval mirrors and lights add a fluid rhythm to the bathrooms.

SAL CURIOSO

Stefano Tordiglione Design

The bar's colourful ceramic tiles were inspired by the Spanish architect Gaudi.

At the bar and dining establishment Sal Curioso, guests are transported to what feels like a curious corner of Spain, courtesy of an intriguing interior design by Hong Kong-based Stefano Tordiglione. The concept is based on the life of imaginary inventor and traveller Sal Curioso.

The design team began by slicing the space visually to create a distinctive split effect. Cement – a neutral material – is used for lower and upper areas, while the middle sections contain more elegant materials. In essence, the luxurious contrasts with the gritty.

Each of the distinct zones in the space has its own unique design. The lounge is welcoming and cosy, echoing clubs of the 1970s with its optical wallpaper, sofas covered in colourful fabric and stand-out black and red stools. The bold pattern of cut Spanish tiles on the bar is in keeping with the overriding construction-and-deconstruction theme and was inspired by Spanish architect Gaudi. The mixed-era furniture, including 1950s chairs, custom 1960s-style banquettes and 1970s vintage lamps, makes the bar a stylish mix of eras.

Details are expressive of an imagined journey. Evoking the ocean, wave-like sand-blasted mirrors surround the sleek, stainless steel open kitchen. Large central columns in the dining area are decorated with patterns and prints inspired by the Islamic palace and fortress complex of Alhambra in Granada, Spain. Opposites attract in the bathrooms, where the bottom and top of the space is finished in simple monochrome tiles, while a strip of stark cement runs around the middle. Like the curious Sal Curioso himself, this space is full of surprises.

WHERE **Wyndham Street, Hong Kong**
OPENING **November 2012**
CLIENT **Woolly Pig Concepts**
DESIGNER **Stefano Tordiglione Design (p.550)**
FLOOR AREA **300 m²**
WEBSITE **n/a**

MINIMUM AGE **n/a**
SIGNATURE DRINK **Tequila Cocktail**
PRICE OF A CUP OF COFFEE **HKD 45**
OPENING HOURS **12.00–01.00**
CAPACITY **110 guests**

The lounge revisits the 1970s, with optical wallpaper and semi-psychedelic upholstery.

Patterns also adorn the mirror-lined columns in the dining area.

SINGLE ORIGIN ROASTERS

Luchetti Krelle

Some rather eccentric pipework – by contractor Alco Joinery – adds interest to the space without extra clutter.

Asked to create a fresh new design for the cafe Single Origin Roasters – a long time Surry Hills favourite for coffee aficionados – Luchette Krelle decided that what was needed was a cleaner aesthetic to present the serious coffee (and food) on offer. Plus, the design team decided to add a fun element to reflect the quirky side of the brand.

The client's brief was to revitalise the store without alienating loyal customers. The space had not been updated in 9 years, since the original fit-out. Single Origin Roasters has always had close ties to street artists, and this remains a key feature as a changing element within the space. With 'art series' blends of coffee being presented in packaging designed by the street artists four times a year, a part of the very small site reinforces this retail element of the business.

The use of aluminium cladding represents a shipping container and highlights Single Origin's strong connections with producers and commitment to ethical trading. A touch of innovation and fun is provided by a cumulous cloud with paratroopers up-lighting their parachutes as they hover above the patrons' heads. This cloud was finished in cork, part of a palette of sustainable materials. Other clever detailing includes the overhead shelving supports wrapped in leather bicycle handle straps (a nod to the clients who commute to the area by bike).

The end result? A sophisticated revamp with a twist that expresses the character of this fun, left-of-centre brand – and its great coffee.

WHERE **60-64 Reservoir Street, Surry Hills, Australia**
OPENING **June 2013**
CLIENT **Single Origin Roasters**
DESIGNER **Luchetti Krelle (p.546)**
FLOOR AREA **29 m²**
WEBSITE **singleoriginroasters.com.au**

MINIMUM AGE **n/a**
SIGNATURE DRINK **Gourmet coffee**
PRICE OF A COFFEE **AUD 4**
OPENING HOURS **Mon-Fri 6.30-16.00, Sat 7.30-15.00**
CAPACITY **30 guests**

The bar unites cork with corrugated sheet metal, the latter intended to evoke a shipping container.

A streamlined but fun interior for an ethical coffee brand

SPARK
Barzileye Concept & Design

Hollywood glamour adds personality to the sleek, chic lounge area with its neutral palette (the interior was constructed by Woodfever).

The spotlights, illuminated glass shelves and entire lighting concept was by Design Electro Products.

Called in to transform the existing bar of the Hilton The Hague, Angelika Barzilay (of Barzileye Concept & Design) set out to create an environment that would attract non-guests as well as hotel residents. 'The interior design style needed to differ from that of the hotel itself,' she says, 'thereby giving the bar its own individual character.'

The design concept was based on 'images that sprang to mind reminiscent of 1950s Italian cinema'. Her interior would reference 'scenes shot in stylish vintage interiors, interspersed with casual Italian American chic, giving the bar that alluring movie magic. Nothing too slick, but classy nevertheless'.

These ideas were translated into a cinematic play with light, materials and texture. The mosaic wall is a playful combination of contrasting natural stone and copper-glazed tiles from Porcelanosa: this, together with the glass shelves which are individually illuminated by LED lighting creates an intriguing and dramatic effect. The side tables around the bar are inlaid with the same mosaic, which is coated with resin, giving a rich, jewel-like effect.

The design for the dining tables was inspired by retro American patchwork patterns, and executed in different shades of stained wood. The lounge area achieves a touch of 1940s Hollywood glamour, thanks to oyster leather seating, glossy dark tables and flooring, downlighting, and a gallery of Hollywood portraits on the wall. Papa Bear lounge chairs by Hans Wegner and Wendela bar stools and chairs by Cristoph Seyferth complete the effect.

WHERE **Hilton, Zeestraat 35, The Hague, the Netherlands**
OPENING **March 2013**
CLIENT **Hilton The Hague**
DESIGNER **Barzileye Concept & Design (p.541)**
FLOOR AREA **135 m²**
WEBSITE **restaurantpearl.com**

MINIMUM AGE **18**
SIGNATURE DRINK *Spark Cocktail*
PRICE OF A GLASS OF HOUSE WINE *EUR 5*
OPENING HOURS *Sun–Thu 16.00–01.00, Fri–Sat 16.00–02.00*
CAPACITY *60 guests*

The multicoloured mosaic pattern behind the bar was created with Porcelanosa ceramic tiles.

Copper colours with tinges of purple run throughout the interior, including the quilt-inspired tabletops.

STAR ALLIANCE LOUNGE

Barzileye Concept & Design

A richly textured environment welcomes guests to the First Class lounge.

According to Angelika Barzilay, designer of the Star Alliance Lounge at Paris Charles de Gaulle airport, the experience should offer travellers 'a memorable moment of Parisian glamour, sophistication and charming hospitality'. This informs her design for the lounge complex, which sets out to evoke the City of Light. Barzileye chose the Dutch firm Intos Interior Contracting to realise the project and create this ultimate airport experience.

At the entrance, eligible guests can choose the First Class lounge on the eleventh floor, or head to the Business Class lounge on the lower level. Throughout, the floor plan was inspired by an aerial pattern of the French capital created by the 20 spiralling arrondissements of Paris. This layout allowed for flowing spaces and cosy areas offering a refuge for quiet relaxation or a comfortable corner to work on a laptop. The rather organic arrangement ensures a warm, protected composition.

A major challenge of the Business Class zone was the fixed low ceiling height. The designer's solution was to focus instead on the width of the space, by using mirrors on the side walls. French cuisine, of course, is a major part of the Parisian experience and so the food service point play an important role in the space, becoming focal points thanks to their eye-catching organic forms made from Corian.

The upper level lounge is decorated with the black and gold of the Star Alliance logo, threaded with copper browns and white to create a space of unfettered, stylish sophistication. Large, black-and-white photographs depicting nostalgic imagery of Paris at its most glamorous continue the theme of combining the classic with the contemporary.

WHERE **Charles De Gaulle Airport, Terminal 1, Paris, France**
OPENING **April 2014**
CLIENT **Star Alliance**
DESIGNER **Barzileye Concept & Design (p.541)**
FLOOR AREA **900 m²**
WEBSITE **staralliance.com**

MINIMUM AGE **n/a**
SIGNATURE DRINK **n/a**
PRICE OF A GLASS OF HOUSE WINE **Complimentary**
OPENING HOURS **5.30–22.30**
CAPACITY **224 guests**

Pockets of intimacy, like this metal chain curtained oval, help to break up the space.

White room dividers reflect the street plan of Paris which inspired the design and help to articulate the lounge.

Black, copper and white dominates
the First Class space.

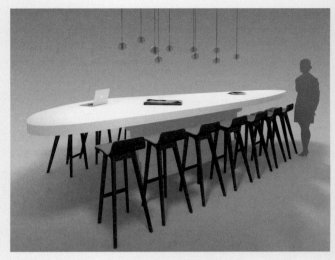

A tall table creates a central island in the Business
Class zone, akin to the Île de la Cité in Paris.

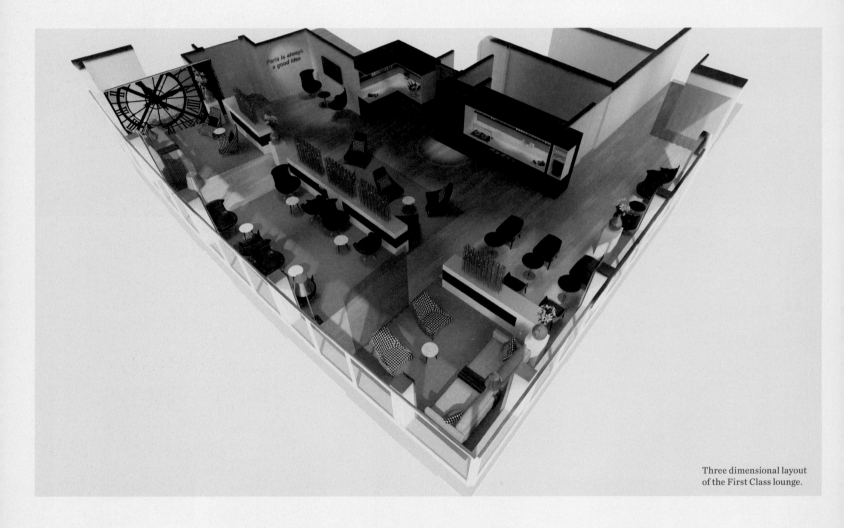

Three dimensional layout
of the First Class lounge.

Each of the laser-cut panels have a
pattern illustrating a different part
of the Paris street plan.

TENTH FLOOR

1 Entrance area of the Business Class lounge
2 Cosy seating niches with metallic curtain
3 Buffet food point
4 Kitchen
5 Entrance to relax lounge
6 Lavatories

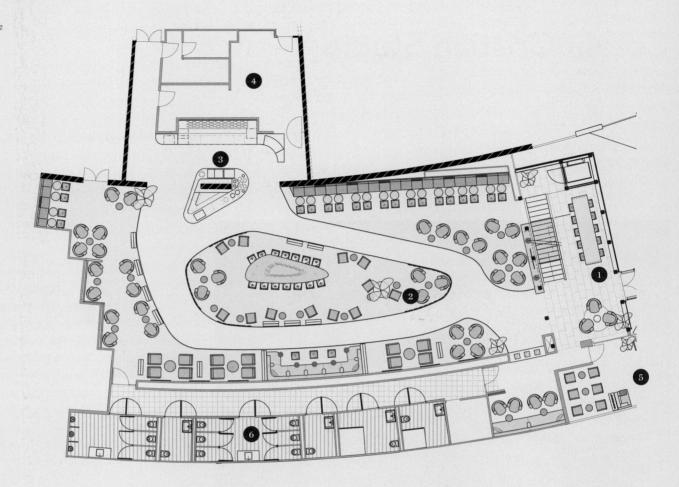

ROOM DIVIDER

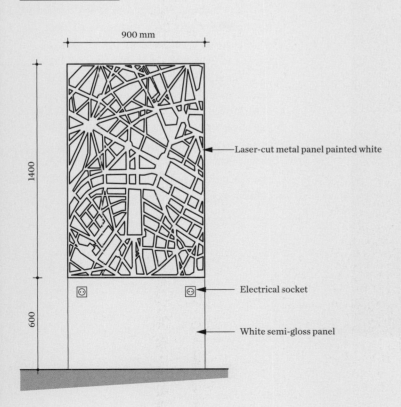

900 mm

1400

600

Laser-cut metal panel painted white

Electrical socket

White semi-gloss panel

The layout was inspired by an aerial pattern of the 20 spiralling arrondissements of Paris

STUDIO HERMES

Corvin Cristian Studio

The curved wooden fins craft an aesthetically pleasing envelope, whilst also having an acoustic function.

Studio Hermes calls itself 'the first social club in Bucharest to blend live music, exquisite drinks, good food and great company with contemporary culture, modern architecture, and multifaceted entertainment'. The venue, a former movie theatre, packs an all-round experience into 600 m², hosting a variety of performances from cabaret to live bands.

The design therefore needed to respond to acoustic requirements according to designer Corvin Cristian who gave the club its cool look, which he explains resembles a 1960s music hall. Mid-century-modern forms and materials are used for an evocative, nostalgic effect. A lush onyx bar makes a luminous focal point, with plush velvet banquettes and walnut wainscoting adding to the warm, luxurious feel.

A dramatic oval void punctures the space, and this is lined with timber fins (for sound absorption, but bang on the mid-century look) creating a sculptural effect. A sweeping staircase echoes these curved lines. Brass pipes and lights are suspended from the concrete ceiling, with a spectacular installation formed from brass cymbals occupying the central position.

Upstairs, a tiled bar and glossy turquoise floor invite guests to enjoy the view from above: the oval void offers a full view of the stage and everything else happening below.

Furnishings take a faultlessly 1960s direction and include Eames' plywood chairs, plus Mather bar stools and Butterfly bar chairs by Autoban. Pedrali table bases are given custom-made marble and solid American walnut tops (matching the walls), and the copper pendant lights are also custom made.

WHERE **16 Selari Street, Bucharest, Romania**
OPENING **October 2013**
CLIENT **Studio Hermes**
DESIGNER **Corvin Cristian Studio (p.542)**
FLOOR AREA **600 m²**
WEBSITE **studiohermes.ro**

MINIMUM AGE **18**
SIGNATURE DRINK *Exclusive wines*
PRICE OF A GLASS OF WINE **RON 20**
OPENING HOURS **12.00–06.00**
CAPACITY **240 guests**

Walnut veneer (for the walls and fins) creates a central ceiling void, filled with the spectacular cymbal installation .

A dramatic oval void of timber fins creates a sculptural effect

Custom-made copper light pendants
and a backlit onyx bar add a real glow
to the expanses of wood.

THE BLACK SWAN

Takenouchi Webb

The chevron pattern in the wallpaper above the bar is a popular art deco motif.

A former bank dating from the 1930s becomes a three-storey art deco-inspired bar and restaurant worthy of *The Great Gatsby*, courtesy of Takenouchi Webb. The focal point of The Black Swan is the stunning horseshoe-shaped bar. Clad in stained timber and marble, with a towering expanse of mirror and brass behind the bar, this centerpiece is topped with a quotation by Scott Fitzgerald: 'Here's to the rose-coloured glasses of life'.

The bar acts as a dividing line: on one side, there is an elegant space to lounge with a cocktail, and on the other there is a dining area, each stylistically united by the materials and motifs used. Reflecting the building and its history, brass, marble and terrazzo, together with high-gloss veneers are repeated throughout the project in varying combinations.

Patterns include the geometric chevron used as a screen over the door and window openings, and a zig-zag patterning of alternating maple, mahogany and black gloss laminate. Light fittings are custom-made: decorated pendant globes of sand-blasted glass with brass fixtures, and wall lights of semi-circular vertical glass rods.

Downstairs is a private dining room, located in the former vault; upstairs is the mezzanine bar called The Powder Room. Dark timber cladding and geometric patterned wallpaper are used here to create a distinct atmosphere. The bar is located at the back of the space and clad with birds-eye maple strips and a marble top. The lounge seating is also covered with a geometric fabric. As the bar is only used at night, lighting levels are low, with the only illumination from the wall lights, bar pendant lights and the bottle display.

WHERE **19 Cecil Street, Singapore**
OPENING **July 2013**
CLIENT **The Lo & Behold Group**
DESIGNER **Takenouchi Webb (p.550)**
FLOOR AREA **443 m²**
WEBSITE **theblackswan.com.sg**

MINIMUM AGE **18**
SIGNATURE DRINK ***Good Night Peru***
PRICE OF A GLASS OF WINE **SGD 15**
OPENING HOURS **Mon–Thu 11.30–01.00, Fri 11.30–02.00, Sat 17.00–02.00**
CAPACITY **200 guests**

The bar, topped by a Scott Fitzgerald quote, makes a dramatic centrepiece in the space.

Shades of Gatsby glamour

The private dining room is located in the basement, in the bank's former vault.

Lighting adds to the period feel and makes the most of high-gloss materials.

THE CLUB
Cloud-9 interior design

Built into the wall, drawers with hand-stitched leather pulls open to reveal screen-printed floral graphics.

When is a showroom not a showroom? When it's The Club, a showroom with a real difference, created for furniture manufacturer Haworth by Cloud-9. What has been designed feels like a luxurious lounge bar, and is much more than a space to showcase Haworth's products – it is also a multifunctional venue for events, workshops and festivities, and the space is also available for hire.

Building on China's long tradition of craft, Cloud-9 emphasised handwork and materiality in its project for Haworth. The showroom is part of Parkview Green, a landmark commercial complex with LEED Platinum certification. The high-tech sustainable ceiling was just one element that Cloud-9 had to keep in mind in designing the interior.

Given a free rein, the designers looked to local history and aesthetics, as they do for many of their projects. Taking a cue from Chinese heritage, the team based their concept on a traditional Qing dynasty wood-and-mirror jewellery box, also known as a 'dowry box'. In their efforts to transform the sterile environment into a warm and tactile space, they concealed the problematic overhead surface behind large circles of mirrored stainless steel, which float just below ceiling level. For wall cladding, they chose a combination of reclaimed oak and *kirei*, a sustainable substitute for wood that is similar to bamboo. Timber panelling is punctuated by porthole windows framed with red bulbs, colourfully reflecting the street life of Beijing.

WHERE **9 Dong Da Qiao Rd, Beijing, China**
OPENING **November 2013**
CLIENT **Haworth**
DESIGNER **Cloud-9 interior design (p.542)**
FLOOR AREA **675 m²**
WEBSITE **haworthxfriends.com**

MINIMUM AGE **n/a**
SIGNATURE DRINK **n/a**
PRICE OF A GLASS OF HOUSE WINE **Complimentary**
OPENING HOURS **By arrangement**
CAPACITY **50 guests**

The wood-lined space has a mirrored ceiling which expands the space upwards.

Designed as a luxurious lounge bar, the showroom is a multifunctional space in an innovative 'green building'.

Drawing on local Chinese culture for inspiration, the coffee bar references typical street-side shops in Beijing.

The designers wanted to create a warm, contrasting atmosphere through the use of wood, colour and decorative detailing.

Furniture products set in a luxurious lounge bar space

Angles for the edges of each piece of glass used for the mirror required meticulous calculation.

Numerous small details in the lounge are like parts of a jewellery box.

Horizontal wood panelling at the entrance creates a graphical pattern that contrasts with the circular window.

Prototypes led to the definitive Diamond Mirror, composed of a large number of facets, all assembled by hand.

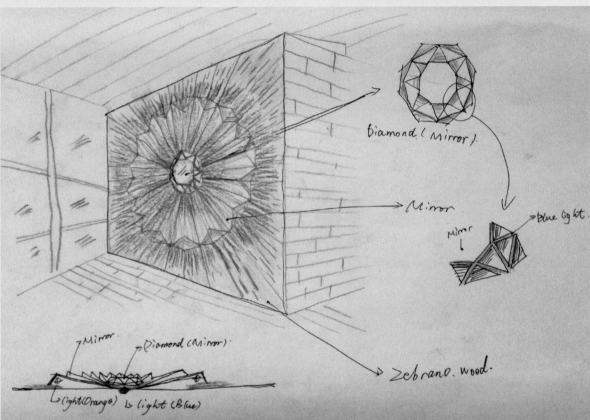

Notes accompany early sketches that detail the construction of the bespoke mirror and include coloured lighting, its source hidden from view.

The facade wall at The Club features porthole windows.

Taking a cue from Chinese heritage, local history and aesthetics

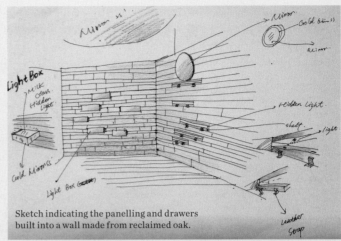

Sketch indicating the panelling and drawers built into a wall made from reclaimed oak.

The coffee bar under construction.

Mirrored, circular panels conceal the air-conditioning in the ceiling.

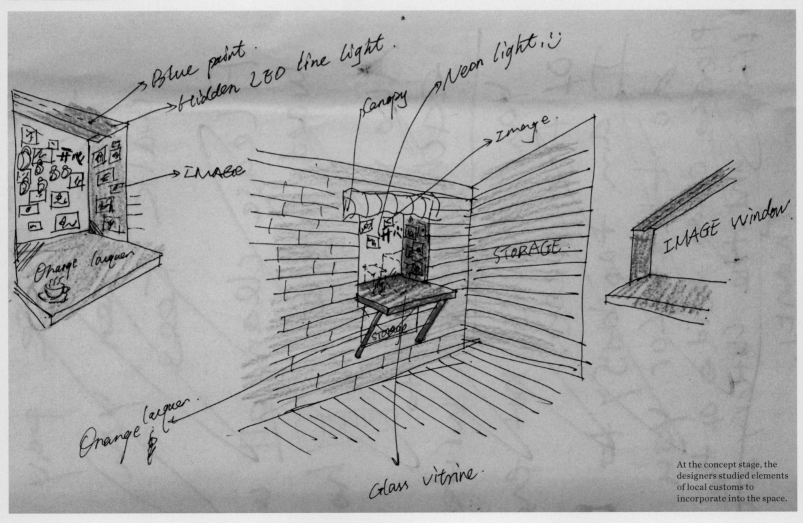

At the concept stage, the designers studied elements of local customs to incorporate into the space.

THE COLLINS

Woods Bagot

The client's aspiration for the bar was to enable a unique offering for visitors, whilst reinvigorating the local market.

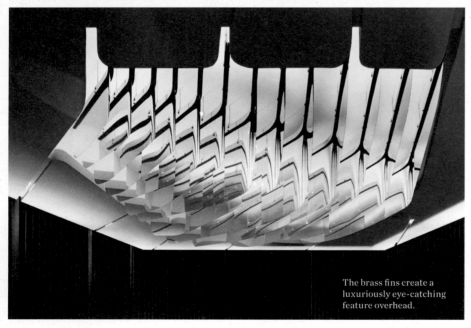

The brass fins create a luxuriously eye-catching feature overhead.

'Cocktails, but not as you know them' – this is the promise of contemporary cocktail bar The Collins, in central Adelaide. On the ground floor of the Hilton Hotel, with its prominent corner of Victoria Square in the very heart of the city, this bar certainly ticks all the boxes for location. Woods Bagot was called in to ensure that the design preserved this local context, while reaching a global level by providing a fresh, modern and urban-chic approach to a hotel bar.

Designed to stand strong as an independent offering within the building fabric of the Hilton Adelaide, glazed doors therefore open the bar to the street and welcome passing patrons. Inside, the space is divided into two distinct areas: a bright active daytime venue with a front bar that provides a sense of theatre, and a secluded cocktail lounge room that can be locked down for private functions.

Inspired by 'the classic form of a tailored suit' no less, the interiors blend precious materials – such as brass and marble – with contrasting wire-brushed, stained timber and saddle leather that promises to age and wear beautifully over time. A spectacular pattern of metallic blades on the ceiling provides a focal point as a combined bespoke art piece and lighting element.

All in all, the venue is a confident concoction of skillfully mixed elements – much like the cocktails served up behind the bar.

WHERE **233 Victoria Square, Adelaide, Australia**
OPENING **January 2013**
CLIENT **Sitehost**
DESIGNER **Woods Bagot (p.551)**
FLOOR AREA **325 m²**
WEBSITE **thecollins.com.au**

MINIMUM AGE **18**
SIGNATURE DRINK **Collins Aussie BBQ Mary**
PRICE OF A GLASS OF HOUSE WINE **AUD 12**
OPENING HOURS **Mon–Thu 16.00–00.00, Fri 15.00–01.00, Sat 16.00–01.00, Sun 16.00–22.00**
CAPACITY **115 guests**

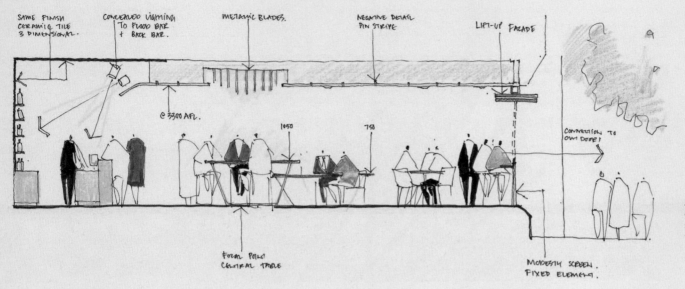

A sketch shows how the design was conceived as a series of public zones, from the street to the bar.

Design for the bar's feature screen with brass detailing.

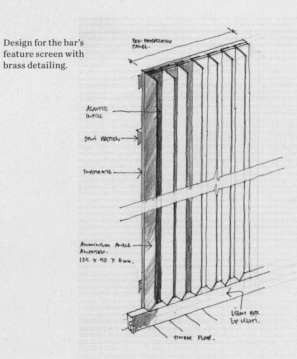

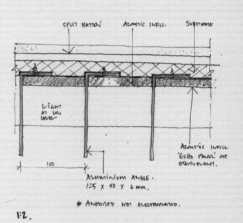

A fresh, modern and urban-chic approach to a hotel bar

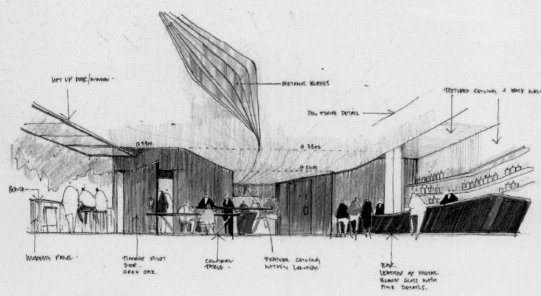

Concept sketch showing the central focus of the brass ceiling fins above the large, communal table.

Rich, dark furnishings create an intimate atmosphere.

The interior also includes solid marble, stained timber and smoked mirrors.

THE MOVEMENT CAFE

Morag Myerscough

The bespoke furniture features bright designs, hand-painted by Morag Myerscough with some of Sissay's tweets.

Myerscough's creative collaborator Luke Morgan designed the bicycle ice-cream cart.

A temporary cafe and performance space in Greenwich was put in place to provide the many visitors of the Olympic Games with an attractive venue in which to hang out. Located next to the central transport hub, it vibrantly filled a void left by demolition in an area that was being regenerated.

The colourful concept came about as a result of a public art collaboration between Morag Myerscough and poet and prolific tweeter Lemn Sissay. Myerscough designed the space based on Sissay's tweet from 27 June 2012. As there were only 16 days to construct the venue (to coincide with the opening of the Olympics), shipping containers were chosen as a base structure. Onto these metallic volumes, hand-painted plywood cladding was applied. The panels created a bright aspect, featuring a multicoloured geometric pattern and the words from Sissay's tweet. Topping it off in a quirky style was a huge cut-out, illuminated letter 'M' and a wind sock.

The furniture and fittings were designed and made by Myerscough and artist Luke Morgan, including reclaimed school laboratory worktops and cushions hand-sewn from kite fabric. A bicycle to sell locally-made ice cream was customised by Morgan as well. Around the structure, a scaffolding amphitheatre with seating area surrounded by planting, provided a place for storytelling, poetry reading and performances.

WHERE **London, United Kingdom**
OPENING **July 2012 (venue has since closed)**
CLIENT **Cathedral/The Movement**
DESIGNER **Morag Myerscough (p.547)**
FLOOR AREA **154 m²**
WEBSITE **themovementgreenwich.com**

MINIMUM AGE *n/a*
SIGNATURE DRINK *Movement Coffee*
PRICE OF A GLASS OF WINE *GBP 5*
OPENING HOURS *11.30–21.00*
CAPACITY *40 guests*

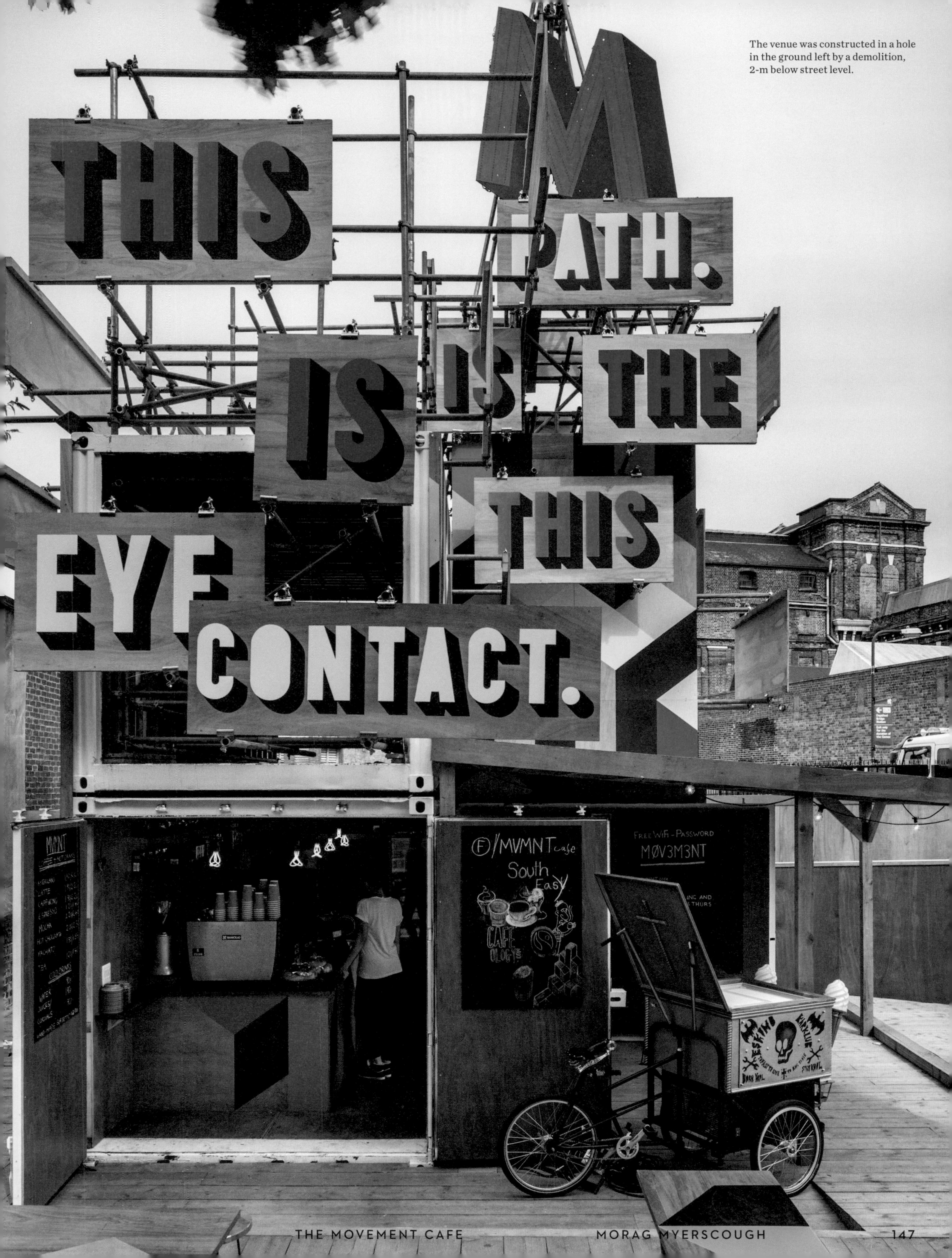

THIS IS THE EYE CONTACT. THIS IS THE PATH. THIS IS

Initial colour studies for the project.

The exterior of the cafe was clad in plywood panels, hand-painted by Myerscough and her team.

On-site installation of the panels.

The painting in progress on-site.

The bare container construction.

'This is the house.
This is the path.
This is the gate.
This is the opening.
This is the morning.
This is a person passing.
This is eye contact.'

Tweet from Lemn Sissay, 27 June 2012.

Model for the
temporary venue.

Placement of the text panels that spell
out the tweet of Lemn Sissay.

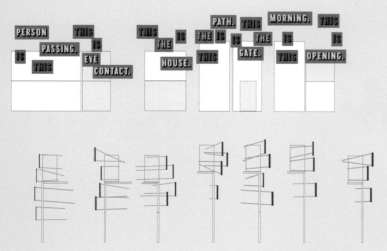

Elevation drawings of the
container construction.

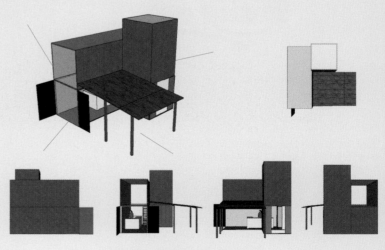

TRUTH COFFEE

Haldane Martin

The brand's retro signage sets the tone for the interior, with its copper, brass and raw steel material palette.

A steampunk theme for a coffee bar? According to designer Haldane Martin, steampunk reflects the old-world technology of coffee roasters and espresso machines – not to mention the romance of the fragrant beverage. David Donde, the man behind Truth Coffee who commissioned Haldane Martin to design his cafe, as well as the behind-the-scenes space (the headquarters of the brand), loved the idea, as it resonated strongly with his 'maverick inventor' personality. Donde, with business partner Mike Morritt-Smith, went on to physically build many of the designs Martin conjured up for the Truth Coffee interior furnishings.

The location is a three-storey, turn-of-the-century warehouse. It was first stripped back to its bare bones, revealing beautiful cast iron pillars, pine roof trusses and floors, and original stone and brick walls. Tall steel and glass doors were added to open up the ground floor facade onto busy Buitenkant Street. Most of the building's natural, aged patina was kept intact and complemented with raw steel, timber, leather, brass and copper.

The ground floor houses Truth's HQ and the cafe, its dining areas and kitchen, as well as the imposing Probat roaster machine, a barista trainee school, public event space, coffee bean warehouse, espresso machine workshop, management office and restrooms. The huge, fully functioning vintage roaster became the kingpin for the space. 'Once this was located centrally on the ground floor plan, everything else fell naturally into place,' says Martin. A leather-top bar, overstuffed armchairs, exposed copper pipes, Victorian tap levers, pull chains and floor tiles help to complete the look – with outlandish steampunk staff uniforms topping everything off.

WHERE **36 Buitenkant Street, Cape Town, South Africa**
OPENING **August 2012**
CLIENT **David Donde**
DESIGNER **Haldane Martin (p.545)**
FLOOR AREA **600 m²**
WEBSITE **truthcoffee.com**

MINIMUM AGE **n/a**
SIGNATURE DRINK **Slayer prepared flat white**
PRICE OF A COFFEE **ZAR 25**
OPENING HOURS **Mon–Thu 7.00-18.00, Fri–Sat 7.00 until late, Sun 8.00-18.00**
CAPACITY **120 guests**

The raised dining area has
steampunk dining chairs and tables,
designed specifically for Truth
Coffee HQ, with waxed steel frames
and antique leather upholstery.

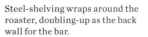
Steel-shelving wraps around the roaster, doubling-up as the back wall for the bar.

A huge, fully functioning vintage roaster is the kingpin for the space

The countertop of the bar is clad in shoe sole leather.

Custom steel shelves are backed by steel mesh.

Raw-tin pressed ceiling panels are fixed to the front of the bar.

FLOOR PLAN

1. Cafe seating area with bespoke 'saw' tables
2. Coffee bar
3. Terrace seating
4. Bike storage
5. Barista training counter
6. Communal table
7. Raised dining seating
8. Lounge area
9. Banquet seating
10. Bar
11. Coffee roaster
12. Coffee packing area
13. Kitchen
14. Barista school area
15. Workshop (with access to upstairs office)
16. Packed coffee storeroom
17. Staff lockers
18. Coffee bean storage
19. Back-of-house
20. Lavatories

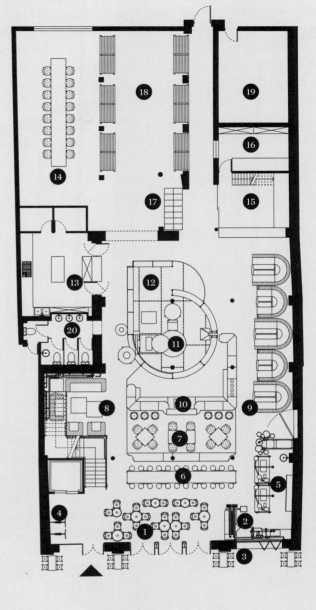

TABLE DRAWINGS

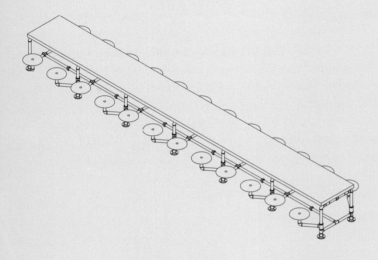

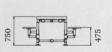

End view

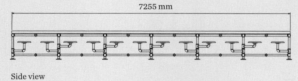

Side view

7255 mm

750   475

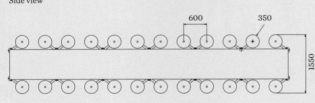

Top view

600   350

1550

Drawing of bespoke communal table with articulated swing-out stools.

FRONT ELEVATION

The custom-cog tables in the cafe are made from zinc-plated steel tops and cast iron flanges and pipes.

Custom details fit in with the steampunk theme.

Bathrooms have waxed raw-steel partitions, with Victorian tiles and brass basins on copper stands.

Custom details add to the sci-fi atmosphere

The bespoke table and stools are made from Oregon pine reclaimed from the building's stripped-out ceilings.

TURKISH AIRLINES CIP LOUNGE

Autoban

With the aim of taking the pre-flight experience to a higher level for commercial clients, Autoban's CIP Lounge for Turkey's national airline sets out to embody Turkish hospitality at its best, in a relaxed and contemporary setting.

For the design, the office returned to the concept of *kervansaray* – the traditional Turkish roadside inn where travellers and merchants once rested on their journeys. The designers also revisited the curvy domes of Istanbul's many mosques and the unique architecture of the Grand Bazaar. Translating the arcade system of such traditional architecture into modern terms resulted in a series of bubble-like portals, which create a structure-within-a-structure in the existing shell of the airport hall. This substructure brings a more human scale to the gigantic airport and lends warmth to the space.

The 5-m-high spherical pods divide the space into sections while maintaining open views of the rest of the lounge and so providing a sense of continuity. Each of these pods serves a specific purpose: there's a library, restaurant, tea garden, piano area, screening room, meeting room, kids' playground and rest rooms. From the entrance, they are organised in order of the priority of passenger needs.

The black elements that frame the modules hide all the mechanical and electrical systems, while bringing a visual balance to the all-white backdrop of the arches. Autoban also installed a white cage featuring a traditional Turkish Seljuk pattern and covered one of the concave walls with a map of the world. Wood floors and pieces of Autoban's signature furniture collection, such as the Throne chairs and the Cloud table, complete the picture.

As passengers begin their journey around the globe (or stop-off in transit), they can catch up in the 'news lounge' portal on world happenings.

WHERE **Istanbul Atatürk Airport, Turkey**
OPENING **July 2011**
CLIENT **Turkish Do&Co**
DESIGNER **Autoban (p.541)**
FLOOR AREA **4200 m²**
WEBSITE **turkishairlines.com**

MINIMUM AGE **n/a**
SIGNATURE DRINK **Turkish coffee**
PRICE OF A GLASS OF HOUSE WINE **Complimentary**
OPENING HOURS **24/7**
CAPACITY **2000 guests daily**

Spherical cut-outs in the domes allow for a flowing series of interconnecting spaces.

Delicate Ottoman patterns lend lightness to a number of the portal structures.

The designers revisited the curvy domes of Istanbul's many mosques

The initial sketch of the concept portrays a kaleidoscopic spherical portal.

CONCEPT

The design scheme concept started with a sphere that gradually morphed into a pod-like portal.

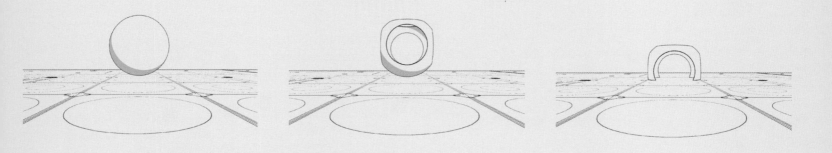

DRAWINGS

A series of interconnecting portals create a visual illusion within the vast interior of the airport, each one is a new space to be discovered.

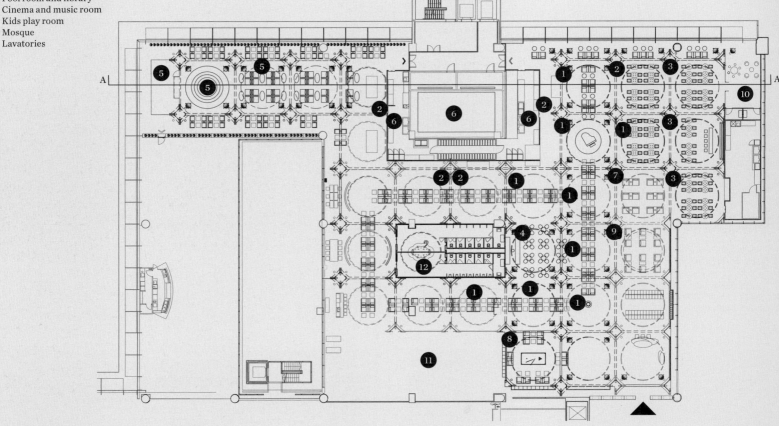

5-m-high spherical pods divide the space into sections while maintaining open views of the rest of the lounge

SECTION A

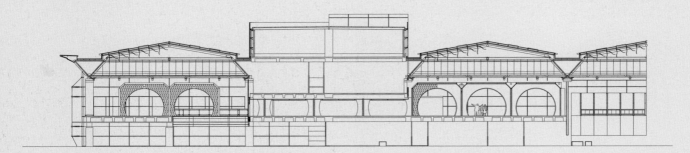

The portals bring the airport's gigantic proportions to a more human level.

One space serves as a mini-cinema, with surfaces upholstered with leather and suede for acoustic purposes.

VERSUZ

Pinkeye

The concrete appears to have been chiselled away specifically to create a light feature to highlight the bottles on display.

For the Versuz club in Hasselt, Pinkeye was called on to design a trio of bars, each one sponsored by a different drinks brand – Coca-Cola in cooperation with Bacardi, Stella Artois and Jupiler – and each one requiring its own distinctive look.

The Coca-Cola Bacardi bar links the entrance lobby of the club with the main hall and features a remarkable chandelier – made from brass tubes and sphere-shaped lights which stands over the black and gold facetted oval-sculpted bar like a radiant crown.

Further down the main hall, the Stella Artois bar displays oversized golden lamps and a mirrored back wall incorporating a diamante pattern. The giant lamps have bases shaped like the classic Stella chalice glass and appear to be emitting a golden glow, radiating a golden circular pattern on the black expanse of the bar counter below. The back wall of facetted cut mirrors also has integrated displays for 360-degree-lit Stella bottles. The mirror pattern is repeated on the ceiling, with multiple reflections recurring seemingly into infinity.

The Jupiler bar is located in the 'bunker hall' of the club and exudes the brand's earthy masculine values. The part of the bar that catches the eye is the concrete form that rises above the heads of customers like a rocky outcrop, running all the way up to the balcony. The looming shape appears to have been chiselled out of one piece of concrete into seven blocks with the Jupiler bull embossed across the front of them. The bar itself is clad with Corten steel to create a colour contrast with the ceiling – completing Pinkeye's achievement in shaping three very different, but equally high-impact spaces.

WHERE **Gouverneur Verwilghensingel 70, Hasselt, Belgium**
OPENING **December 2013**
CLIENT **Yves Smolders**
DESIGNER **Pinkeye (p.548)**
FLOOR AREA **3100 m²**
WEBSITE **versuz.be**

MINIMUM AGE **18**
SIGNATURE DRINK **n/a**
PRICE OF A GLASS OF HOUSE WINE **n/a**
OPENING HOURS **Thu 23.00-06.00, Sat 22.00-07.00, Mon 23.00-06.00**
CAPACITY **3000 guests**

With its radiant solar crown, this bar is like a shining beacon, giving it star appeal.

A golden glow emanates from the Stella bar.

Angular shapes carve
out an imposing volume.

Three bars, three brands, three dramatic looks

Painted metalwork shaped into
the diamante pattern reflect the
facetted cut mirrors behind.

JUPILER BAR ELEVATION

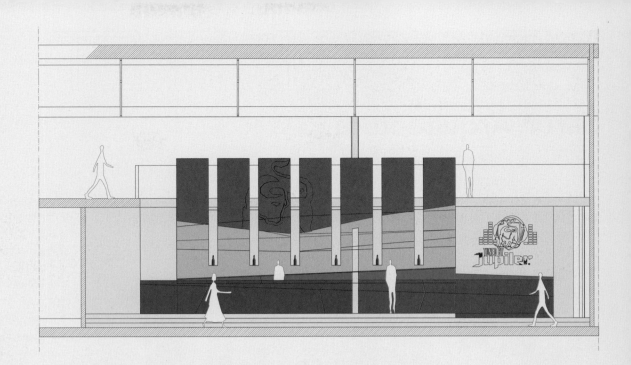

CCB BAR ELEVATION

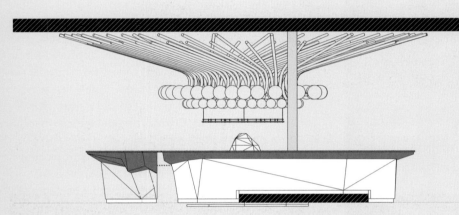

CCB BAR DRAWING

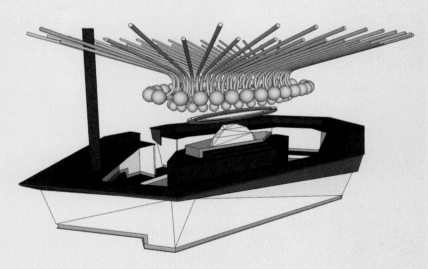

STELLA ARTOIS BAR ELEVATION

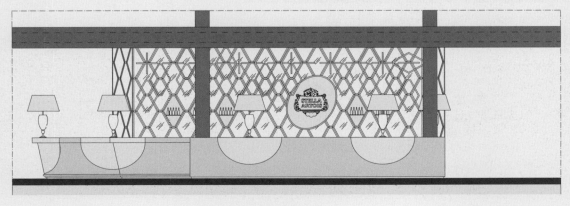

VEX CABARET

Sarur Arquitectura

Bespoke furniture in oak and velvet suggest
oversized chess pieces and baroque footstools.

Commissioned by a private investor to design a new Mexico City nightspot, Sarur Arquitectura aimed to make Vex Cabaret exclusive and elegant, while diverging from the classic idea of a nightclub. Approaching the main entrance, which is reminiscent of a lonely alley, the visitor seems to encounter a glamorous club from the past, now rediscovered for a new age, as several intricate layers of design are grafted one onto another.

The design team – inspired by the dramatic qualities of circuses, carousels, Parisian cabaret and theatre – achieved a fine equilibrium between modern and antique. Careful attention is paid to creating a sense of refinement, like that of 'old money'. The custom-made furniture manufactured in solid oak and thick floral tapestry is suggestive of heavy baroque thrones and blown-up chess pieces, while contrasting amicably with a sleek metallic installation wall – made up of a collection of fridges – that changes colour dramatically in a dizzying waltz of lights.

However, the main features of the venue are the restored carousel horses scattered throughout the space. Lacquered in black and suspended on golden poles as if in mid-leap, each one acts as a platform around which dancers can release their inhibitions. A further horse, hanging from the ceiling and cloaked in mirrors in disco-ball fashion, cries out to be the centre of attention.

An intense, saturated colour palette of red, fuchsia, purple and blue mixes with metallic elements such as the asymmetric, gold covered DJ stand. It's an exaggerated and rococo mix that adds up to an astonishing anachronistic space.

WHERE **Bosques de las Lomas, Mexico City, Mexico**
OPENING **December 2012**
CLIENT **Vex Cabaret**
DESIGNER **Sarur Arquitectura (p.549)**
FLOOR AREA **380 m²**
WEBSITE **n/a**

MINIMUM AGE **25**
SIGNATURE DRINK *Old-School Champagne Cocktail*
PRICE OF A GLASS OF HOUSE WINE **USD 10**
OPENING HOURS **23.00–05.00**
CAPACITY **300 guests**

Rich, brocade fabrics in jewel-bright shades bring the antique-looking sofas up to date.

An exaggerated mix that adds up to an astonishing anachronistic space

Restored carousel horses in black lacquer prance through the space.

DRINK

Behind the bar, a rainbow wall of fridges for drinks changes colour in a dazzling light show.

FLOOR PLAN

1 Welcome desk
2 Club/dance area
3 Seating area
4 DJ booth
5 Bar
6 VIP area
7 Kitchen
8 Storage
9 Lavatories

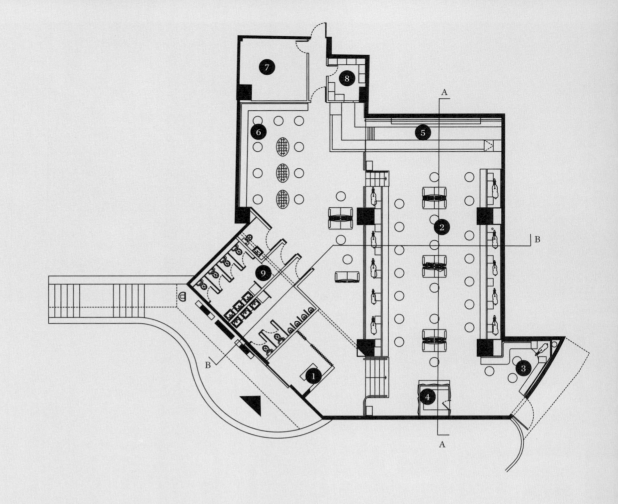

SECTION A

SECTION B

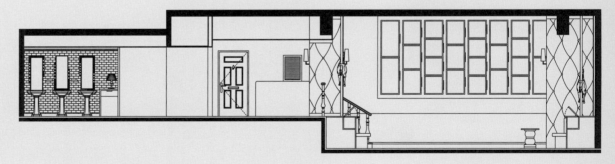

A club inspired by circuses, cabaret and all things theatrical

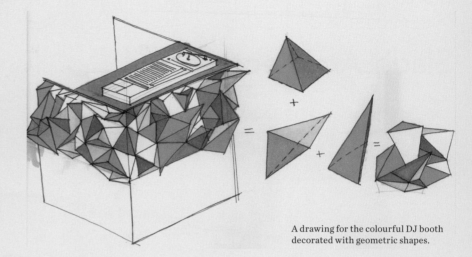

Sketch for the wall of
technicolour fridges
behind the bar.

A drawing for the colourful DJ booth
decorated with geometric shapes.

The music emanates from a booth
located at one end of the club.

A line drawing indicates
the position of the horses.

One of the many restored carousel
horses that populate the space.

VIRGIN ATLANTIC CLUBHOUSE AT JFK

Slade Architecture

Access to the luxurious clubhouse is exclusive
to Virgin Atlantic upper-class passengers.

The sinuous, walnut slatted-wall separates
off the quiet lounge, making a secluded space.

The Virgin Atlantic Clubhouse at JFK Airport functions as a private members club, boutique hotel lobby, restaurant and (in the evening) chic bar. Bounded on two sides by expansive views over the jet ways, with a direct view of the iconic TWA terminal, the lounge picks up on the glamour of 1960s air travel.

Slade Architecture collaborated with Virgin Atlantic's in-house design team to create distinct areas for different passenger activities and interactions, organised in acoustic and temporal levels: there are quiet and talking areas, while activities that require less time are closer to the entrance.

Cloud shaped in plan, the central cocktail lounge is enclosed by a diaphanous, curving screen of stainless steel rods and walnut fins. The rods and fins mediate views and create an internal skyline. At the heart of the lounge, 2000 powder-coated, golden cylinders hang from the ceiling, creating a glowing, sculptural topography.

Furnishings help define the character of each area. There are custom grey, amorphous pebble sofas and a red ball sofa forming a seating landscape in the cocktail lounge. The talking area includes the restaurant and is furnished to encourage groups and interaction. The quiet area emphasises individual seating. Aluminium walls perforated with a pixelated cloud pattern are cut out to create 'floating' seating pods. Spa and hair salons complete the amenities.

Details reinforce the 'uptown' theme of the lounge. Two custom wallpapers portray New York icons: the Chrysler Building and the Empire State Building create one pattern; the other features hot-dog cart punctuated by red apples. In the bathrooms, white subway tiles and large-scale black-and-white Sanborn maps of New York City complete the picture.

WHERE **JFK Airport, Terminal 4, United States**
OPENING **February 2012**
CLIENT **Virgin Atlantic Airways**
DESIGNER **Slade Architecture (p.549)**
FLOOR AREA **1000 m²**
WEBSITE **virgin-atlantic.com**

MINIMUM AGE **n/a**
SIGNATURE DRINK **Virgin Redhead cocktail**
PRICE OF A GLASS OF HOUSE WINE **Complimentary**
OPENING HOURS **24/7**
CAPACITY **220 guests**

Guests move through the
curvaceous cocktail lounge in
a rhythmic, syncopated flow.

Brushed stainless-steel rods create a see-through partition.

Subway maps adorn the bathroom walls.

The lounge evokes the glamour of 1960s air travel

Flow Chairs in grey fabric are positioned alongside the perforated metallic walls with their cosy seating niches.

Designer furniture in the central lounge accompanies bespoke items, such as the spherical red-ball sofa.

The 'talking lounge' area includes the restaurant and is furnished to encourage groups and interaction.

VIRGIN ATLANTIC CLUBHOUSE AT NEWARK

Slade Architecture

The bar's display cabinet is a central feature, standing proud like a giant crystal-cut diamond.

The Virgin Atlantic Clubhouse at Newark Airport brings together New York City's downtown flair and the airline's warmth and individuality. Slade Architecture collaborated with Virgin Atlantic's in-house design team to realise a space that lives and breathes lower Manhattan – evoking Soho boutiques, Tribeca lofts and Meatpacking District chic.

A constellation of sparkling pinpoint lights draws guests into the sculpted entrance, with its specular reception desk, which acts as an extended decompression zone between the busy terminal and the relaxed luxury inside the clubhouse. The interior is organised around a facetted bar that rises in the centre of the lounge, culminating in a crystalline bottle display under the central skylight.

A series of distinct, downtown-inspired spaces revolve around the bar. Each space references an iconic downtown typology: cafe, theatre, art gallery, restaurant, club, bar and lounge. Grab a coffee and read a book or magazine in the wood-lined cafe. Venture into the curtain-wrapped screening room to catch the latest arthouse video. Curl up in an upholstered pod, carved into the protective facetted concrete of the passion pit. Pull up to the bar at the liquid lounge. Sit down for a delicious meal in the gallery-like brasserie. Or simply catch up on your email or listen to music in the colourful origami lounge.

Art is central to the downtown vibe, so digital finger paintings of lower Manhattan, commissioned from New York artist Jorge Colombo, animate the cafe. The brasserie features three mixed media works by New York artist Garrett Pruter, inspired by discarded travel photographs found in various downtown junk shops. Works by Kate Hazell, Galia Rybitskaya, Mille Marotta and Jonny Moss are displayed throughout the space.

WHERE **Newark Airport, Terminal B, United States**
OPENING **November 2012**
CLIENT **Virgin Atlantic Airways**
DESIGNER **Slade Architecture (p.549)**
FLOOR AREA **500 m²**
WEBSITE **virgin-atlantic.com**

MINIMUM AGE **n/a**
SIGNATURE DRINK **Virgin Redhead cocktail**
PRICE OF A GLASS OF HOUSE WINE **Complimentary**
OPENING HOURS **24/7**
CAPACITY **130 guests**

A first-class sparkle welcomes guests in the reception area, with its glossy-black wall tiles and recycled-glass terrazzo flooring.

Summer berry hues pop out in the passion pit, with its facetted concrete walls in folded forms.

Big Apple references abound, with graffiti-inspired wallpaper leading to the bathrooms.

A flash of colour comes in the form of illuminated resin sinks.

The lounge lives and breathes lower Manhattan

The brasserie adopts a gallery style, with New York art on show.

Guests can wile away the hours at the chic cocktail bar.

A regular schedule of movies are screened in the cinema zone.

WASBAR

Pinkeye

Socialising is central to the concept, as is washing.

Adding a new dimension to the phrase 'good clean fun', Wasbar combines a bar with a laundry salon, so young folk can get their routine chores done whilst socialising at the same time. Pinkeye, the studio called in to do the design, decided that a concept like this required a unique setting. A fun and eclectic mix of vintage furniture, custom objects and, naturally, washing machines, was the result.

The design team notably opted to put the washing machines on full display, instead of trying to hide them. A blue-tiled bar balances the rows of washers and dryers. The main goal was to create a 'living room' feel throughout the entire space, with custom decorations being inspired by all things laundry-related. The second-hand furniture and one-off fixtures take the concept of upcycling to heart: lamp shades are created from the cheapest wire clothes hangers and old cabinet drawers from second-hand stores are fastened to the walls to provide frames for objects and the menu boards.

The designers admit they faced a couple of tough challenges. On a technical level, a laundromat needs a lot of plumbing, and all of this had to somehow be concealed. In design terms, Pinkeye reckoned that it was crucial to devise a really strong identity for Wasbar, as others would quickly copy the idea. The design studio created the graphic identity as well as the interior concept using a jolly, pastel colour palette and the upcycled drawer frames as a motif.

WHERE **Graaf Van Egmontstraat, Antwerp, Belgium**
OPENING **August 2013**
CLIENT **Make Them Talk**
DESIGNER **Pinkeye (p.548)**
FLOOR AREA **130 m²**
WEBSITE **wasbar.com**

MINIMUM AGE **n/a**
SIGNATURE DRINK **Aperitivo Prosecco**
PRICE OF A REGULAR COFFEE **EUR 3**
OPENING HOURS **Mon–Fri 10.00–22.00, Sat–Sun 10.00–18.00**
CAPACITY **55 guests**

The bar is covered with tiles from Winckelmans, their colours picked out in the painted recycled chairs.

A laundry salon that combines routine chores with socialising

Old drawers are upcycled into frames above the washing machines.

The Wasbar logo makes its mission clear.

WHITE RABBIT
Genesin Studio

The birdcage DJ booth, sits between the private ensuite VIP area and the mirror-maze dance floor.

For a club launched by three friends, the brief to design office Genesin Studio was simple: 'We want a fun environment, serving great drinks and solid house music!' The name White Rabbit quickly came up in a meeting, introducing an *Alice in Wonderland* theme of a journey through a mind-altering environment.

The project itself proved to be something of an interesting trip. The existing site was an old nightclub and the bar was partially reused and remodelled to save money. The rest of the site was demolished, which was unfortunate for the designers, 'We came into some costly base building and structural repairs that we had no choice but to fix,' says Ryan Genesin. 'After that, the budget was very strategically allocated to ensure we were still on track.'

Despite these complications, the project lives up to its intention to express all sorts of fun. The space carries a designed narrative all the way from the rabbit warren mirror-maze entrance; through the tea-garden lounge with patterned botanical upholstered fabrics and green carpet; past the tropical cabana bar with upholstered ceiling and polished brass shelf and blue-tiled bartop; and onto the enchanted dance-floor with its mirror-web wall.

'White Rabbit offers a progressive experience starting from the entry all the way to the toilets,' says designer Ryan Genesin. 'From drinking champagne in tea cups in the tea-garden lounge, to dancing or entertaining mates in the VIP suite with its private butler, this club offers every level of fun to patrons.'

WHERE **Adelaide, Australia**
OPENING **December 2012 (venue has since closed)**
CLIENT **n/a**
DESIGNER **Genesin Studio (p.545)**
FLOOR AREA **300 m²**
WEBSITE **whiterabbitdisco.com.au**

MINIMUM AGE **18**
SIGNATURE DRINK *Alice Iced Tea*
PRICE OF A GLASS OF HOUSE WINE **AUD 9**
OPENING HOURS **21.00–05.00**
CAPACITY **250 guests**

If in need of a rest from dancing, guests can lounge on the oversized furniture in the 'green room'.

Thonet bentwood bar stools have
been painted a vibrant colour.

The *Alice in Wonderland* theme imagines a journey through a mind-altering environment

White-painted lattice lines the walls, custom-made from 70 x 9 mm timber.

Fringe benefits: retro lighting adds further eccentricity.

A comic-strip mural dorns one wall behind an imitation hedge.

Patrons can drink champagne from tea cups in a tea-garden lounge

A white tiered, scalloped pelmet is an eye-catching statement in the bathroom.

The club's logo was applied in a graffiti style around the venue.

Clubbers encounter a surreal tableau of homely furnishings, which adds to the mind-bending concept.

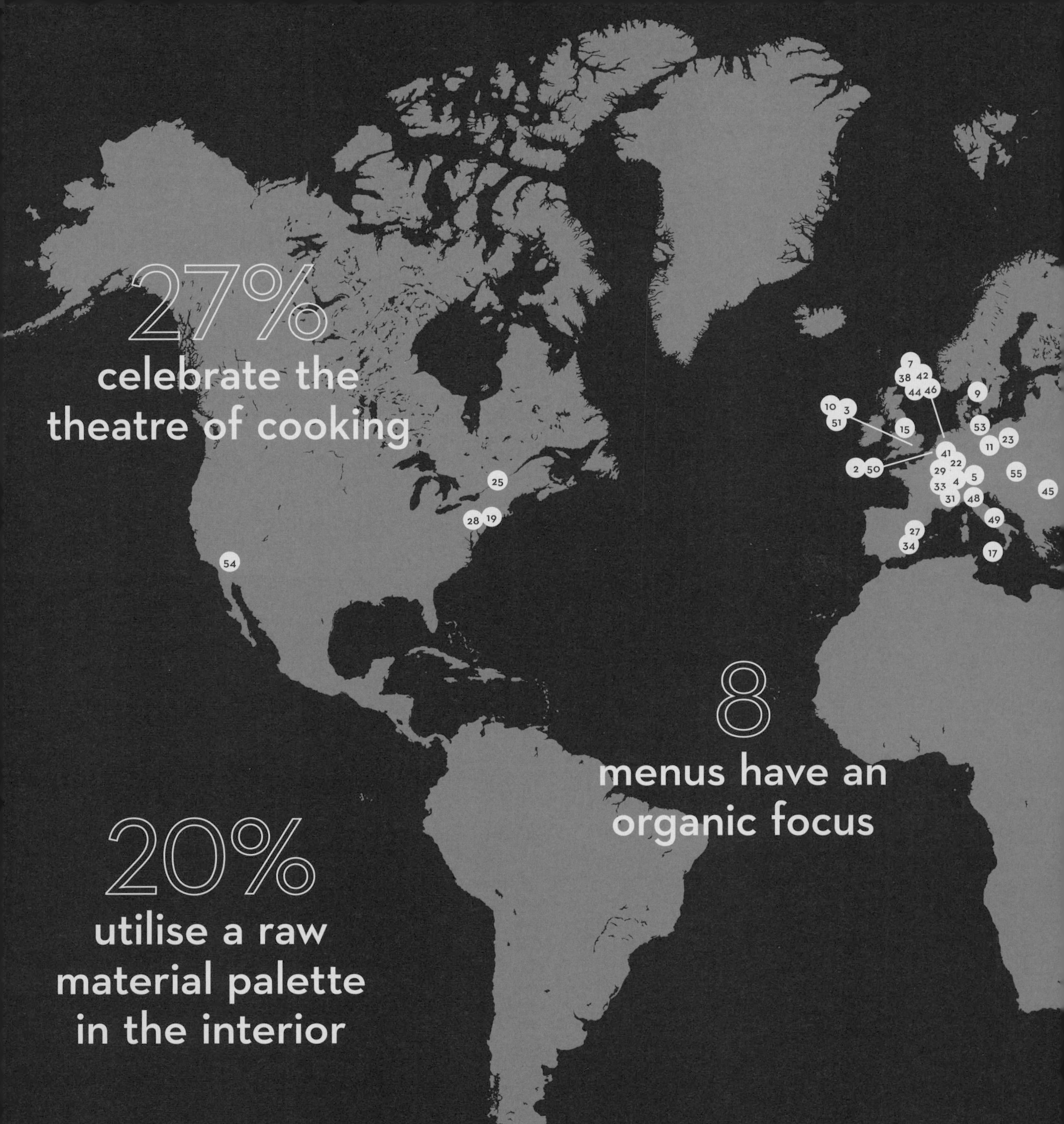

27%
celebrate the theatre of cooking

20%
utilise a raw material palette in the interior

8
menus have an organic focus

EAT

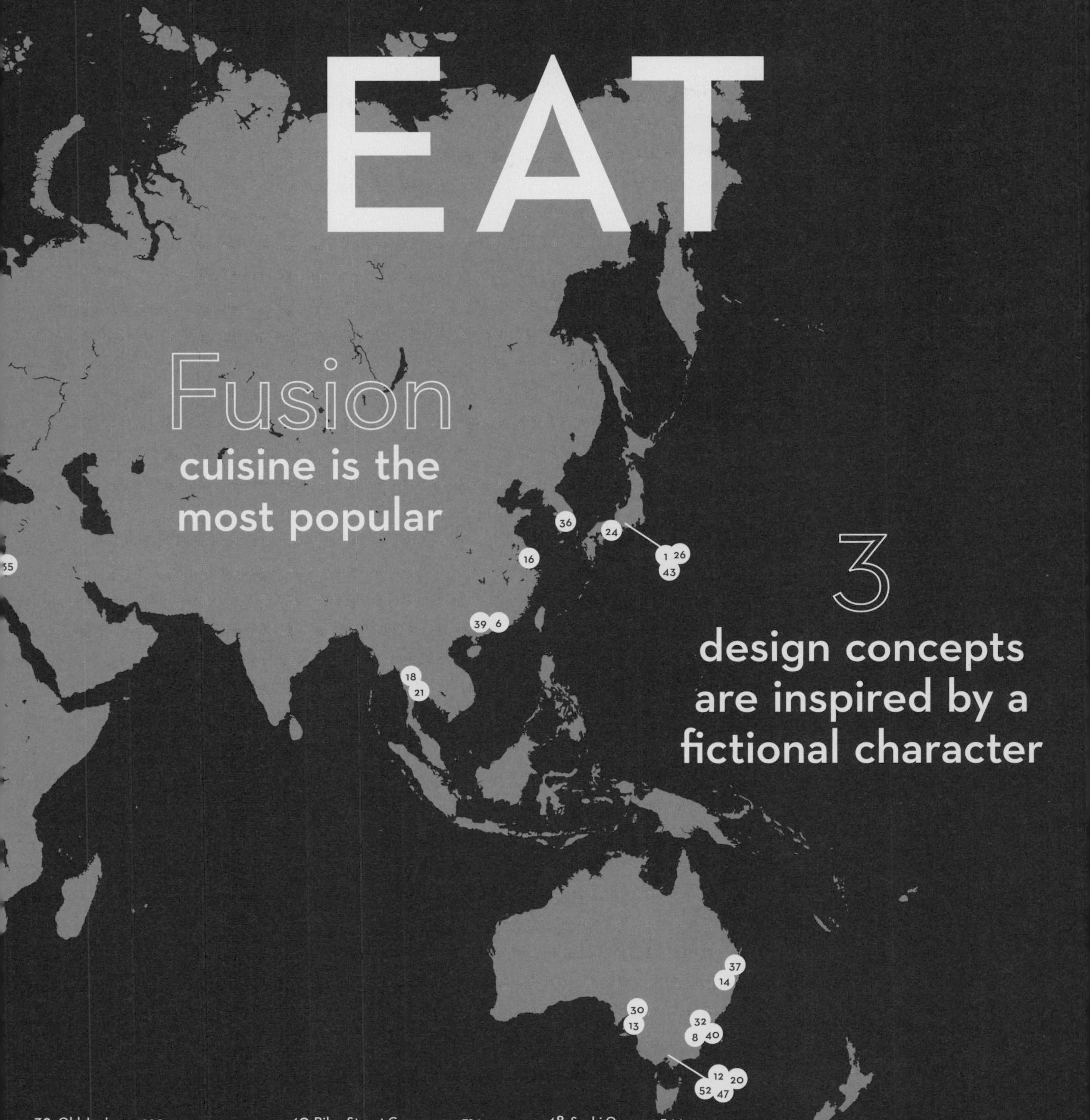

Fusion
cuisine is the
most popular

3
design concepts
are inspired by a
fictional character

ARCANA TOKYO KARATO

brownbag lab.

A message from the proprietor is stencilled on the wall in a simple format, with the words – aspiring to the great tradition of healthy food – forming an outline of his facial profile.

For this restaurant offering a new kind of French cuisine with the theme of 'vegetable gastronomy', the brownbag lab. design team came up with the concept of a Japanese *auberge*. This combined the four seasons and references to nature, especially the forests and pristine natural scenery of Japan's Izu peninsula.

The space therefore has natural and simple materials: stone slate and rich, glossy walnut flooring, with stainless steel for the kitchen. The table settings are kept simple and white, in order to highlight the food, while the chairs are given four different shades of warm grey.

The decorative details that accentuate the space are designed with traditional Japanese craftsmanship in mind. At the entrance, visitors are greeted by a green acrylic installation of big bubbles, meant to evoke both water and forest plants. The partition panel that divides up the dining area is embellished with an *ayasugibori* pattern, a kind of herringbone carving. The chef's table is made of a stunningly beautiful solid wood – Japanese zelkova (a type of elm) – that is found in Izu's forests. In the main dining area, there are original acrylic paintings with Izu's four seasons as a theme, created by Kyoto artist Beniko Motonaga. Finally, behind the bar, a textured wall features a jaunty bottle-shaped relief pattern crafted by Japanese artisans.

Outside on the terrace, circular tables constructed around growing trees and delicate lighting create a fairy-tale atmosphere and add to the varying moods and possibilities of this very versatile space. Two private rooms, which can be used separately or in combination, further extend the options.

WHERE **JP Tower Kitte 6F, Tokyo, Japan**
OPENING **March 2013**
CLIENT **Asada**
DESIGNER **brownbag lab. (p.541)**
FLOOR AREA **405 m²**
WEBSITE **arcana.co.jp**

AVERAGE PRICE OF MAIN COURSE **JPY 6400**
TYPE OF KITCHEN **Modern French cuisine**
OPENING HOURS **Mon–Sat 11.00–16.00, 18.00–23.00, Sun 18.00–23.00**
CAPACITY **150 seats**

The chef's table is made from a solid piece of Japanese zelkova wood, one of the references to nature that recurs in the design of the restaurant.

The water-inspired bubble theme is evident in the glass doors of the entrance, as well as in the bottle-green installation that illuminates the interior.

One of the four original acrylic paintings by Kyoto artist Beniko Motonaga is like a waterfall cascading behind the diners.

The terrace is like an 'enchanted forest', with circular tables placed around growing trees with soft lighting adding to the atmosphere.

In a fairly minimal interior, wine shelves assume a decorative role.

Decorative details display traditional Japanese craftsmanship

The screen at the far end of the dining room is embellished with a Japanese-style herringbone carving.

BAR MARIE
Creneau International

Words figure prominently in this canteen for a publishing company in Belgium, as do magazines – with one wall made entirely of back issues.

For media company Sanoma Belgium, Creneau International set out to design a canteen/bar with the fluid feel of a magazine – conveying the same blend of storytelling and inspiration. In order to reference the idea of looking through the different sections in a magazine, the designers created a variety of zones in the space, which serves company staff and visitors.

There's a 'gossip lounge', where you can chat without being disturbed, and a 'home zone' which is a relaxed, lounge space. The 'meet and greet' area has a long table for large or formal gatherings, and in the centre of the whole thing is a very visual focal point: the 'greenhouse', a wooden frame structure sheltering a collection of plants and herbs. Finally, for good old-fashioned cosiness, there is the 'DIY' zone.

Graphic and typographic elements are used throughout the collage-like space to further the magazine metaphor, and there are even accessories that visitors can actually buy. The tables and chairs are vintage design items, while the rugs are from a local manufacturer. The meet and greet area is separated from the rest of the space by a custom-made tapestry curtain, in a thick jacquard fabric in a striking design, custom made by the Textilelab in Tilburg. The bar itself is finished with the Dtile system: ceramic tiles in undulating forms themselves resembling textiles. The finishing touch is the food – fresh, healthy and mostly organic. Like the space itself, it suggests anything but a classic media cafe.

WHERE **Stationstraat 55, Mechelen, Belgium**
OPENING **September 2013**
CLIENT **Sanoma Media Belgium**
DESIGNER **Creneau International (p.542)**
FLOOR AREA **370 m²**
WEBSITE **barmarie.be**

AVERAGE PRICE OF MAIN COURSE *EUR 10-15*
TYPE OF KITCHEN *Organic, healthy*
OPENING HOURS *Mon–Fri 8.30-17.30*
CAPACITY *70 seats*

The focal 'greenhouse' breathes life and energy into the space thanks to its central purpose of sheltering a range of plants.

The food and beverage bar is unusually sinuous for a tiled object (courtesy of the Dtile system).

The informal space is dotted with different zones, the 'meet and greet' area having a blackboard wall and a sign that appears to invite patrons to apply their own chalk creations.

PLEASE DO WRITE

THE ONES WHO THINK THEY ARE CRAZY ENOUGH TO CHANGE THE WORLD, ARE THE ONES WHO DO.

A collage-like space with the fluid feel of a magazine

The raised 'gossip lounge' is laid out with retro furniture positioned so you can grab a coffee and have a good natter.

Much of the space is furnished with second-hand items and quirky thrift-store finds.

Text statements supply food for thought.

BARNYARD
Brinkworth

A material palette that could have been lifted straight from a farm includes distressed corrugated metal used for the walls.

Drinks can be served in old milk bottles, personalised with the Barnyard logo.

Barnyard is the latest project from Ollie Dabbous and his business partner Oskar Kinberg. Following the success of their Brinkworth-designed restaurant Dabbous, the duo decided to welcome back the studio to create a concept for this new eatery also. The food is inspired by the nostalgia of traditional farming environments and the decor took on a definite metallic theme once again.

The design was developed to suit the menu of simple yet exquisitely made British dishes and together they create a distinctive and easy dining experience. The whole restaurant is clad with various materials commonly found in lightweight farm buildings, such as old (in fact, rusty) corrugated metal sheets and reclaimed timber panelling. These materials are not often used in a restaurant, but work well with this concept, adding plenty of texture to the interior, as well as a rustic vibe that's distinctly rough around the edges.

High bench tables and stools in the front area create a welcoming and social space, and wooden booth style seating has been positioned to the rear on a mezzanine level.

Food is served in a style fitting with the interior vibe – on enamelled metal white and blue plates, while drinks are presented in old milk bottles. It all helps to emphasise the idiosyncratic, almost outdoor mood of the venue. A real-life tree, planted within the staircase that sits in between the bar and the mezzanine area, contributes to the overall rural aesthetic of the concept.

WHERE **18 Charlotte Street, London, United Kingdom**
OPENING **March 2014**
CLIENT **Ollie Dabbous and Oskar Kinberg**
DESIGNER **Brinkworth (p.541)**
FLOOR AREA **163 m²**
WEBSITE **barnyard-london.com**

AVERAGE PRICE OF MAIN COURSE **GBP 12**
TYPE OF KITCHEN **Modern British**
OPENING HOURS **Mon–Sat 12.00–00.00, Sun 12.00–16.00**
CAPACITY **32 seats**

The rustic space uses reclaimed planks for the tables and some seats are made from oil drums.

The bare industrial-style lighting fits perfectly with the design concept.

BERUFSSCHUL-
ZENTRUM
FRIEDRICHSHAFEN

atelier 522

The writing is literally on the wall at
the cafeteria of the vocational school of
Friedrichshafen on Lake Constance, in the
form of intriguing facts – such as 'lemons
swim, limes sink'. Fun trivia like this, painted
onto the walls, is part of the concept from
atelier 522, which brought the cafeteria back
to life (it had burnt down in 2012).

The idea was to create a social space
that appeals to students and goes beyond the
actual purpose of a cafeteria. The new space
was designed to be the centre of school life,
where people can eat, meet and relax. Like the
menu, the atmosphere offers variation. There
are 48 seats outside, while indoors, there are
several seating options: small, individual
seating areas offer peace and quiet, there are
regular tables for lunch meetings with friends
and colleagues, and a very large table for
spontaneous get-togethers. Varied furniture
and lighting creates a lively effect. A focal
point is the blackboard-style bar for food
and beverages.

The new cafeteria can seat twice as
many guests as the previous one, but five
cash registers have been integrated into the
concept to ensure a smooth, fast check-out
process. Throughout, a neutral colour
palette contributes a restful feeling to the
often busy space.

All in all, this interior shakes off the
old-fashioned, dusty school atmosphere to
become a space of social interaction.

Seating options for smaller groups
contribute to the flexibility of the space,
with blackboard walls an eye-catching
feature of the cafeteria.

WHERE **Steinbeisstrasse, Friedrichshafen, Germany**
OPENING **April 2013**
CLIENT **Landratsamt Bodenseekreis**
DESIGNER **Atelier 522 (p.541)**
FLOOR AREA **365 m²**
WEBSITE **atelier522.com**

AVERAGE PRICE OF MAIN COURSE **EUR 3.50**
TYPE OF KITCHEN **Snacks, pastries and lunch specials**
OPENING HOURS **Not open to the public**
CAPACITY **200 seats**

Students can sit at the long, central table on
Tabouret Haut natural wood stools, with
Bolich pendant lights hanging overhead.

BUSINESS CLUB ALLIANZ ARENA

Clemens Bachmann Architekten

Clemens Bachmann (head of design), Ben Rinkens (project leader) and Nuno Mendes (project architect) worked on the interior; the food concept is by Area One.

When Clemens Bachmann Architekten was called in for the renovation and redesign of the Business Club in the Allianz Arena, the football stadium of FC Bayern München, the team had a hard act to follow: the original space was designed by Herzog de Meuron. After 7 years running, however, the interior design needed a fresh look. The club is at the heart of the dining experience for visitors to the stadium, with a total floor area of 3500 m².

The design team decided to replace the original, monumental food counters by smaller units, which are intended to bring to mind contemporary market stalls. By repeating these elements across the area, the designers gave the space a different rhythm and a more intimate quality. Highlighted by a unique lighting concept, these individual islands invite guests to enjoy the experience of watching their food being prepared and served.

The counters are covered by wavy wooden panels, which give a dynamic feel to the space and, say the designers, reflect the ever-changing emotions that, as every fan knows, can be experienced during a football match. The waves with their different sizes and curved profiles cut across each other horizontally and create a strongly 3D image. The smooth, neutral colour provides a modest yet effective backdrop for the food and beverages.

Round tables and pillars surround the counter islands, continuing the curved theme and ensuring that the space continues to flow. While the floor is wood, the ceiling offers a different texture and warm, metallic surface, with rounded forms once again creating a smooth and eye-catching impression. Sleek furniture by Rolf Benz is the finishing touch.

WHERE **Werner-Heisenberg-Allee 25, Munich, Germany**
OPENING **August 2013**
CLIENT **Allianz Arena München**
DESIGNER **Clemens Bachmann Architekten (p.542)**
FLOOR AREA **3500 m²**
WEBSITE **allianz-arena.de**

AVERAGE PRICE OF MAIN COURSE **n/a**
TYPE OF KITCHEN **European/speciality dishes**
OPENING HOURS **Open at match time**
CAPACITY **2200 seats**

Members of the club can dine in the vast space at any time of day when there is a match on, with all food included in the ticket price.

The metallic gold installation overhead is a sight to behold, covering the full expanse of the ceiling across the 3500-m² space.

The designers replaced the original, imposing
food counter with smaller units which are
reminiscent of little market stalls.

The service islands invite guests to get an intensive experience of food preparation.

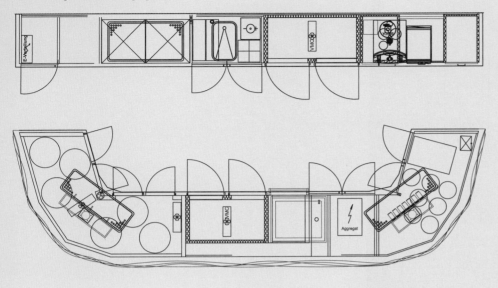

Curved profiles cut horizontally create a strong 3D image

Drawings depicting the development of the service island concept.

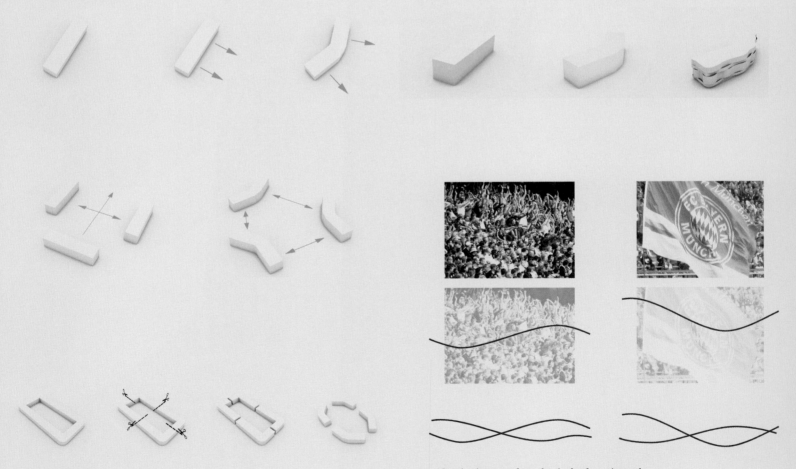

Inspiration came from the ripple of emotion and the waving of fan flags during a football match.

The wavy, natural wood from the model (above) features in the final units, positioned in front of real tree trunks (below).

FLOOR PLAN

1   Food preparation/service points
2   Dining area with high tables
3   Relaxed, round-table dining area
4   Seating area with a view over the pitch
5   Lavatories

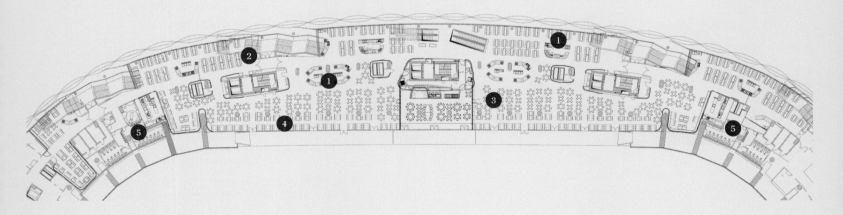

CAFE BORD DE MER

Kinney Chan & Associates

The white column is like a huge scroll of paper, about to be dispatched as a giant message in a bottle.

Located in the Auberge Discovery Bay resort, Cafe Bord de Mer occupies a striking coastal site. The design objective, therefore, was to create a relaxing and serene dining space that showcases the spectacular waterfront as a principal feature.

To maximise the dramatic view of the South China Sea, full-length windows are framed in all-natural components, inviting the sunlight to stream in and creating a bright, seaside feeling. An open layout with interactive cooking stations adds to the fresh and spacious atmosphere. The ceiling is partly topped by broad wooden blinds, which extend to the windows, splitting and scattering the sun's rays to attractive effect. The same treatment is applied to the decorative partitions which articulate the large space.

The feature columns are the signature of the restaurant, based on the concept of the traditional 'message in a bottle', tossed into the ocean. The imposing white columns take on the form of rolls of paper tied with a metal string, with lighting effects highlighting the surfaces of the columns.

Beyond the eatery is a casual, family-friendly lounge bar. The decor is cosily modern with soft carpet, wooden shelves, a marble bartop and counter, and subtle accents of blue in the glassware dotted around on the tables. Guests can relax on the soft, leather sofas with shell-themed cushions.

The outdoor terrace, meanwhile, is designed to bring diners closer to nature. All the spaces feature many organic elements including light wood tables and floors, natural shell displays on dining tables and food menus with wooden covers.

WHERE **88 Siena Avenue, Discovery Bay, Hong Kong**
OPENING **February 2013**
CLIENT **Hong Kong Resort Company**
DESIGNER **Kinney Chan & Associates (p.546)**
FLOOR AREA **597 m²**
WEBSITE **aubergediscoverybay.com**

AVERAGE PRICE OF MAIN COURSE **HKD 500**
TYPE OF KITCHEN **Fusion**
OPENING HOURS **6.30–22.00**
CAPACITY **478 seats**

Clusters of delicate lamps created a starry effect.

Natural wood is a key feature throughout, in particular in the timber fins which are functional as well as decorative.

A serene dining experience showcasing a spectacular coastal site

From the outside, the restaurant layout with its open cooking stations, shows itself to full advantage through a huge glass facade.

CATCH BY SIMONIS

Ferry Tabeling

Rippling forms reinforce the watery theme of a seaside restaurant.

The restaurant owner Alain Simonis commissioned Ferry Tabeling to be in charge of creating the new layout for his family business. Design Electro Products (DEP) was then brought on board to create a lighting scheme in keeping with the overall design. The concept of this fish restaurant in Scheveningen, located next to the old harbour, was inspired by the perpetual movement of the sea and the waves.

The interior combines a wide range of different settings and table furniture, divided over four storeys, including a basement and a spacious outdoor terrace, with a centrally-located lift connecting all the floors. The watery design concept unites all the fittings: the curved wooden plates on the wall, rosewood-veneer furniture finished with a high-gloss epoxy coating, curvacious benches in various dimensions, undulating bar fronts with a polished sheen, and details in the ceiling shaped like ripples in sand, all engineered and constructed by Kroeze Interiors (located in the Dutch city of Oldenzaal).

In order for the lighting to complement the fluid forms of the architecture and interior, DEP custom-designed organically-shaped lighting armatures for outside the restaurant, and followed the same principle inside. The interior elements comprised a material palette that was a challenge to light – including the lift doors and their luxurious surround of coral-red mosaic tiling – and DEP responded by emphasising the corrugated ceiling with a lighting form suggesting the tide line. This ribbon of light pulls together the entire interior design and is bang on theme. DEP also designed and installed a high-end sound system, which was produced by Seven Sound.

WHERE **Dr Lelykade 43, Scheveningen, the Netherlands**
OPENING **June 2013**
CLIENT **Alain Simonis**
LAYOUT **Ferry Tabeling (p.545)**
FLOOR AREA **600 m²**
WEBSITE **catch-bysimonis.nl**

AVERAGE PRICE OF MAIN COURSE **EUR 21**
TYPE OF KITCHEN **Fish**
OPENING HOURS **12.00–23.00**
CAPACITY **500 seats**

Polished rosewood, white plaster and ceramic tiles and white, fish-printed leather comprise the material palette.

Organic shapes complement the fluid forms

The design makes a virtue of irregular forms.

The ceiling evokes ripples in sand.

CLAUDE'S
Pascale Gomes-McNabb Design

In the upstairs dining room, swathes of
colour and angular shapes did the talking.

When acclaimed chef/owner Chui Lee Luk
invited Pascale Gomes-McNabb Design to
breathe new life into Claude's – a 36-year-old
Sydney fine-dining institution – she wanted
a design that would shake up its staid image
and echo her fresh and innovative culinary
language. The challenge was to create two
different dining experiences to work together
as a whole, while taking budget and spatial
constraints into consideration.

The design team responded with a
clearly divided space: a downstairs bistro
that was casual and accessible, with a more
luxurious, fine-dining room above. The
downstairs bistro was based on the notion
of flux: customised furniture sitting at
varying heights, providing playful contrasts
and engaging a sense of movement within
the small room, while also allowing
different dining choices. The wooden floor
was arranged in diagonal sections, with
the complex geometric shapes in the wall
patterns, colours and mirrors referencing the
camouflage of WW1 'Dazzle Ships', employing
plays on visual perception. The furniture
choice was classic, but in offbeat mixes of
black and wood.

Upstairs, bronze mirrors and vibrant,
geometric colour blocks created a sense
of rhythm and helped expand the space of
the more formal dining room. The dark
carpet, marble-topped dressers, glittering
drapery and brass joinery conveyed a luxe
sophistication. A sculptural display of
heirloom Napoleonic Limoges dinnerware
paid homage to the restaurant's history whilst
a feathery Ingo Maurer chandelier was added
as a whimsical touch.

While the two dining spaces were
treated quite differently, the swathes of bright
colour and dynamic geometry in both served
to underline the family resemblance.

WHERE **Sydney, Australia**
OPENING **July 2012 (venue has since closed)**
CLIENT **Chui Lee Luk**
DESIGNER **Pascale Gomes-McNabb Design (p.548)**
FLOOR AREA **125 m²**
WEBSITE **n/a**

AVERAGE PRICE OF MAIN COURSE **n/a**
TYPE OF KITCHEN **French cuisine**
OPENING HOURS **n/a**
CAPACITY **n/a**

Blocks of bright blue, zig-zagging shapes, mirror strips, dining plates on the wall and a customised Ingo Maurer lamp with feathers all added up to a dynamic interior.

Downstairs, the bistro and bar took on an offbeat 'dazzle' camouflage.

CUCKOO'S NEST

Stylt Trampoli

A model biplane brings to mind just one of the many technological advances on show at Cuckoo's Nest.

'You don't have to be mad to be a scientist, but it sure seems to help!' That, according to design office Stylt Trampoli, is the concept behind Cuckoo's Nest, the restaurant and bar of a Radisson Blu Hotel in Lindholmen. This particular locality in Gothenburg, Sweden has been called 'the most exciting place in Europe' – thanks to its technology and innovation cluster, rather than its nightlife attractions – hence the 'mad scientist' connection. Stylt Trampoli set out to make the pure genius of the area visible in the design studio's interior for the restaurant.

'It wasn't just that the hotel needed a restaurant,' says Stylt Trampoli's Erik Nissen Johansen. 'It was that the people of Lindholmen, the thinkers, innovators, coders, contrarians and creatives (and their friends), needed a meeting place – somewhere warm and home-like, where they could brainstorm, write, mingle, drink, laugh, eat and hatch new ideas.'

The interior is a happy clash between an old-fashioned library and the most comfortable natural history museum imaginable, with plenty of whimsical touches – such as the mysterious collection of scrap paper surrounding the TV-screen, the chalked Einsteinian notes on the bar and the small banner-toting biplane suspended from the ceiling.

'Creative minds have a very serious need for whimsy,' explains Erik Nissen Johansen. 'Playing is the best way to have an idea, and this place is all about new ideas. And old ones! We wanted to help tell the story of this place, of industry and innovation and technology, and the people who made it all happen.'

WHERE **Lindholmspiren 4, Gothenburg, Sweden**
OPENING **March 2013**
CLIENt **Winn Hotels**
DESIGNER **Stylt Trampoli (p.550)**
FLOOR AREA **375 m²**
WEBSITE **cuckoosnest.se**

AVERAGE PRICE OF MAIN COURSE **SEK 250**
TYPE OF KITCHEN **International**
OPENING HOURS **11.30–22.00**
CAPACITY **200 guests**

PHOTOS Erik Nissen Johansen

A happy clash between old-fashioned library and natural history museum

Even the furniture
has a seriously
studious look about it.

Comfy but academic-looking seating is surrounding by science-related knick-knacks – even the TV screen sits in the middle of what appears to be a montage devoted to some arcane theory.

FLOOR PLAN

1 Library/lobby
2 Bar
3 Dining area
4 Buffet area
5 Kitchen
6 Back-of-house

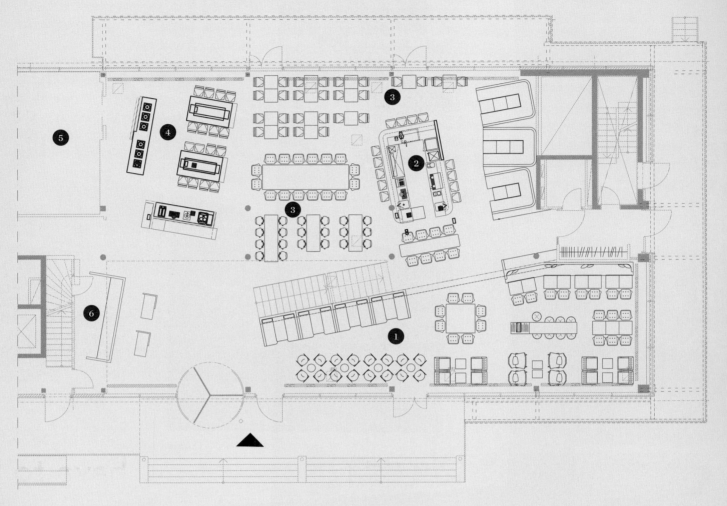

Drawing showing the shelving
installation, inspired by the shape
of the periodic table.

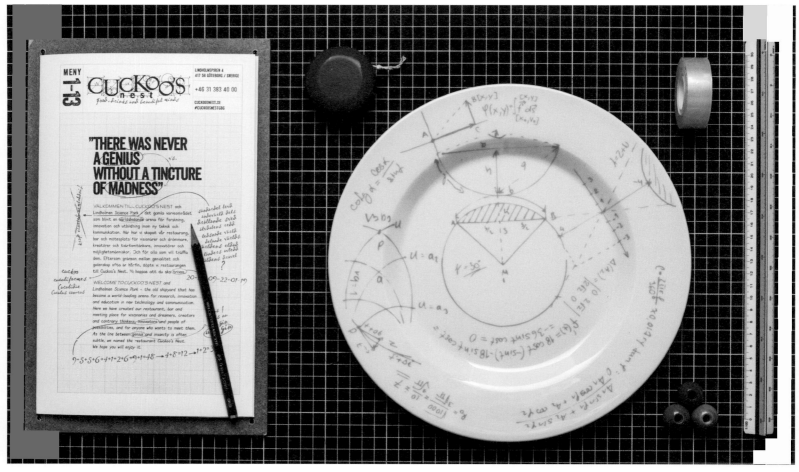

Graph-paper tablecloths and an equation theme for the plates help apply the concept in the finest of detail.

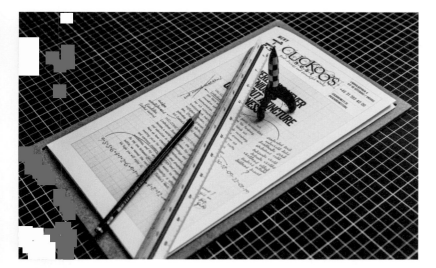

'You don't have to be mad to be a scientist, but it sure seems to help!'

The menu too is based on a scientific paper, complete with 'Fundamental Principles' and 'Sweet Conclusions'.

DABBOUS
Brinkworth

Industrial, yet surprisingly delicate, steel-framed mesh screens form partition walls and act as an acoustic buffer.

Briefed to create both branding and interior for Dabbous restaurant, Brinkworth took inspiration from the minimal and natural food presentation to create a raw, industrial space and a contemporary, restrained identity.

Working from a shell site, the design team used authentic materials – steel, reeded glass, concrete, exposed brick and wire mesh – to define the architecture of the space. With select walls lined in burnt wood, the restaurant area is decked out with custom-designed furniture, including waxed-wood tables and black-leather chairs. An eclectic selection of light fixtures, including bespoke blown-glass fittings, soften the otherwise almost brutal material palette.

The wire mesh screens are used to discreetly separate the wine store, waiter station and stairwell from the main space. The kitchen is partly screened by reeded glass. A cluster of tiered, clear-glass light fittings highlight the staircase to the lower ground floor, creating an immediately recognisable route to the bar area. The bar is kept raw and minimal. Custom wood and steel benches and large tables predominate with high seating at the bar. Leather and steel armchairs and a banquette furnish the 'snug' under the stairs.

The large windows of the corner site flood the space with light in the daytime and at night reflect the sparkly image of the blown-glass lights. Above the door, the word Dabbous is picked out in simple typography, the logo developed by Brinkworth and used across all media to present a cohesive and confident overall identity for this acclaimed restaurant.

WHERE **39 Whitfield Street, London, United Kingdom**
OPENING **January 2012**
CLIENT **Ollie Dabbous**
DESIGNER **Brinkworth (p.541)**
FLOOR AREA **207 m²**
WEBSITE **dabbous.co.uk**

AVERAGE PRICE OF MAIN COURSE **Tasting menu GBP 59**
TYPE OF KITCHEN **Modern European**
OPENING HOURS **Tue–Sat 12.00–14.00, 18.00–22.00**
CAPACITY **32 seats**

PHOTOS Louise Melchior

The free-standing metal framework gives a sense of division, set against the bare wall with its purposefully-raw finish.

A raw, industrial space with a restrained identity

The restaurant has a mix of bespoke timber and steel furniture in the dining area.

The design team was also responsible for the typography, which reflects the industrial yet quirky character of the interior.

DAS BROT.
Designliga

The textured plasterwork of the ceiling suggests the tiled roof of a farmhouse.

Vistors to the theme park and education centre Autostadt – the Volkswagen car collection and museum in Wolfsburg, Germany – can now experience this organic bakery. All restaurants at Autostadt are operated by Mövenpick with a catering concept that focuses on regional produce, the majority of which is grown or farmed according to ecological and seasonal principles. Designliga was asked to take care of the interior for this new in-house bakery.

The design team's concept was built on the basic philosophy of baking bread. 'From field to counter' was utilised as the thread for the design. This idea is especially visible in the design of the ceramic floor tiles connecting the dining area with the shop. The shapes in the pattern represent the metamorphosis from the field: to wheat, to flour and, with added water, to bread. Simultaneously, this flooring is an example of high-quality craftsmanship combined with modern computer technology as all of the 25,000 tiled elements in the floor have subtly different shapes.

Sustainable, renewable materials as well as craftsmanship were clear priorities in the brief the designers were given. Local timber, tiles and fabric make sure these criteria are met. Textured plasterwork above the communal table of the dining area suggests the form of a farmhouse roof and the open shelving was inspired by traditional half-timbered buildings. Furthermore, local weavers created the panels that are positioned on the front of the wall unit.

The ambience which abounds in the dining space is that of a welcoming living room, which is filled with a homely cosiness, moving to a more functional atmosphere in the busy bakery and shop area.

WHERE **Autostadt, Stadtbruecke, Wolfsburg, Germany**
OPENING **December 2012**
CLIENT **Autostadt**
DESIGNER **Designliga (p.543)**
FLOOR AREA **190 m²**
WEBSITE **autostadt.de**

AVERAGE PRICE OF MAIN COURSE **EUR 5**
TYPE OF KITCHEN **Organic baked goods**
OPENING HOURS **8.00–18.00**
CAPACITY **16 seats**

A long wooden table
where guests eat together,
dominates the dining area.

BUTTERBROT
MIT SAUERRAHMBUTTER 1.50 EUR

KLAPPSTULLE
MIT SAUERRAHMBUTTER 1.80 EUR

BUTTERBROT
MIT SCHICHTKÄSE 2.90 EUR

KLAPPSTULLE
MIT SALAMI 3.20 EUR

BUTTERBROT
MIT BERGKÄSE 2.90 EUR

KLAPPSTULLE
MIT SCHINKEN 3.20 EUR

WARM GERÖSTETES BROT 3.10 EUR
AUFSTRICH MIT KÜRBIS & INGWER

SAUERRAHMBUTTER 3.60 EUR
250 GR.

SAUERRAHMBUTTER 1.80 EUR
125 GR.

The bakery, located on the ground floor, turns
the spotlight on artisanal baking traditions.

Half-timbered houses served as
inspiration for the open shelving.

The design concept was built on the basic philosophy of baking bread

The pattern of the ceramic-tiled floor echoes the bread making process.

A wardrobe is located in the back for the use of customers.

Designliga also did the branding, including packaging.

The open displays behind the counter allow customers to see through to the bakery itself and create a feeling of transparency.

ECOVILLE

Hachem

The interior of the venue is light and airy
thanks to the all-glass facade and solid
bleached oak furnishings.

The Ecoville Project is a civic development,
which involved the integration of a residential
estate. Ecoville is now an active site which
engages its residents in community activities,
and enables them to contribute to the
sustenance and growth of their environment.

The client, Resimax, directed Hachem
to transform the site, which was essentially
a large paddock (west of Melbourne), into
inviting, usable parkland, and to create
public areas for recreation and interaction.
As architects, Hachem wanted to work
sensitively with the natural elements that the
land offered, and develop concepts that would
invigorate the area, and provide residents with
a sense of belonging and responsibility.

Eco-sustainable practices needed to be
integrated into the project from the start. This
meant thinking small and local, and enacting
simple, effective ideas. Ecoville, today,
comprises a landscaped park and gardens, a
sports arena, barbecue areas and playground
equipment. At its centre is a restaurant and
cafe nestled beneath a soaring pavilion.
It acts as a community hub, encouraging
outdoor activities and casual get-togethers
all year round. Eco-sustainable practices
were also incorporated into the venue's
kitchen: meaning a menu of simple food
offerings, utilising local produce. A beautiful,
organic vegetable garden invites communal
participation and promotes a healthy lifestyle.

The wind turbine park is a source of
clean energy for the neighbourhood, as well
as being a sculptural asset and a totem for the
progressive nature of the project. In addition,
large underground water storage tanks collect
rain and storm water, which subsequently
irrigate the gardens and parklands and service
the community's toilets.

WHERE **Mazel Drive, Tarneit, Australia**
OPENING **January 2013**
CLIENT **Resimax**
DESIGNER **Hachem (p.545)**
FLOOR AREA **1450 m²**
WEBSITE **n/a**

AVERAGE PRICE OF MAIN COURSE **n/a**
TYPE OF KITCHEN **Variable**
OPENING HOURS **Bookings only**
CAPACITY **300 seats**

At the heart of Ecoville, a soaring pavilion stretches over the amphitheatre.

The eating area extends outside, with seating provided around the social arena.

The dining area is furnished with white Skitsch chairs having solid oak legs.

Eco-sustainable practices were integrated into the soaring pavilion

Thinking eco: well-shaded spaces in natural tones blend into the environment.

SITE PLAN

1 Civic garden amphitheatre
2 Pavilion and restaurant
3 Seating
4 Car park
5 Bike racks
6 Sand pits and playground
7 Paving

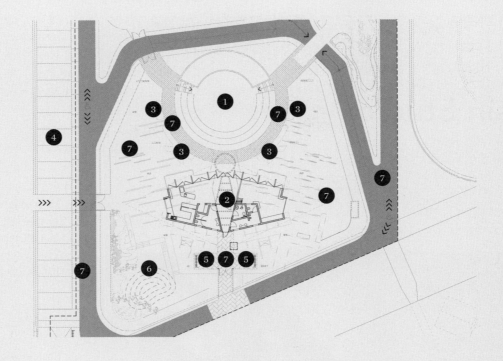

FLOOR PLAN

1 Foyer
2 Dining area
3 Office area
4 Prep area
5 Warm up kitchen
6 Kiosk
7 Lavatories

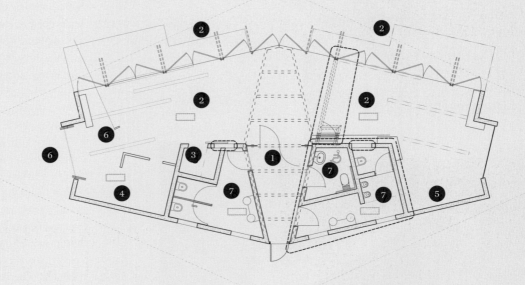

SOUTH ELEVATION

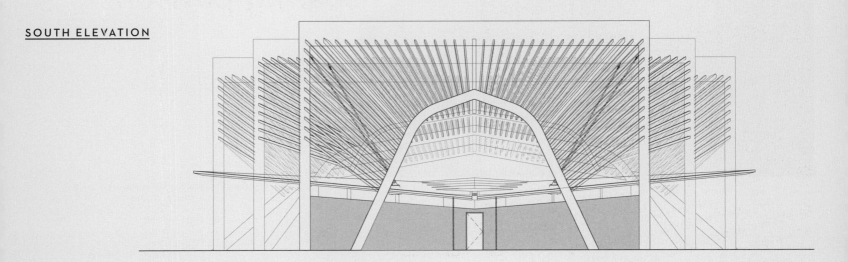

EDEN
Genesin Studio

A neutral-timber treatment throughout the interior creates harmony with the material and a less-is-more palette.

How to give year-round appeal to a seaside venue – that was the challenge Genesin Studio faced with the new beachfront eatery Eden. The design approach took its cues from the 1960s, using wood to create an organic interior that is cool in summer, but warmly welcoming in winter. A major challenge of the project, which has an all-glass facade, was the harsh Australian sun. This is blocked and filtered by a facade screen which gives shade during the day and creates allure when illuminated at night.

The black, patterned facade creates an appealing entrance to the venue, with a long tiled bar which offers options for casual eating or simply enjoying a drink. There's also a black-on-grey upholstered lounge area for lingering over a cocktail. The wall panelling is executed using cost-effective marine ply, which is also used for the tailor-made tables and banquette, giving a highly bespoke feel.

The dining area is tucked away and offers either banquette seating or a choice of large tables. There is also a wine-blending room boasting unique, climate-controlled local wines in vats or bottles for tasting. Patrons can even try their hand at making their own blend.

Two outdoor terraces complete the picture, offering the ideal way to enjoy balmy summer nights. One is casual, while the other is a more formal extension of the dining room.

WHERE **Lights Landing, Glenelg, Australia**
OPENING **December 2012**
CLIENT **Jason Makris and Chad Hanson**
DESIGNER **Genesin Studio (p.545)**
FLOOR AREA **450 m²**
WEBSITE **edendiningroom.com**

AVERAGE PRICE OF MAIN COURSE **AUD 23**
TYPE OF KITCHEN **Contemporary Australian**
OPENING HOURS **Mon–Thu 11.00–24.00,
Fri–Sun 8.00–01.00**
CAPACITY **160 seats, 350 guests**

Marine ply details the walls and furniture in a
way that brings about a simplistic charm that
is poetic and appreciated.

The brief asked for a space that felt timeless, making use of natural materials.

The facade's patterned screen is made of laser-cut marine ply.

Wood makes for an organic interior that is cool in summer, but warmly welcoming in winter

The polished-brass pendant lights are from the studio of Michael Anastassiades.

With 75 per cent of the venue walls glazed, the facade screen offers shade yet still allows views of the ocean beyond.

FAT NOODLE

Luchetti Krelle

From the exterior of the historic Treasury Building, the illuminated chopstick installation that lights up the restaurant interior grabs the attention of passers-by.

For a new dining destination showcasing the talents of head chef Luke Nguyen, design office Luchetti Krelle was inspired by the culture of food in many Asian countries, and by the mix of colonial and vernacular architecture throughout the continent. The elegance and grand proportions of the historic building in which the restaurant is located certainly evokes a colonial air, and to this backdrop the designers brought ideas generated by 'hawkers markets' with their open kitchens and lively buzz. The space is densely layered with contemporary takes on iconic Asian artefacts and symbolism.

The bar front takes on the form of an ancient scroll unravelling itself, while a new basket-weave parquet floor references Asian steam baskets while also respecting the heritage-building context. With dual entrances to the restaurant, a street presence was essential. Due to heritage restrictions, this could only be achieved through glimpses of the interior. The soaring ceilings provided the opportunity to dazzle with super-scaled suspended elements in the dining space and backlit vertical installations in the bar area.

In this rich and playful interior, everything except the chairs was custom designed and often crafted by artisans. An abstract fire-dragon light sculpture bursts from the entry corridor and dives into the open kitchen, while a custom chandelier of woks with uplighting to thousands of golden chopsticks delicately dances overhead in the dining room (these two complex elements were realised with the help of Armature Design Support). Custom materials include hand-painted mah-jong-style tiles and a stunning gold wallpaper in the private dining room – rich fare indeed.

WHERE **130 William Street, Brisbane, Australia**
OPENING **November 2012**
CLIENT **Echo Entertainment**
DESIGNER **Luchetti Krelle (p.546)**
FLOOR AREA **552 m²**
WEBSITE **treasurybrisbane.com.au**

AVERAGE PRICE OF MAIN COURSE **AUD 17**
TYPE OF KITCHEN **Asian fusion**
OPENING HOURS **Sun–Thu 11.30–23.00, Fri–Sat 11.30–01.00**
CAPACITY **150 seats**

Rumour has it that the restaurant is a stage of mythical creatures from the 'Forbidden City', with guests entranced by the overhead fire dragon immediately on entering the venue.

A storybook landscape climbs up behind the central bar area.

The lofty ceilings of the heritage building are used to maximum effect.

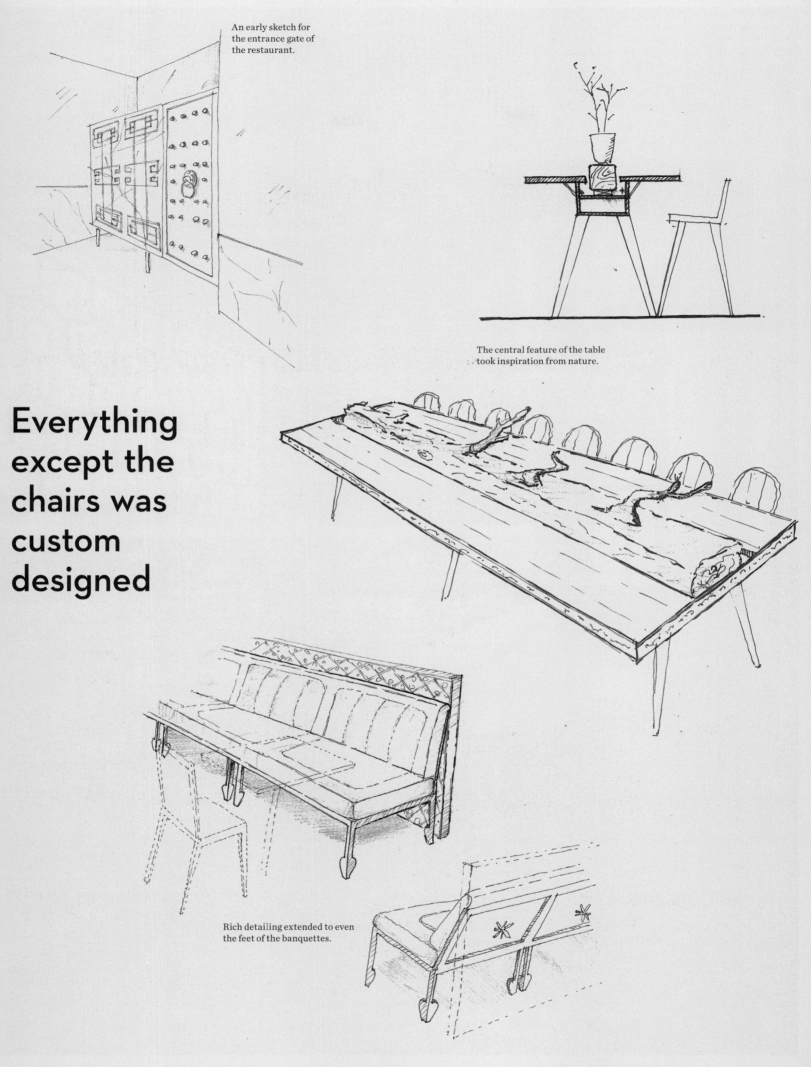

An early sketch for
the entrance gate of
the restaurant.

The central feature of the table
took inspiration from nature.

Everything except the chairs was custom designed

Rich detailing extended to even
the feet of the banquettes.

Wrapping around the tall space over the bar is an eye-catching illuminated feature, reminiscent of an ancient Japanese scroll.

The space is densely layered with Asian artefacts and symbolism, all with a modern twist

Couldron Lion Heads were sculpted by Rosemonts and placed on the mirrored wall to act as guardians of the space.

The custom wallpaper in the dining area was by Quercus & Co.

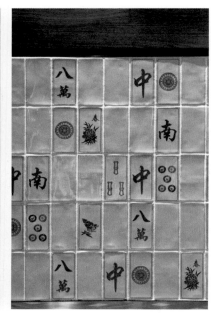

The delicate hand-painted tiles were decorated by Cone 7.

FLOOR PLAN

1 Welcome station
2 Dining area
3 Private dining
4 Outdoor dining
5 Bar
6 Waiters' station
7 Kitchen
8 Lavatories

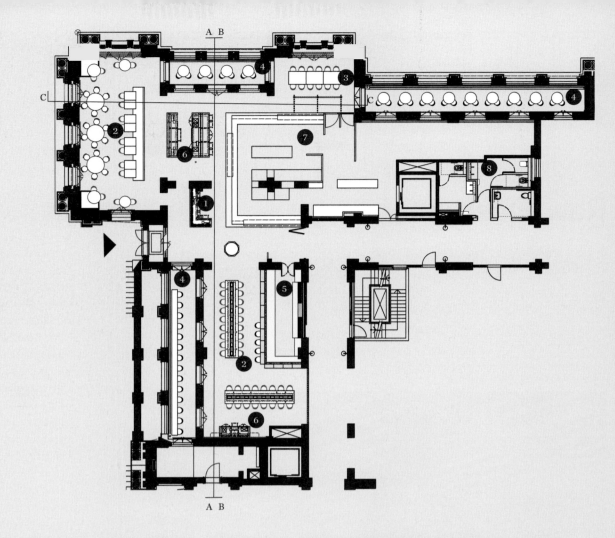

SECTION A

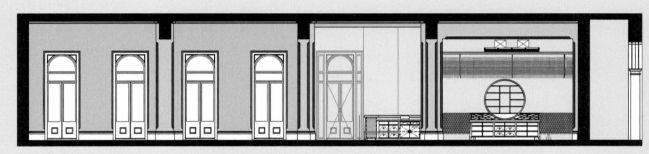

SECTION B

SECTION C

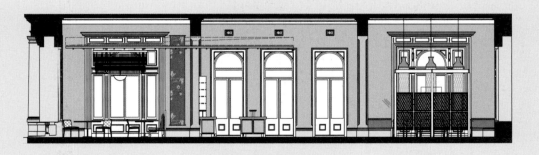

FLEET STREET KITCHEN

Raw Design

Bespoke steel lampshades and high marble
tables combine to idiosyncratic effect in
this bright and breezy interior.

Fleet Street Kitchen occupies the ground and
basement floors of a modern apartment block
in a central, city location. The space suffered
from a lack of natural light and a paucity of
any features – Raw Design was called in to
change this, and to produce a contemporary,
sociable restaurant and bar space.

Raw Design's initial act was to remove
the front facade, replacing it with full-height
glazing to ensure maximum light flooded
into the space. The ground floor was then
defined as three zones: formal dining, relaxed
dining and a bar area. A series of demountable
shutters were taken internally up over the
existing windows and across the ceiling to
define the dining areas within the space, these
being up-lit with colour-changing LEDs to
dramatically change the atmosphere from
day to evening.

The cooking area was deconstructed,
with a back-of-house kitchen and a custom-
made Barbacoa char grill brought to the front
of house. This was then complemented with
meat-ageing fridges and a large prep-space
of a marble counter and wooden butcher's
block, thus allowing customers to experience
the cooking process and highlighting the
restaurant's locally-sourced products. The
furniture is an eclectic mix of loose tables,
chairs and benches, with a casual dining
experience created by a long, feature marble
table near the bar.

Heading to the lower level, guests enter
the late-night lounge through a luxurious gilt-
edged door. Downstairs feels a little bit more
daring, with its interior of marble mosaic
floors, battered leather furniture and fashion-
inspired illustrations in graphic monochrome.
There is a stage for performances, and
the icing on the cake is the eye-catching
chandelier that makes a stunning statement.

WHERE **Summer Row, Birmingham, United Kingdom**
OPENING **April 2013**
CLIENT **Town and Country Inns**
DESIGNER **Raw Design (p.549)**
FLOOR AREA **876 m²**
WEBSITE **fleetstreetkitchen.co.uk**

AVERAGE PRICE OF MAIN COURSE GBP 18
TYPE OF KITCHEN Grill
OPENING HOURS 12.00–02.00
CAPACITY 200 seats

Glass bottles and jars add colour to the windows, giving a stained glass effect to an otherwise fairly monochrome space.

Plants contribute an important touch of both colour and nature to the formal dining area.

The tiled logo and marble table, topped by cute accessories, reference vintage interiors.

A series of demountable shutters define the dining areas

Louvred panels act as partitions and also filter the light effectively, making for a soft effect.

PENCIL SKETCHES

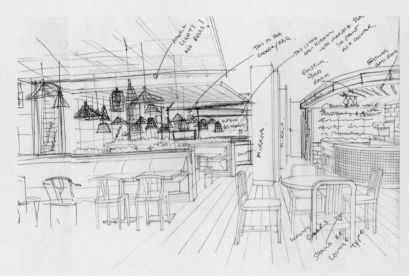

Sketches showing the first ideas for the bespoke steel lights.

COLOURED SKETCHES

The design team's plan for the dining areas was always to use greenery as a way to weave an organic thread through the eatery.

GROUND FLOOR

1   Bar
2   Casual dining
3   Formal dining
4   Terrace
5   Meat fridge
6   Butcher's block
7   Barbacoa char grill
8   Kitchen
9   Wine store
10 Waiters' station
11 Bar wash-up
12 Seating
13 Stage area
14 Lavatories

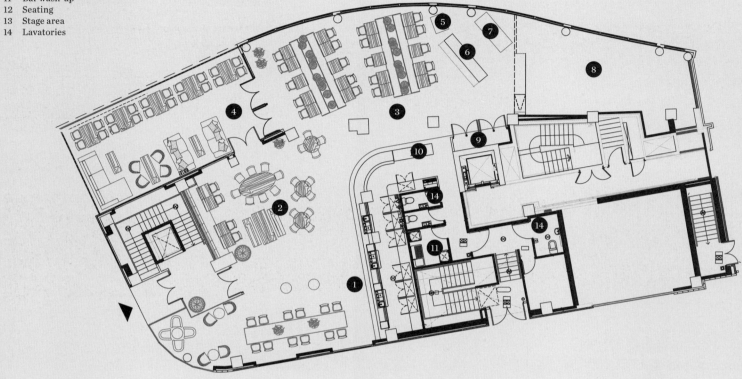

LOWER FLOOR

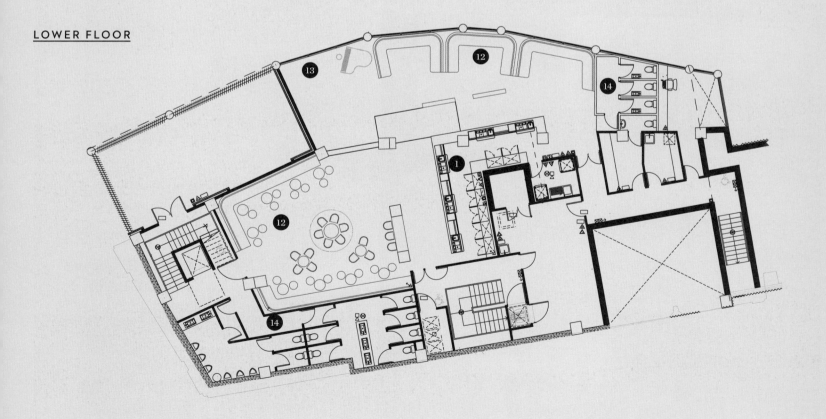

A change of mood for the downstairs late-night bar: dark, rich shades and fabrics are applied for a more nocturnal, cabaret-friendly effect.

Guests can lounge on the banquettes in front of the tongue-in-cheek wall paintings.

GREEN KITCHEN
A00 Architecture

For the established Taiwanese brand Green+Safe, the green architecture specialists at A00 created the interior for Green Kitchen, collaborating with Studio 1:1. The fusion-food eatery forms part of this brand's flagship location in Shanghai, set apart from the rest of the retail space by the more intimate ambience that has been instilled by the design team, thanks to soft lighting, built-in sofas and the use of wood for flooring and furniture.

The restaurant is housed in an industrial brick complex in the city's former French concession. To limit the environmental impact of the project, A00 took a minimalistic approach, allowing the industrial shell to shine, setting off the wholesome natural food on offer.

The main intervention is a dramatic steel staircase linking the main dining space on the lower floor and the lounge area upstairs. 'Wrapping the stairs in steel creates an experience of surprise by hiding the direct views upstairs,' says A00's Sacha Silva. 'The stairs rise up into the upper lounge area, with its low ceiling to really contrast with the full-height ceiling in the main dining area. Once we positioned the staircase, the rest of the layout fell into place.'

Although there are full windows along the south side, the team decided to internalise the design by creating full metal screens on the exterior to filter the light. These provide one of the interior's few decorative touches. Contrasting to the lower level restaurant area, which is set within the retail space and boasts long, communal tables, the lounge has a continuous sofa along the walls, creating cosy and sociable niches.

The expansive glass facade has decorative metal screens to filter the light and create intimacy inside.

WHERE **6 Dongping Lu, Shanghai, China**
OPENING **June 2012**
CLIENT **Yuen Foong Yu Group**
DESIGNER **A00 Architecture (p.540)**
FLOOR AREA **250 m²**
WEBSITE **green-n-safe.com**

AVERAGE PRICE OF MAIN COURSE **RMB 220**
TYPE OF KITCHEN **Fast food, fusion, tapas**
OPENING HOURS **17.30–23.00**
CAPACITY **60 seats**

A sweeping steel staircase adds a touch of dynamism and links the main ground-floor dining space to the lounge area upstairs.

Long communal tables make for a social space in the dining room.

An industrial shell sets off the natural, wholesome food

A quirky light installation makes the most of the angular roof.

IL-BARRI RESTAURANT

Galea&Galea Architects

A celebration of light, craftsmanship and fine detail, the bar is a legacy to a longstanding local tradition of decorative intricacy.

In the small Maltese town of Mgarr, Il-Barri offers a serene dining experience. Located on the first floor, the mainly white interior was designed by local studio Galea&Galea Architects utilising a concept that seeks to merge parallel worlds in a microcosm of detail. Straight lines meet circular forms in a newfound contemporary expression revealing various degrees of decorative intricacy. Grasping the essence of a longstanding tradition that transcends time or cultural context, the designers drew upon a repertoire of Maltese symbols using ornamentation as a device of transformation.

The local crafts of lacemaking, filigree, wrought ironwork, fretwork and patterned concrete tiles all inspired the interior. In collaboration with Japanese tattoo artist Emico Hatakeyama, the team – led by Monica Audrey Galea – explored a fusion of cultures in the playful yet conceptual reinterpretation of form and pattern. The result is a series of laser-cut, hand-finished backlit metal screens that impart a precious fragility to the interior. This detail is attractively applied to the bar front.

As guests enter up the seemingly floating, illuminated stairs, they see the minimal handrail that morphs into a coat hanger. Playing on the careful juxtaposition of materials that impart character, the identity of the interior unfolds. Animated by shadowy effects in the wall niches, the main space is lit up by a random arrangement of seamless circular light fittings that echo the radial screen patterns. At the far end, the bar and service areas cut through the space in a series of powerful volumes expressed in a rich array of warmer tones. The reddish hues of the copper, the maple accents and the vibrant blue–green glass pose a dramatic backdrop to the structure of the bar, instilling balance and poetic harmony.

WHERE **Church Square, Mgarr, Malta**
OPENING **April 2014**
CLIENT **Stephen Sammut**
DESIGNER **Galea&Galea Architects (p.544)**
FLOOR AREA **150 m²**
WEBSITE **il-barri.com.mt**

AVERAGE PRICE OF MAIN COURSE **EUR 20**
TYPE OF KITCHEN **Traditional Maltese cuisine**
OPENING HOURS **Tue-Sun 9.00-23.30**
CAPACITY **120 seats**

Copper, maple and glass combined with accurate illumination contribute to the calm ambience in the restaurant.

Exploring a fusion of cultures in a conceptual reinterpretation of form and pattern

The floating stairs lead to the first floor dining space.

Transformation of function as the handrail morphs into the branch-like coat hooks.

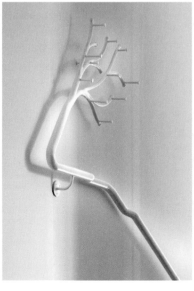

Details on the laser-cut screen reinterprets form and pattern.

KAGUYA
OpenAir Studio

Natural materials of wood, stone and bamboo deck out the entrance patio.

For Kaguya, a restaurant serving French-influenced Japanese food in Bangkok, design office OpenAir Studio set out to showcase the cuisine in a what founder Wit Chongwattananukul calls 'a simple and elegant space'.

The entrance makes a welcoming statement, with low stone walls and stairs fronting an expanse of glass that offers glowing views of the delights within. From the inside, diners can enjoy street views through the glass on two sides. The floor plan meanwhile divides the restaurant into two distinct spaces: a lower dining area with a sake bar, and an upper area with a sushi bar.

Traditional craft techniques are used for the interior, and really make the most of the simple, honest materials used: stone, wood and bamboo shine thanks to a rustic yet sophisticated set of treatments. Traditional Japanese fencing is the inspiration for the custom bamboo wall screens, which are tied together with scarlet cords. Double layers of these add depth and texture to the space. They also continue the theme of translucency, offering views of other parts of the space and of the greenery outside. The ceiling, meanwhile, uses Jenga-like wooden blocks, installed in a chequered pattern. The pattern adds texture and lends depth to the rather low space. At 10-cm thick, the wooden blocks give a sculptural, solid and earthy feel to the interior.

Materials and design create a supremely tactile, warm and intriguing space, somewhat reminiscent of a puzzle cube. The finishing touch? A bespoke wooden chandelier, its form inspired by grains of rice, which lends further detail with its interplay of light and shade.

WHERE **Sukhumvit Rd, Bangkok, Thailand**
OPENING **July 2013**
CLIENT **Sukit Khunsiwawong**
DESIGNER **OpenAir Studio (p.548)**
FLOOR AREA **200 m²**
WEBSITE **n/a**

AVERAGE PRICE OF MAIN COURSE **THB 660**
TYPE OF KITCHEN **Japanese gastro bar**
OPENING HOURS **19.00–00.00**
CAPACITY **70 seats**

The upper mezzanine's opening to the lower level allows a glimpse of the rice-inspired ceiling installation.

Cubic shapes abound in the furniture and fittings.

The chequered pattern overhead was installed to compensate for the room's low ceiling height.

Japanese fencing is the inspiration for the custom bamboo wall screens

Lit from within, the contemporary chandelier was inspired by a conglomeration of rice grains.

Behind the sushi bar, the marble surround has elongated slits of illumination.

KUTSHER'S TRIBECA

Rafael de Cárdenas / Architecture at Large

Serge Mouille inspired custom
pendants hang over the bar.

The beautiful craftsmanship of the birch fins
with their brass detailing is clearly evident.

This 100-person restaurant and bar, located in the heart of Tribeca, is a modern interpretation of Kutsher's Country Club – a classic destination for Jewish cuisine in the Catskills, upstate New York. Run by a fourth-generation Kutsher, this Manhattan venue channels the communal spirit of Kutsher's historic dining room. The design is a fresh and urban take on the 1960s canteen, complete with bold geometry and rich materials.

The warm, neutral palette is punctuated by jewel-tone accents of honey onyx and bronze mirror. Baltic birch plywood fins, subdivided and joined by elegant brass rods, surround the dining room to create an interesting geometric backdrop. These screen-like interventions help to create an atmosphere of intimacy within the 260-m² space. The relative openness of the interior is ideal for the large family parties that tend to congregate here.

Though the overall effect is mid-century modern, the white-painted brick walls and dark-green banquettes add casual, contemporary touches. Bespoke diamond-shaped pendant lights in two varieties – upholstered and open with exposed bulbs – cast a warm glow over the restaurant and bar area.

The big achievement of this interior is the way that it alludes to the past while instilling a modern air– a good match for the food offered, which consists of classic Jewish American dishes updated with some current, playful touches to appeal to the next generation of diners.

WHERE **186 Franklin St, New York, United States**
OPENING **December 2011**
CLIENT **Kutsher's Tribeca**
DESIGNER **Rafael de Cárdenas / Architecture at Large (p.549)**
FLOOR AREA **260 m²**
WEBSITE **kutsherstribeca.com**

AVERAGE PRICE OF MAIN COURSE **USD 20-45**
TYPE OF KITCHEN **Jewish/American**
OPENING HOURS **Day: Mon–Fri 11.45-14.30, Sat–Sun 10.00–15.00; Eve: Mon–Wed 17.30-22.00, Thu–Sat 17.30-23.00, Sun 17.00-22.00**
CAPACITY **100 seats**

Custom-designed parallelogram pendants illuminate the main dining room.

Slabs of carrara marble define the horizontal surfaces, while geometric strips of blonde wood act as vertical partitions.

LA SVOLTA PRAHRAN

Insider Outsider

A sharp, linear bar space brings
the pizzeria bang up to date.

This restaurant and bar is the second that Insider Outsider designed for the La Svolta brand. It is the inner-city sibling of the larger, more family-oriented original, designed and opened the year before. The new venue in Prahran unites two formerly separate properties but, as the brief called for a conceptual contrast between two types of dining, the majority of the separating wall was retained, resulting in two distinct areas: a traditional pizzeria with open kitchen, and a sharper, more linear bar space. The material palette is limited to black or white painted brick and timber, concrete and brass. Finishes were selected to complement the minimalist approach while adding tactility.

A tunnel-like entrance adds drama for visitors entering the space, and delivers them into the heart of the action. The bar area is defined by a single brick element running the length of the space with overhead, folded brass-box light fittings. Constructed of white-painted brick with a brass countertop, the bar accommodates various features along its length: a traditional drinks bar, cold-cuts display fridge, waiters' station and seating on both sides for 20 people.

The pizzeria area, seating a further 20 guests at the back of the venue, is similarly minimal with a well-scrawled blackboard wall – and more framed blackboards, in lieu of art, on the white wall opposite – provide a lively human touch. Simple wooden furniture completes the picture.

The entire project was delivered from conception to completion in less than 2 months, and the designers describe the budget as 'small but workable'.

WHERE **3–5 Cecil Place, Melbourne, Australia**
OPENING **September 2012**
CLIENT **Valerio Calabro and Pino Russo**
DESIGNER **Insider Outsider (p.545)**
FLOOR AREA **190 m²**
WEBSITE **lasvolta.com.au**

AVERAGE PRICE OF MAIN COURSE **AUD 20**
TYPE OF KITCHEN **Traditional Italian pizzeria**
OPENING HOURS **17.30–21.30**
CAPACITY **60 seats**

The entrance has been shaped with painted wooden planks into a dramatic, tunnel-like space.

A minimalist yet textural approach

A bespoke brass-box light fits the venue's linear theme.

The bar counter, of whitewashed brick with a brass countertop, runs the whole length of the front section.

LAEM CHA-REON SEAFOOD

Onion

Backlighting makes an illuminating feature behind the stone-coloured banquette.

Laem Cha-Reon Seafood has become a famous feature of the Thai seaside province of Rayong, where it has been serving its popular Thai-style seafood dishes for over 30 years now. Building on this success, the restaurant has made an appearance in several locations in bustling Bangkok. Luckily for its customers, each branch has a particular character, avoiding the one-design-fits-all approach.

At the location created by the team at Onion, a family-style eatery welcomes hungry diners with a restful and thoroughly-modern design. The open plan layout is bordered on one side by a 13-m-long wall – this expanse of oak-coloured plywood, has been laid with the wood panels creating a delightful pattern of diagonal stripes. This creates a light and cheerful backdrop for the rest of the interior, with its custom backlit banquette in a chic stone hue and its simple wooden tables and chairs. A floor of coffee-coloured ceramic tiles keeps things cool and grounded.

So far, so low-key – but the designers took advantage of the high ceiling in the space to add visual interest to the restaurant. The ceiling is studded with geometric rows of black eyelets, which provide the basis for an intricate three-dimensional grid of criss-crossing black ropes and custom-made iron hanging lamps. Matching iron standing-lamps hover in a row alongside the long banquette. The bespoke furnishings, mixed with the subtle patterns and texture give a contemporary air to the space.

WHERE **Central Plaza, Ladprao, Bangkok, Thailand**
OPENING **September 2011**
CLIENT **Laem Cha-Reon Seafood**
DESIGNER **Onion (p.548)**
FLOOR AREA **300 m²**
WEBSITE **laemchareonseafood.com**

AVERAGE PRICE OF MAIN COURSE **THB 650**
TYPE OF KITCHEN **Thai seafood**
OPENING HOURS **10.00–21.00**
CAPACITY **142 seats**

The private dining room features a round table under a super-sized black bell-shaped lampshade.

Criss-cross patterns of the black cords, passing through eyelets on the ceiling, form a graphic, geometric pattern.

Bespoke furnishings, patterns and texture give the space a contemporary air

The back wall is finished in oak-coloured plywood creating a pattern of diagonal stripes.

LAUBE LIEBE HOFFNUNG

acre and Franken Architekten

The function room has a cosy air, created by tables of recycled oak and classic chairs, plus clusters of hanging lamps.

A unique feature is the restaurant's adjoining 14-m-high viewing tower, ideal for admiring views of the surrounding park.

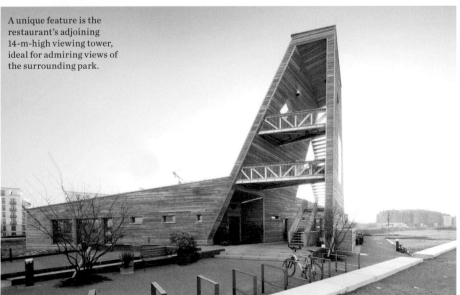

At the heart of Frankfurt's new Europaviertel district, Laube Liebe Hoffnung provides a much-needed meeting point and a sense of identity for the fledgling neighbourhood. The park eatery, which boasts an adjoining 14-m-high viewing tower, was designed by Franken Architekten as a sculptural wooden pavilion with three wings: one each for the restaurant, function room and viewing tower.

The interior design and restaurant concept were undertaken by the team at acre, setting out to create exactly what the new area needed: a sense of soul. Laube Liebe Hoffnung recalls a wooden house in a garden. The 'heart' takes the form of an open kitchen, evoking the homely atmosphere of family gatherings around the table. The use of recycled oak for the tables and classic chairs – such as the Frankfurt Kitchen Chair (a homage to the restaurant's home city) and the Tolix – give the place a warm and familiar feel, complemented by the daylight which floods in thanks to full-length windows.

The focal point is the open kitchen, framed by mosaic tiles with a floral pattern. Adding to the nostalgia are the old Central European kitchen lamps, original specimens from the 1920s and 1930s, which hang throughout the dining and bar areas, creating a theme in the space.

The multifunctional lounge, with views of the Frankfurt skyline, boasts original Eames Plastic Side Chairs from the 1960s and 1970s, vintage rugs and lots of Akari paper lanterns. Throughout, wood is the dominant material, harmonising with the building's timber-frame and larch facade. Fresh, seasonal home cooking adds the crowning touch.

WHERE **Pariser Str. 11, Frankfurt am Main, Germany**
OPENING **November 2013**
CLIENT **aurelis Real Estate**
DESIGNERS **acre (p.540), Franken Architekten (p.544)**
FLOOR AREA **450 m²**
WEBSITE **laubeliebehoffnung.de**

AVERAGE PRICE OF MAIN COURSE **EUR 16**
TYPE OF KITCHEN **German**
OPENING HOURS **Mon–Sat 10.00–00.00, Sun 10.00–23.00**
CAPACITY **46 (restaurant), 96 (terrace/beer garden), 50 (function room)**

The concept saw the kitchen as the 'heart' of the homely restaurant, hence it dominates with its surround of nostalgic, floral-patterned tiles.

LIESCHEN MUELLER

dan pearlman

Located in a historic building, fitting in with a sense of heritage.

The patterns that adorn the upholstery in the homely location was a mix of traditional textile designs from Lusatia, a historic region in Central Europe.

'Lieschen Mueller' is a synonym for the average German *hausfrau* – and therefore for culinary skill, down-to-earth values and warm hospitality. The brand itself was developed based on the myth of Oma Liesegang, whose culinary and baking artistry was well known throughout Berlin. The concept's goal was to translate the idea of the good old days into the present, and in this way to create a brand which combines both craftsmanship and modernity.

The approach of the design team was to create an interior concept based on authenticity. Lieschen Mueller stands for tradition and local ingredients, ideas which are integrated into many playful details in the space. Recycled vintage ceramic and wooden kitchen furniture is integrated into the bar counter. The seating is covered with real Lusatia kitchen linen in cheery traditional patterns, while the walls display a collection of old kitchen implements and equipment, from a vintage clock to a wooden spoon collection. A corporate pattern based on the first page of Oma Liesegang's cookbook subtly recurs throughout the space, and all the products are marked with custom-designed labels featuring grandma-style handwriting. A 'Kiez gallery' of photos depicting local neighbours and friends adds a family air to the space.

Such nostalgic detailing combines with a crisp approach which keeps the result fresh. Lots of white and grey, bare lightbulbs and cottage-style pine tables, combined with modern chairs, make for an effect which is clean and unfussy. The message is clear: Lieschen Mueller is authentic and contemporary.

PHOTOS Guido Leifhelm and Peter Medilek

WHERE **Schönhauser Allee 134 A, Berlin, Germany**
OPENING **February 2013**
CLIENT **Lieschen Mueller**
DESIGNER **dan pearlman (p.543)**
FLOOR AREA **50 m²**
WEBSITE **lieschenmueller-restaurants.com**

AVERAGE PRICE OF MAIN COURSE **EUR 8**
TYPE OF KITCHEN **Culinary and baking artistry, local ingredients**
OPENING HOURS **Mon–Sat 8.00–18.00, Sun 10.00–18.00**
CAPACITY **20 seats**

The counter was made of wood reclaimed from drawers and doors, that originally served as kitchen cupboards.

Nostalgic detailing combines with a crisp approach which keeps the result fresh

Original artefacts and photos adorn the walls, with portraits of neighbours and friends, adding a personal touch.

LUMIÈRE OSAKA KARATO

brownbag lab.

Screens and pendant lights incorporate pinkish glass, adding warmth and contrast to the cool tones of the furnishings and flooring.

Who said beige was boring? Certainly not the designers at brownbag lab. The team saw to create an elegant, neutral space with its gorgeous panoramic views and open kitchen presenting a lively culinary theatre. Lumière Osaka is located on the eighth floor of a busy commercial complex and, unusually for an eatery, is targeted mainly at women. As it is not the only restaurant in this location, the entrance boasts an eye-catching artwork – a chef's face, made up of the restaurant's name in 'vitamin' colours.

Even before entering the restaurant, guests can see the lively kitchen – in fact they have to walk through it into the lofty 4-m-high dining space. From every seat, there's an impressive view of Osaka, as well as the chefs performing in their own theatre.

While the kitchen is in sleek stainless steel, the dining space is decked out in warm but pale, natural hues: ash-coloured wood flooring is paired with textured, painted and stucco walls in creamy shades. The seating is in either multi-faded beige fabric or classy greige leather. A pinky-brown hue appears in the glassware of the restaurant, from the sleek pendant lampshades to the screens dividing up the space.

During the day, sheer curtains filter the sunlight comfortably. At night, the illuminated city views provide a glittering backdrop. Meanwhile, the counter space acts almost like a frame, showcasing the bustling kitchen with the chefs hard at work. With both panoramic views and kitchen capers to entertain diners, decoration can be kept to a minimum. The only artwork is subtle and unobtrusive – a painting in (what else?) shades of beige.

WHERE **Grand Front Osaka 8F, Osaka, Japan**
OPENING **April 2013**
CLIENT **K-Coeur**
DESIGNER **brownbag lab. (p.541)**
FLOOR AREA **144 m²**
WEBSITE **k-coeur.com**

AVERAGE PRICE OF MAIN COURSE **JPY 3750**
TYPE OF KITCHEN **Modern French cuisine**
OPENING HOURS **11.00–23.00**
CAPACITY **54 seats**

The sleek, stainless steel kitchen is fully visible, allowing diners to view the chefs as if they were actors on a stage.

The striking visual of a chef's portrait at the entrance – composed of the restaurant's name, repeated in varying colours – is an artwork by Shoji Koyabu.

MISTER STEER

Igloo

New decorative details add impact to a fairly traditional burger joint, with seating upholstered with an unexpected textile pattern by designer Paul Smith.

After 50+ years in the business, Mister Steer – Montreal's oldest and perhaps best-loved burger joint – was in need of an update (the last having taken place in 1988). Local design office Igloo was called in to give the eatery a makeover, refurbishing the interior and revitalising Mister Steer's branding into the bargain.

The challenge was to add modernity to the mix, while retaining the iconic burger joint's familiar and nostalgic appeal. The design team kept the layout traditional and crisply-organised, and focused on adding new interest to the space by using a range of high-impact materials to layer pattern and texture throughout the space. These are unexpectedly ornate: there are beautiful Bardelli tiles designed by Marcel Wanders, resembling a patchwork quilt, plus Paul Smith's detailed textiles for Maharam, and elegant Artek lighting fixtures. These combine to add a surprising richness to the space. Materials like these are combined with the more typical diner-style combination of timber panels, monochrome floor tiles and red leatherette banquettes.

It all adds up to a formula guaranteed not to alienate Mister Steer's loyal customers – many of whom have been coming here since childhood – while capable of attracting a new generation of design-savvy clients.

Attention to detail creates a seamless effect – Igloo also updated the eatery's entire brand, including the website, packaging and signage, right down to the condiment trays and uniforms. The result is retro yet fresh – just right for a city institution dating back to 1958, but still very much alive and kicking.

WHERE **1198 Ste-Catherine Ouest, Montreal, Canada**
OPENING **February 2012**
CLIENT **J Gaspar & A Blanchette**
DESIGNER **Igloo (p.545)**
FLOOR AREA **325 m²**
WEBSITE **mistersteer.com**

AVERAGE PRICE OF MAIN COURSE **CAD 20**
TYPE OF KITCHEN **Casual dining**
OPENING HOURS **8.00–22.00**
CAPACITY **132 seats**

Bardelli ceramic wall tiles, designed by
Marcel Wanders, add another surprise
in the interior, set off beautifully by the
traditional red leatherette booths.

Monochrome tiles were selected for
the flooring throughout, with various
patterns created in different areas of
the diner.

From the initial concept, the design team sketched out the various options for the seating banquettes.

Pattern and texture was layered throughout the space

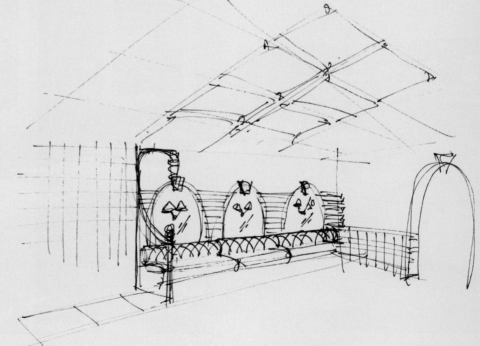

FLOOR PLAN

1 Dining area
2 Service station
3 Hostess station
4 Bar
5 Kitchen
6 Access to storage
7 Dishwashing room
8 Lavatories

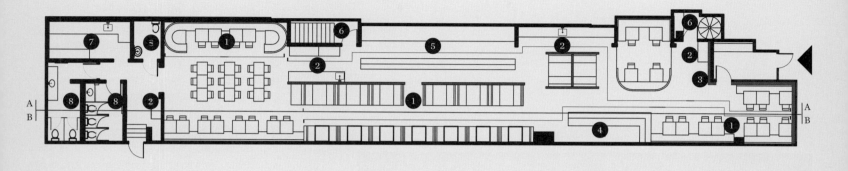

SECTION A

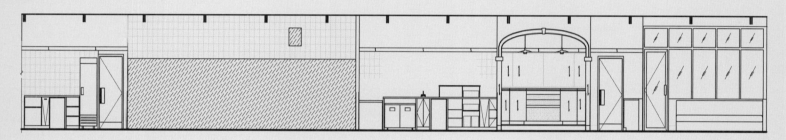

SECTION B

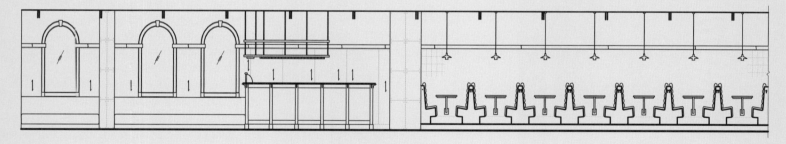

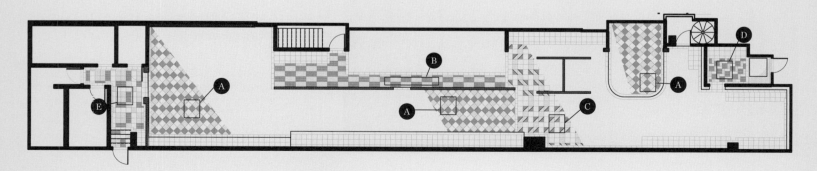

Five different floor tile patterns can be seen
in the diner (options A–E).

N_1221 AOBADAI
Ito Masaru Design Project/SEI

A wooden deck provides a discreet, intimate entrance for the restaurant.

This project involved transforming a former private house into a cosy restaurant, based on the themes of 'ecology' and 'naturalness', according to the client's ethos – this and other similar venues, all have the same name, distinguished only by the associated code that 'marks the spot' in their neighbourhood. The themes also reflect the food on offer: the restaurant serves grilled vegetables and other dishes as small plates, making the most of the natural taste of healthy ingredients from choice locations.

Designer Ito Masaru, called in to effect the transformation, began by reinforcing the original structure of the building and removing all the partition walls. New walls and screens created an airy new layout, more in line with the space's new function. The building faces a road with a row of cherry trees along a river – a beautiful and classically Japanese view. The whole wall facing the road was therefore replaced by a huge window in order to allow customers a chance to enjoy seasonal changes of the landscape. In addition, a deck terrace was added to both floors, enabling diners to enjoy fresh air whenever the weather allows.

The interior is kept simple and low-key, echoing the natural theme and reflecting the wholesomeness of the food on offer. Playfulness is added in the furniture, which illustrates the keyword 'recycled'. In addition to collecting used furniture for the space, the designer even custom-made chairs and tables from waste materials. The chandeliers on the ground floor are a spectacular example, with each being made from the wheel of an abandoned bicycle, becoming the focal point of the restaurant. On top of all this, the open-style kitchen allows customers to watch their vegetables being cooked.

WHERE **1-22-1 Aobadai, Meguro-ku, Tokyo, Japan**
OPENING **February 2013**
CLIENT **Natural Door**
DESIGNER **Ito Masaru Design Project/SEI (p.546)**
FLOOR AREA **210 m²**
WEBSITE **n1155.jp**

AVERAGE PRICE OF MAIN COURSE *JPY 550 per small plate*
TYPE OF KITCHEN *Tapas/small plates, mainly vegetable dishes*
OPENING HOURS *11.00–00.00*
CAPACITY *70 seats*

Literal recycling: the chandeliers on the ground floor were made from old bicycle wheels.

Lighting makes the big statement in this subdued wood-filled interior.

The interior is kept simple and low-key, echoing the naturalness theme

The venue has an all-front facade where diners can sit and have a view of the nearby river and the passing seasons.

Furniture is either recycled, or custom-made using discarded materials, with delightfully whimsical touches added.

Wood-lined stairs are in keeping with the organic concept.

NICKY'S FOOD & DRINKS

Oscar Vidal Studio

Retro metallic chairs are teamed up with neutral wood furnishings.

For regular client Hispabowling, Oscar Vidal Studio was asked to redesign the restaurant and bar of a bowling centre in Gandia, on the Mediterranean coast. The designers repeated the highly appropriate motif, used in an earlier project, of reclaimed bowling lanes – but in this case, they added used pins, too.

The first step, however, was to cover the whole interior with dark grey paint, to obliterate any traces of its previous incarnation and create a unified space. Then the old maple bowling lanes were added to top the bar and to make benches and create one of the doorways, plus – most spectacular of all – super-long tables. Underlying the material's origins, pins were fixed at the end of the table, allowing customers to examine them up close – naturally, bowlers normally see them only from a distance. Worn-out pins were also placed in blocks, then suspended from alcoves in the ceiling.

As the space is used as a cafe, restaurant and sports bar, the tables and seating are flexible and diverse, ranging from the large communal tables and benches to individual tables which are accompanied by replicas of the 1950s French Chair by Jean Pauchard, and finishing with bar stools for casual use. Some old-fashioned leather armchairs also make an appearance to create a pubby, clubby atmosphere. The custom lamps – designed using old washtubs in galvanized steel – add an unexpected and humorous touch. It all adds up to a coolly contemporary take on the traditional American-style bowling alley bar.

WHERE **Camp de Morvedre, Gandia, Spain**
OPENING **June 2012**
CLIENT **Hispabowling**
DESIGNER **Oscar Vidal Studio (p.548)**
FLOOR AREA **340 m²**
WEBSITE **ozonegandia.com**

AVERAGE PRICE OF MAIN COURSE **EUR 8**
TYPE OF KITCHEN **Fast food**
OPENING HOURS **Mon–Sun 12.00–23.00**
CAPACITY **130 seats**

A dividing line was clear in the wall and ceiling treatments: aged dark-grey paint vs pale-wood strips.

Customised lamps add a humorous touch

Fun lighting installations make use of upturned washtubs and an eye-catching cluster of bowling pins.

NIKO RESTAURANT
Rafael de Cárdenas / Architecture at Large

The luxurious bartop is made from a slab of white onyx marble, edged in brass.

On Mercer Street in SoHo, New York City, a slender staircase leads up and into the heart of sushi restaurant Niko. Overt symmetry dominates the spatial organisation, while natural materials lend warmth and nuanced irregularity. A network of ropes intricately stitches across the ceiling and onto the walls, creating a graphic foreground to the exposed brick walls. Banquettes wrap the perimeter of the room, extending towards dramatic double-height windows at one end of the space. On the opposite side of the dining room, an onyx and brass sushi bar sits across from its cocktail bar double, separated by a herringbone travertine floor. Above the bars, two art pieces created by Jim Drain suspend brass, tinted wood and glass overhead like vibrant, primitive chandeliers.

De Cárdenas drew inspiration from Japanese Shinto design aesthetics for this dramatic interior. This is most noticeable in the various latticed installations on the walls, and in Drain's colourful ceiling structures and elaborate dyed-wood screen. These pieces add movement and excitement, focusing attention upwards and outwards in the space.

Double-height windows bathe the restaurant in natural light and offer great city views, while materials are both humble (brick, rope) and luxurious (walnut, oak, onyx). To provide a restful backdrop for all the geometric wall and ceiling installations in the restaurant, De Cárdenas kept the furnishings in the dining room simple and low key. These include a custom-made bar, black-leather upholstery and simple wall mirrors.

WHERE **170 Mercer St, New York City, United States**
OPENING **2011 (venue has since closed)**
CLIENT **Niko Restaurant**
DESIGNER **Rafael de Cárdenas / Architecture at Large (p.549)**
FLOOR AREA **1220 m²**
WEBSITE **helloniko.com**

AVERAGE PRICE OF MAIN COURSE **USD 30–60**
TYPE OF KITCHEN **Japanese**
OPENING HOURS **Mon–Fri 12.00–01.00, Sat 18.00–02.00**
CAPACITY **70 seats**

PHOTOS Floto + Warner

Close-up view of the geometric, cable wall display.

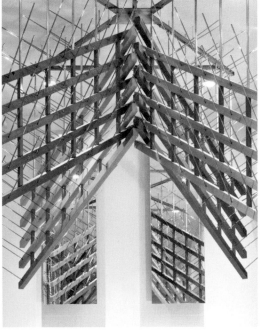

The artwork is constructed from coloured timber and glass components.

Japanese Shinto design aesthetics inspire this dramatic interior

Guests emerge into the heart of the restaurant behind the pastel-hued latticed wall.

NONNA MARTHA

Franken Architekten

The design sets out to reflect the simple, yet elegantly-rustic cuisine that is served in the restaurant.

For Franken Architekten's second restaurant for Brauhaus Goldener Engel in the centre of Ingelheim, the designers channelled the homely kitchen of the archetypical Italian grandmother. The concept of Nonna Martha was to create a combination of food and interior based on the down-to-earth traditions of rural Italy. The cuisine is a hommage to the Italian grandma – *la nonna* – and her rustic yet delicious home cooking.

As a main aim for the designers was to convey authenticity, the interior features a material palette of coarse untreated wood, white tiles and industrial enamel. All the walls are covered with a patchwork of wooden boards, both in stained pine and oak, which create a rich, relief-like texture. This is framed above and below by a white strip, with the exposed ceiling painted in an expanse of black.

The plain, concrete-grey floor underscores the simple nature of the interior and fits in with the radically reduced colour spectrum. The rather graphic effect is enhanced by a lighting concept which features, bare light bulbs, as well as black and white pendant luminaires in various sizes. This interior-design equivalent of *la cucina povera* is also emphasised by the simple chairs and tables, as well as tableware.

The interior avoids predictability by offering a large choice of seating at various heights and in various combinations, ranging from long tables for groups to grey, upholstered sofas and bar stools and more intimate tables for two. Franken Architekten collaborated with Stereoraum Architekten on the project, and with Surface on the graphic concept.

WHERE **Binger Str. 84, Ingelheim, Germany**
OPENING **April 2012**
CLIENT **Brauhaus Goldener Engel**
DESIGNER **Franken Architekten (p.544)**
FLOOR AREA **208 m²**
WEBSITE **nonnamartha.de**

AVERAGE PRICE OF MAIN COURSE **EUR 14**
TYPE OF KITCHEN *Rustic Italian*
OPENING HOURS **Mon–Sat 10.00–00.00**
CAPACITY **95 seats**

PHOTOS Würmli Fotograf

Patchwork wood panelling wraps around the space to enhance the down-to-earth ambience.

A patchwork of wooden boards creates a relief-like texture

A calming colour palette is underlined by the pale grey flooring, making a soft and neutral base for fittings and furniture.

NORDBURGER

Genesin Studio

The metal aspects of the bespoke stools
were painted a corporate green colour.

Nordburger's interiors and branding approach is seamless thanks to Genesin Studio's collaboration with designer Peter Jay Deering, which ensured a uniform comfortable-yet-street look for house style and restaurant space.

With a client brief to create a comfortable, affordable burger and hotdog store that didn't look like a diner, Genesin took its design inspiration from old-school New York street diners – but deconstructed and reinterpreted for the modern age. Instead of leatherette and formica, therefore, the team opted for warm timber, white tiles and raw concrete – a material palette that is modern in the extreme.

Classic, gloss-white tiles envelop the space except for the oak veneer wall behind the serving counter, which also acts also as the main seating aspect. From here, guests get a front-row theatrical view of the cooks at work. As the space is very narrow, the stools were fixed to avoid the messy furniture syndrome and keep the space sleek and streamlined. Additionally, an all-concrete, industrial-style washbasin was incorporated at the back of the space for the use of customers. All this combined creates an understated, approachable fast-food experience which is nevertheless high on style.

The result is that rare thing – a burger joint with plenty of contemporary class. Ryan Genesin reports that the big hit of this project was incorporating the hand-wash basin into the retail food experience. 'People have loved the idea of eating with clean hands or even washing after eating – simply leaving a fast-food store feeling clean and not dirty, which is half the stigma with fast food,' he says. Why did nobody ever think of it before?

WHERE **168 The Parade Norwood, Adelaide, Australia**
OPENING **March 2013**
CLIENT **Nordburger**
DESIGNER **Genesin Studio (p.545)**
FLOOR AREA **60 m²**
WEBSITE **nordburger.com.au**

AVERAGE PRICE OF MAIN COURSE **AUD 7**
TYPE OF KITCHEN **Fast food**
OPENING HOURS **From 11.30 until late**
CAPACITY **20 seats**

The sink at the far end of the diner is for the use of customers, to freshen up before tucking into their burger.

A burger joint with plenty of contemporary class

The lighting adheres to the streamlined aesthetic (Oluce Fresnell wall lights).

White tiles and oak veneer is also applied to the eatery's facade.

NOT GUILTY
Ippolito Fleitz Group

Simple materials and forms together with light, pearly tones live up to the restaurant's name.

A 'little heaven on Earth' is the idea that design office Ippolito Fleitz Group sets out to convey with its interior for this fast food restaurant chain, where the focus is firmly on honest and nutritious foods, imaginatively prepared into many different salads and snacks. The chain's downtown Zurich location, the third in the series, is no exception.

The long, open space welcomes guests with a range of natural tones and textures. Pastel hues, including pearly beige, soft terracotta and dusky pink, combine harmoniously with the natural, oak wood herringbone flooring. The focal point on entering is the colourful salad bar – colour of course coming from the wide range of vegetables on offer (fresh daily from a local farmer), and is accompanied by a graphic, easy-to-read menu board.

The restaurant is alluring from the outside, thanks to the view from the street of a long, central, communal table canopied by curving, white-lacquered branches of the floor-to-ceiling tree installation. Nearby, several other types of seating are also available – offering something for everyone. Curved lines contrast with rectilinear ones, as round tables and sofas are combined with rectangular tables and stools. The dominant materials within the space suggest purity and wholesomeness, as do the simple, flowing lines. It's all perfectly on brand for the chain with its natural and healthy values. Playful and unexpected elements, like the taut, twisted canvas ceiling bands, and hemp twine-embellished wall graphic of clouds, add an element of gentle surprise.

WHERE **Badenerstrasse 29, Zurich, Switzerland**
OPENING **April 2013**
CLIENT **not guilty Management**
DESIGNER **Ippolito Fleitz Group (p.545)**
FLOOR AREA **230 m²**
WEBSITE **notguilty.ch**

AVERAGE PRICE OF MAIN COURSE **EUR 14**
TYPE OF KITCHEN **Natural foods (salads, soups, etc.)**
OPENING HOURS **Mon–Fri 6.30–21.00, Sat–Sun 8.00–21.00**
CAPACITY **91 seats**

A lacquered white floor-to-ceiling tree installation attracts attention and adds drama to the communal table.

A colour palette of white, beige and dusky pink enhances the oak herringbone parquet floor and the wooden furniture.

A ceiling installation of canvas bands weaves its way throughout the space.

Alcove seating provides the option of privacy for customers.

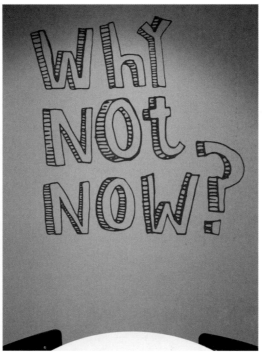

Fun, graphical statements on the wall offer food for thought.

Playful and unexpected details add an element of surprise

Extras like treats and magazines for guests to peruse maximise the restaurant experience.

OLD JOE'S

The Society Inc.

Colourful tiles, timber planks and painted concrete – ideal floor coverings for sand-strewn customers heading inside for refreshments, straight from the beach.

Old Joe's, says designer Sibella Court, was 'named after the old milk bar that everyone from the area remembers, covered in old advertising and run by Joe'. This new version, a casual cafe and eatery, is located directly across the road from the beach, and the design revolves around the idea of bringing the outside in. The aim was to create a bright, relaxed place to eat and hang out, 'straight from the beach, sand on your feet kinda feel,' says Court.

The outdoorsy atmosphere is helped along by the recycled wooden floor, which mimics the beach boardwalk. Wooden picnic tables painted in pastel blue, and lampshades made from deckchair-stripe fabrics, continue the beachy references.

Drawing on the beach culture she grew up with in the 1970s, as well as on her research into local social history and surf culture, the designer discovered the Old Joe's milk bar cropped up time and time again in the stories associated with the Cronulla area of Sydney. This inspired her to use elements and finishes associated with milk bars in the interior, such as terrazzo bartops, soft sorbet colours, striped awnings and hand-painted signage.

'I worked with a talented team of builders, sign writers, blacksmiths, furniture makers, dyers and print makers to create a detailed space that reveals both the history and legacy of Cronulla and universal seaside culture,' she continues. Indeed, the many custom elements add to the idiosyncratic impression made by this bright, airy space, which has all the freshness of a sea breeze.

WHERE **135 Elouera Road, Cronulla, Sydney, Australia**
OPENING **November 2013**
CLIENT **BSB Holdings**
DESIGNER **The Society Inc. (p.551)**
FLOOR AREA **320 m²**
WEBSITE **oldjoes.com.au**

AVERAGE PRICE OF MAIN COURSE **AUD 18–25**
TYPE OF KITCHEN **Fast food**
OPENING HOURS **12.00–00.00**
CAPACITY **100 seats**

Miami turquoise tiles and tropical fabrics create a vibrantly fresh feel.

The venue has maintained some of the original vibe of Old Joe's, hence the nostalgic signage.

Retro metallic furniture sits beneath faded graphics, heralding idyllic days gone by.

Terrazzo bartops meet soft sorbet colours

The venue has striped lampshades referencing deckchairs, as well an intriguing light installation made from timber lobster pots.

OPUS V

Blocher Blocher Partners

A glass-walled wine store and sleek lounge greet diners at this sixth-floor restaurant.

Opus – the Latin word for a successful composition – is a fitting name for this restaurant above the city rooftops in Mannheim, with its unusual architecture, stylish interior and unique cuisine. Lots of natural materials, especially wood, and an open feeling create a Nordic-style space, uniting simplicity and sophistication.

The restaurant is in an exclusive location, at the top of the elegant Engelhorn department store. Guests ascend to the sixth floor, where they are welcomed by a glass-walled wine store at the entrance to the lounge, an ideal spot for pre-dinner aperitif.

The parquet floors, cherry wood furniture and brick walls of this area continue in the harmonious restaurant interior. Tables are arranged parallel to the panoramic windows and are complemented by ceiling and wall panels of expanded metal in warm-brown tones. The continuous parquet flooring and sliding glass elements open out to a 6-m-wide passage, ensuring a smooth transition to the veranda with its inviting dining terrace. With its array of plants and herbs, this is a green oasis in the middle of the city.

Another highlight is the chef's table, a private room that shares a wooden wall with the kitchen; the wall can be slid aside on request for a direct view into the art of creative cuisine. Other visitors, too, can follow the goings-on in the kitchen through a glass panel in the main dining room, where white volcanic stone meets beige walls and black tiles.

WHERE **O5, 9–12, Mannheim, Germany**
OPENING **November 2013**
CLIENT **Engelhorn Gastro**
DESIGNER **Blocher Blocher Partners (p.541)**
FLOOR AREA **430 m²**
WEBSITE **restaurant-opus-v.de**

AVERAGE PRICE OF SET THREE-COURSES **EUR 60**
TYPE OF KITCHEN **Gourmet, regional with international influences**
OPENING HOURS **Tue–Sat 12.00–14.00, 18.00–22.00**
CAPACITY **50 seats**

PHOTOS Fabian Aurel Hild

Brick walls, wooden floors, cherry-wood furnishings and ceiling panels of expanded metal in warm tones create an earthy, comforting interior.

An open space uniting simplicity and sophistication

The chef's table, a private dining room, offers diners a touch of luxurious privacy.

A shaded veranda opens seamlessly from the main space, thanks to sliding glass elements.

OZONE
Oscar Vidal Studio

The design concept aimed to create long, lean lines.

A bowling alley restaurant in a Spanish seaside town with a large population of retired foreigners called for what designer Oscar Vidal terms 'a more adult character'. For the interior of the eatery in Moraira, he took advantage of the availability of old wooden bowling lanes, beautifully crafted from maple and pine. As the basic structure of the space was concrete, these wooden boards, measuring 4-m long and 7-cm thick, were a welcome addition to the premises, adding the warmth and texture of a natural, and timeworn, material.

The reclaimed wood was used to craft a sleek bar with a canopy, creating a welcoming focal point, plus a large central table alongside some smaller individual ones, as well as bar stools and benches. Simple, sleek forms recall the material's origins and enhance its inherent organic qualities, contrasting effectively with the concrete walls, floor and ceiling and evoking bowling history. The effect is restrained but relaxed, and creates the feeling of a fairly expansive space in the restaurant, helped by the rhythmic hanging lamps around its periphery.

The design team went to some lengths to keep the material palette simple, using Tecnocemento, a cement and resin-based coating which resembles concrete, for the bar structure, so as not to depart from the concept's formula. There's one exception to the wood-plus-concrete rule: the recycled-plastic chairs designed by Barcelona-based Estudio Mariscal, in neutral tones that complement the overall greige colour scheme.

WHERE **Centro Comercial El Planet, Teulada, Spain**
OPENING **April 2012**
CLIENT **Hispabowling**
DESIGNER **Oscar Vidal Studio (p.548)**
FLOOR AREA **218 m²**
WEBSITE **hispabowling.com**

AVERAGE PRICE OF MAIN COURSE **EUR 8**
TYPE OF KITCHEN **Fast food**
OPENING HOURS **Mon–Sun 12.00–23.00**
CAPACITY **84 seats**

Seating comes in the form of wooden benches and contemporary Green Chairs, so-called due to their 100 per cent recycled seats.

Simple, sleek forms recall the material's origins

Simple pendant globe bulbs illuminate the space.

The furnishings have an eco-aesthetic, making use of reclaimed wood from bowling alleys.

PASTEL
Baranowitz Kronenberg Architecture

A futuristic, facetted white ceiling is paired with a monumental marble bar complete with fixed, retro-style lamps.

Pastel is Baranowitz Kronenberg's new brasserie on Tel Aviv's cultural block, located in the new wing of the Museum of Art. The design team realised the restaurant in an exclusive setting: a square on the ground level, facing the museum's sculpture garden and its grove of eucalyptus trees.

The narrative for Pastel is inspired by two opposite worlds: one represented by the hyper-geometric architecture of the new wing, and the world of the brasserie, an almost two-centuries-old culinary bastion of the western world. These two worlds have been juxtaposed in a straightforward yet appealing way, with classic meets contemporary style in a high-contrast space.

The restaurant consists of three areas: a central space, a terrace overlooking the museum's sculpture garden, and the intimate, almost entirely secluded Cocoon bar. The dynamic shape of the new wing is sucked into the space to become the interior envelope of Pastel. In the main dining area, endless shades of white loom over guests in the form of the architectural ceiling with its vigorous geometry. The southeasterly light bounces off the grey stone flooring and creates a soft, welcoming atmosphere, a must-have mood for socialising.

The furniture and fittings are the embodiment of classic brasserie style: booth seating, crystal chandeliers, voluptuous marble tops, and Thonet chairs in a dark-red hue sitting atop a herringbone wood platform – an island of sorts evoking different times and places.

WHERE **Museum of Art, Tel Aviv, Israel**
OPENING **July 2013**
CLIENT **Ma'adana**
DESIGNER **Baranowitz Kronenberg Architecture (p.541)**
FLOOR AREA **530 m²**
WEBSITE **pastel-tlv.com**

AVERAGE PRICE OF MAIN COURSE **ILS 100**
TYPE OF KITCHEN **Modern brasserie**
OPENING HOURS **12.00–00.00**
CAPACITY **172 seats**

The expansive geometric walls and ceiling is a response to Preston Scott Cohen's new wing of Tel Aviv Museum of Art.

Classic meets contemporary in a high-contrast space

An angular terrace offers the option of sitting outside.

Inside, tall windows maximise the effect of daylight.

FLOOR PLAN

1 Dining area
2 Waiters' station
3 Kitchen
4 Cocoon bar
5 Outdoor terrace
6 Lavatories

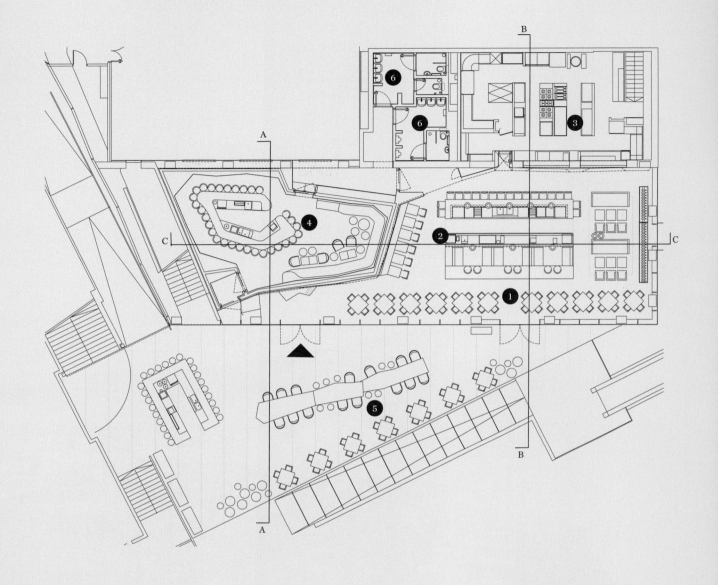

SECTION A

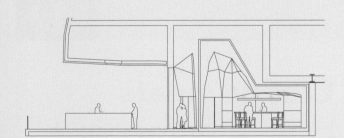

SECTION B

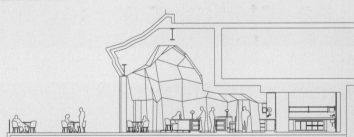

SECTION C

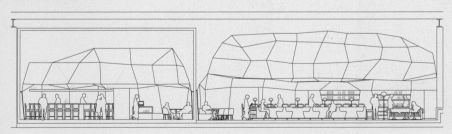

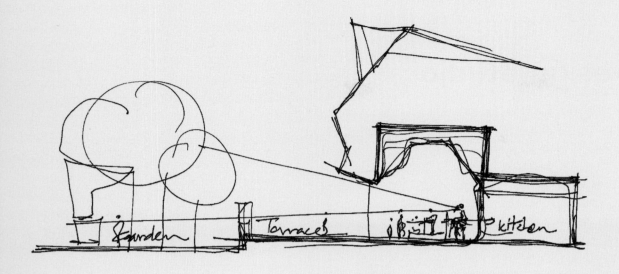

Sketch indicating the view both from within the bar (below) and out onto the terraces (left).

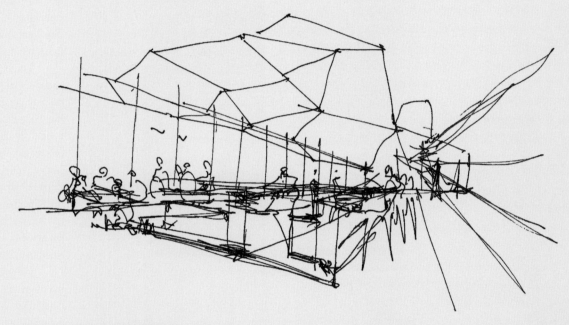

The interior envelope has an architectural ceiling with vigorous geometry

A metallic framework was first installed to shape the ceiling, followed by the asymmetric panels of Barrisol (stretched sheets of polymer).

PLAY POT
Limtaehee Design Studio

Sheets of translucent tarpaulin form the bespoke cupboard fronts, rolled-up to reveal shelves for pots and condiments.

Play Pot is a *boonsik* restaurant offering Korean street food in a snack-bar setting. However, there is a twist: professional hotel chefs prepare the tasty traditional snacks, transforming them into trendy and stylish dishes. This concept, with its combination of hotel cuisine with low-priced yet high-quality food, inspired designer Lim Tae Hee to emulate the 'best of both worlds' idea. 'If this can be done with food, why not with interior design?' she says.

Therefore, the concept set out to create a high-quality version of the Korean *pojangmacha*, a unique type of mobile snack bar based on a modified wheeled cart and a tent. 'It's interesting to express the comfort of an indoor space even though it is installed in the open,' says the designer. 'In order to express this fine line between inside and outside, we decided to project the front sign of the restaurant to give the feeling that the interior is extending outwards into the street, diluting the border between them.'

The *pojangmacha* has another interesting feature. A vinyl tarpaulin is typically used as the tent material, and is glowingly illuminated at night by rows of light bulbs, creating a totally different feel than by day. The design team copied this effect using tent-like swathes of bright yellow striped fabric. Sheets of tarpaulin also cover rows of shelves as improvised storage cupboards. Naked light bulbs and lots of plants placed on the floor help to further the inside–outside feel.

WHERE **Seocho-gu, Seoul, South Korea**
OPENING **July 2012**
CLIENT **Moon Sung Jin**
DESIGNER **Limtaehee Design Studio (p.546)**
FLOOR AREA **77 m²**
WEBSITE **n/a**

AVERAGE PRICE OF MAIN COURSE **SKW 8000**
TYPE OF KITCHEN **Korean street food**
OPENING HOURS **11.30–15.00, 17.00–22.00**
CAPACITY **35 seats**

PHOTOS **Park Young Chae**

Street furniture-style fittings and a raw concrete floor underline the origins of this restaurant's local street food cuisine.

Inside, the bright stripey pattern flows through the space, running across walls, fittings and floor.

The yellow and white material pinned to the ceiling references the striped fabric of *pojangmachas*, street stalls based on modified wheeled carts and tents.

Simple furnishings and bare bulbs enhance the street atmosphere.

A counter of plywood cabinets is painted in a palette of pastels and limes.

A stylish take on Korean street food stalls

The designer sought a cost-effective and unique solution for the diner's interior.

PONY RESTAURANT

Woods Bagot

The theatre of food preparation is at the heart of the forge-inspired concept.

Brisbane's Pony restaurant aims to indulge the senses with sights and smells of food theatrically prepared on the charcoal grill – only here, the grill is composed of huge spits, on which whole sides of meat are roasted on leaping flames. No wonder then that Woods Bagot chose to build the design narrative around the idea of a farrier's forge (where a blacksmith shoes horses).

Many earthy raw materials were incorporated, including an imposing 2-m-wide blackened steel ribbon that winds its way spectacularly through the space, a prime example of the blacksmith's art. Colours and textures are dark and rich but warm, in keeping with the theme.

The object of the design team was to construct an instant sense of history in the space, evoking an emotional experience. Materials are therefore based on raw authenticity: there's an abundance of exposed brick, raw steel, rough-sawn timber and exposed copper pipework, combined with leather upholstered furniture. The effect is kept sophisticated, however, thanks to some careful spatial choreography when it comes to grouping materials and forms.

The people who work here are beautifully framed by the design, since the restaurant is also a stage for the spirited chefs and waiting staff who go about their business in full view of the guests, animating the dramatic scene.

The restaurant features a number of versatile dining spaces, with indoor transitioning to outdoor via an open, timber-decked interior space. The result is a series of dining options, from open, communal spaces, to more intimate banquettes and booths, plus the full dining experience of the kitchen.

WHERE **Eagle Street Pier, Brisbane, Australia**
OPENING **November 2012**
CLIENT **Steel Espresso**
DESIGNER **Woods Bagot (p.551)**
FLOOR AREA **510 m²**
WEBSITE **ponydining.com.au**

AVERAGE PRICE OF MAIN COURSE AUD 38
TYPE OF KITCHEN Authentic charcoal grill
OPENING HOURS 12.00–15.00, 17.30 until late
CAPACITY 200 seats

A blackened-steel 'ribbon' winds its way above the diners through the eatery.

The effect is sophisticated thanks to some careful spatial choreography

Decorative metalwork, mainly overhead, is the major theme.

FLOOR PLAN

1 Welcome station
2 Bar
3 Dining area
4 Open kitchen
5 Back of house
6 Lavatories

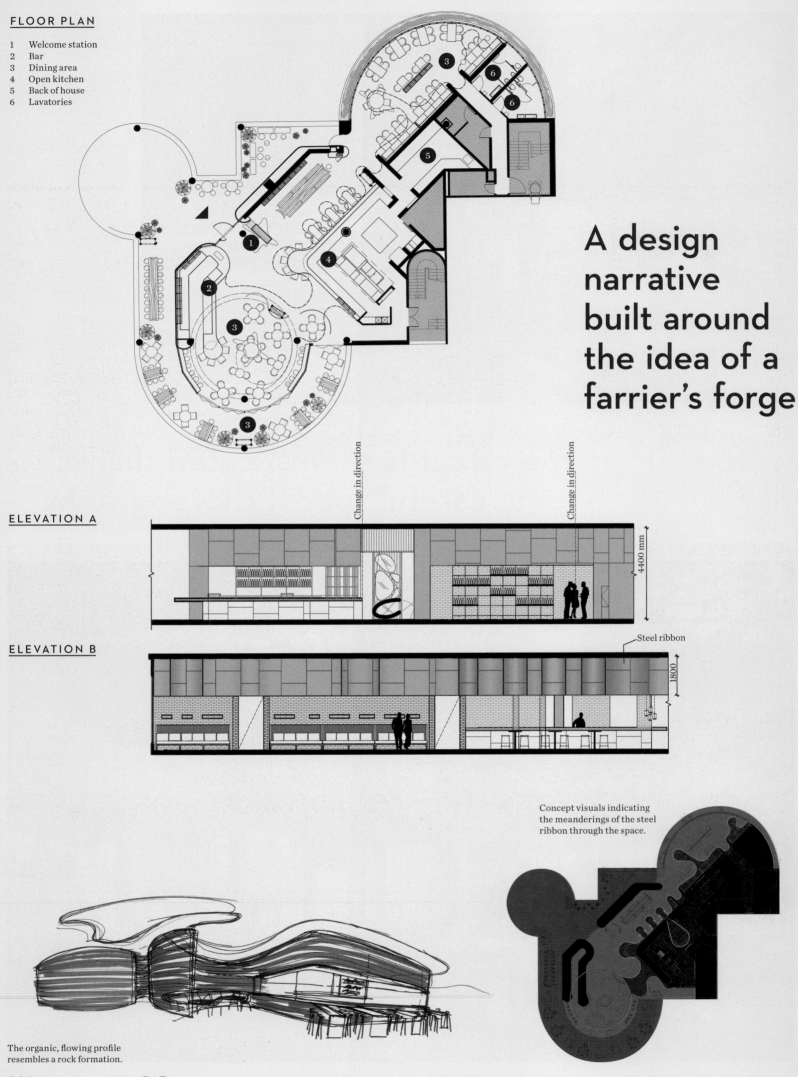

A design narrative built around the idea of a farrier's forge

ELEVATION A

Change in direction

Change in direction

4400 mm

ELEVATION B

Steel ribbon

1800

Concept visuals indicating the meanderings of the steel ribbon through the space.

The organic, flowing profile resembles a rock formation.

Brick, wood and leather add a richly earthy ambience.

Long sightlines throughout the space ensure the dark materials avoid a feeling of claustrophobia.

RESTAURANT VANDAAG

D/Dock

Following the success of Restaurant Vandaag Utrecht, owners Jim and Michelle Xu decided to open a second establishment in Amsterdam. The design studio responsible for the Utrecht project, D/Dock, was asked to create the new restaurant.

Offering seven different cuisines, this venue is no ordinary all-you-can-eat restaurant. According to D/Dock the restaurant is 'like a market place where you can shop around for food'. Since chefs at the various live cooking stations prepare your dish on the spot, there is more than a touch of theatre in this concept.

The variety of cooking counters and cuisines makes the restaurant appealing to a wide range of guests – families, visitors from the nearby congress centre and locals. Children play an important role in the concept: there is a separate playroom and a special counter where kids can bake their own cookies.

Diversity is the main ingredient of the signature dishes, and was also the starting point for the interior design. The large space asked for a warm ambience and a transparent layout. Various seating typologies are integrated to divide the whole space into different areas, creating pockets of intimacy.

The light in the venue features balanced bright and dark areas. The specially designed 'moodscape', a light installation that suggests a natural environment through light and movement, is an effective eye-catcher. The pattern simulates an abstracted stone landscape which is visible throughout the restaurant and buffet area. The contrast between the yellow-toned moodscape and the black industrial ceiling draws attention from the outside and invites passers-by inside.

Contrasting geometries, divided by a metallic curtain: spherical forms on the left, cubic shapes on the right.

Each cooking zone represents a different cuisine, with one eye-catching canopy indicating the fish counter.

WHERE **Europa Blvd 1, Amsterdam, the Netherlands**
OPENING **October 2012**
CLIENT **XU Family**
DESIGNER **D/Dock (p.542)**
FLOOR AREA **1250 m²**
WEBSITE **restaurantvandaag.nl**

AVERAGE PRICE OF MAIN COURSE **Pay per hour**
TYPE OF KITCHEN **World kitchen, live cooking**
OPENING HOURS **11.30–22.00**
CAPACITY **500 seats**

PHOTOS Alan Jansen

The light and dark areas have numerous seating options, creating cosy enclaves.

RICE HOME

AS Design

The designers have dubbed the creative concept as 'playful honeycomb'.

Located in Guangzhou City, China, Rice Home is a newly launched premium casual dining brand, originally from Hong Kong. As the name suggests, the menu is based on rice, and while this is essentially fast food, the emphasis is also on style and good service.

Four Lau and Sam Sum, chief designers of AS Design, chose a design language which they believe will appeal to young people – based on the hexagon as a form and bright yellow as a colour, both evoking the idea of a beehive. 'We distributed this natural structure in every corner, representing a dynamic home/living space,' says Four Lau.

Irregularly placed hexagons enhance the spatial layering of the venue's entrance, where 3D black hexagons mediate between inside and outside. The interior features graphic yellow hexagons on a black background, creating a warm, intimate atmosphere and giving a spacious feel to the restaurant. The furnishings mirror the black and yellow colour theme, with plenty of neutral, warm wood adding a restful element to the young, lively scheme.

The hexagonal shapes on the ceiling add depth and texture, while concealing the air conditioning and framing the lighting. There are more playful 3D details on the curved wooden wall, where sculpted bowls contain yellow spheres that rise from them like the aromas of delicious food. Meanwhile, the restaurant's menus are displayed on TV screens, a detail which gives a high-tech touch to the venue.

WHERE **Hengbao Plaza, Guangzhou, China**
OPENING **April 2013**
CLIENT **Hung's Management Service**
DESIGNER **AS Design (p.540)**
FLOOR AREA: **117 m²**
WEBSITE **n/a**

AVERAGE PRICE OF MAIN COURSE **CNY 25**
TYPE OF KITCHEN **Fast food**
OPENING HOURS **10.00–22.00**
CAPACITY **46 seats**

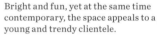

Bright and fun, yet at the same time contemporary, the space appeals to a young and trendy clientele.

On the glazed wall, hexagons appear to float upwards.

Graphic yellow hexagons on a black background, create a warm, intimate atmosphere

RILEY STREET GARAGE
RAD Studio

Once a full-service garage, now an elegant restaurant, Riley Street Garage is a casebook example of repurposing an industrial landmark as a contemporary nightspot. Located in a beautiful, art deco building, the striking original features called for a light but decisive touch, which is exactly what RAD Studio's Richard Alexander provided. The team, which included Quinton Lloyd as the architect, maintained the original industrial warehouse elements while incorporating some spectacular – but quite cost-effective – design finishes, including rich leathers, steel, brass and copper detailing.

'Heritage-building constraints had a strong bearing on the architectural responses,' says Alexander, who decided to concentrate on keeping the space open and uncluttered. 'A restaurant of this size always requires an intricate network of services – plumbing, electrical, and so on. Ensuring this is done with minimal interference with the building fabric was a real challenge.'

In the streamlined space, key furnishings and lighting were custom-designed, with a nod to the deco context. 'The building was and is very raw and honest in its rough state of preservation,' continues the designer. 'It was important that the new materials presented somewhat of a counterpoint to the old work but were also raw and intricate – unlacquered brass tiles, hand-glazed tiles and custom lighting shrouds made from folded metals.' These details add up to a rich, crafted look, in keeping with the atmosphere of the original architecture. Lighting plays a role, with carefully directed spots and up- and down-lighters on the brick walls adding a certain vintage drama.

The staircase was constructed from spotted gum timber with a custom stain finish.

WHERE **55 Riley Street, Sydney, Australia**
OPENING **October 2013**
CLIENT **The Parlour Group**
DESIGNER **RAD Studio (p.549)**
FLOOR AREA **660 m²**
WEBSITE **rileystreetgarage.com.au**

AVERAGE PRICE OF MAIN COURSE **AUD 25**
TYPE OF KITCHEN **Relaxed shared food/oyster bar**
OPENING HOURS **Tue–Sun 12.00–00.00**
CAPACITY **190 seats**

Mechanical elements are gathered into a graphic overhead rig, which enhances the original industrial architecture.

A glowing brass-tiled bar, and other custom furniture and fittings, nod to the building's art deco origins.

All the furniture and fittings were custom-designed for the interior, using rich, earthy materials of wood, leather and metal.

Repurposing an industrial landmark as a contemporary nightspot

Folded metal wall lights illuminate the exposed brickwork.

A simple yet effective lighting scheme adds drama to the restaurant interior.

FLOOR PLAN

1　Bar
2　Casual seating
3　Dining area
4　Kitchen

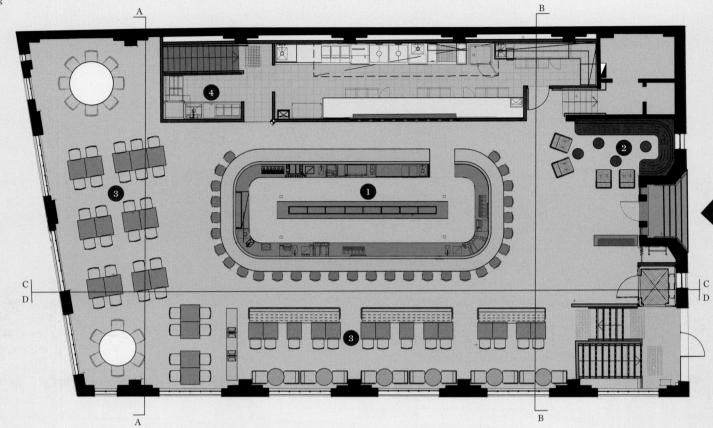

Once a full-service garage, now an elegant restaurant

SECTION A

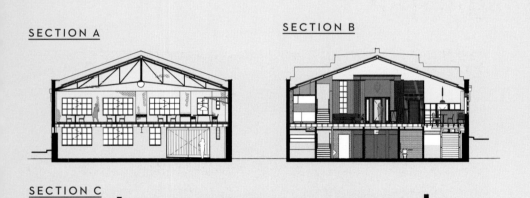

SECTION B

SECTION C

SECTION D

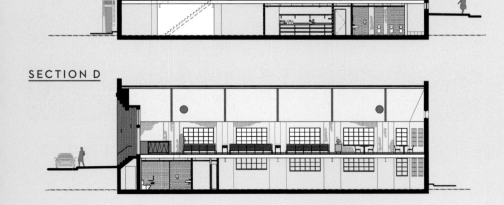

ELEVATION

Carefully modulated colours, forms and materials create a richly-textured space in this repurposed restaurant interior.

SANSIBAR
Dittel Architekten

The furniture and fittings
have a neutral feel, with
walls in matching sand tones.

Recycled wood adds a
washed-out, driftwood effect
for the walls and shelving.

Sansibar, a restaurant located in the new branch of the luxury Breuninger department store in Dusseldorf, was designed by Dittel Architekten and inspired by a taste of sea air.

This is the first mainland branch of the famous Sansibar restaurant, located on the North Sea island of Sylt, which is well known for its seafood menu. The brief was to transfer the relaxed and informal atmosphere of the original restaurant to the Rhine metropolis. In keeping with Breuninger harmony, the restaurant was to radiate a natural, high-class flair and to unify two strong brands, Breuninger and Sansibar.

In order to experience the atmosphere of Sylt, typical materials were used, such as old wood for the panelling and solid oak for the tables. Wine is a key theme for the Sansibar, and this was integrated as a characteristic element – including a cosy enclave where diners can sit amongst the best vintage wines lining the walls.

Two long tables in the middle of the room promote communication and informality, while the contemporary candelabra suspended from the driftwood installation overhead provides pleasant lighting and an eye-catching feature.

Along one side of the space are more cosy booths, where regulars can take up their spot and have time out to escape. The four booths are bathed in indirect lighting. They represent basic wooden huts from the seaside but their design and lighting are simple and modern, again demonstrating a definite link to the Sansibar restaurant on Sylt.

WHERE **Breuninger, Dusseldorf, Germany**
OPENING **October 2013**
CLIENT **Breuninger**
DESIGNER **Dittel Architekten (p.544)**
FLOOR AREA **350 m²**
WEBSITE **sansibarbybreuninger.de**

AVERAGE PRICE OF MAIN COURSE **EUR 20**
TYPE OF KITCHEN **Maritime cuisine meets regional specialities**
OPENING HOURS **Mon–Sat 11.30–00.00**
CAPACITY **130 seats**

Three distinct zones lend interest to the
space as well as allowing diners to choose
from various seating options.

An oak floor and tables are set off by a palette of soft greys and whites.

A driftwood theme meets maritime cuisine

Custom-made crates and cupboards made of driftwood line the walls of this dining area.

SLA
Nicemakers

Passers-by are attracted by the calm ambience radiating from the space.

Wall decorations bring to mind small-scale gardening shears or secateurs.

Sla is the name of an attractive new venture in Amsterdam, as well as being the Dutch word for lettuce. As you might expect therefore, salads feature prominently in this organic, healthy eating joint, along with soups and juices. The restaurant's motto is 'eat, share, live' – so the design of the space had to resonate with this lifestyle philosophy, as well as with the green and natural raw ingredients. Furthermore, it had to result in a formula that could be applied to future branches.

The design team at Nicemakers came up with a greenhouse concept to give the store a strong identity. The greenhouse is where the salads are grown, and so it becomes a repeated motif in the store. A three-dimensional black frame in the shape of a greenhouse forms the heart of the interior – the counter space where customers can place their orders and mix their own customised salad.

At the back of the space, glass doors with skylights above create a conservatory structure that repeats the profile. Greenery is abundant: on the walls, garden trellises support a variety of hanging plants, many placed in terracotta pots which are then playfully positioned in wire baskets. There are plants in pots on the floor and on all the tables too – some in wire baskets shaped like mini-greenhouses.

Behind the counter, wall baskets display an abundance of different fruits. Plants, fruit and food add the main splashes of colour to the simple white and neutral interior. Straightforward patio-style wooden tables and folding wooden chairs complete the rustic, outdoorsy effect.

WHERE **Ceintuurbaan 149, Amsterdam, the Netherlands**
OPENING **July 2013**
CLIENT **Sla**
DESIGNER **Nicemakers (p.547)**
FLOOR AREA **110 m²**
WEBSITE **ilovesla.com**

AVERAGE PRICE OF MAIN COURSE **EUR 8**
TYPE OF KITCHEN **Organic, salads, juices**
OPENING HOURS **Mon–Sun 12.00–21.00**
CAPACITY **40 seats**

Eat your greens surrounded by greenery.

The motto is 'eat, share, live' and the space reflects a green lifestyle philosophy

SOAKS
Ito Masaru Design Project/SEI

Fun signage is an intriguing introduction to this restaurant.

A garden-like terrace sends a clear message about the healthy treats on offer inside.

The owner of this restaurant is a company that makes and sells dried vegetable powder, which it extracts from organic produce using a special technique. The original concept for the eatery was for it to be a means of proposing a whole lifestyle based on supplementing the diet with vegetable powder – a way for the busy people of today to compensate for their often insufficient vegetable intake. The restaurant serves the kind of meals that customers' might make using the powder.

A signature Soaks product is its doughnut range, the director's key food concept, is made using the vegetable powder. The healthy menu also includes nutritious pasta, soups, main courses and sweet dishes with the powder added to the other ingredients. The restaurant interior, by Ito Masaru, was therefore designed to harmonise with this unusually health-conscious concept.

The space conveys the ideas of 'natural' and 'organic' through its use of natural materials, especially lots of wood. Casual furniture and numerous plants create a welcoming, homely atmosphere, while pops of bright, optimistic pink add a certain modern freshness to the project's identity. Apart from the pink, colours are kept neutral and subdued. In one corner of the venue is a sales area, where after a meal customers can hear about how to incorporate the vegetable powder into their own lifestyle.

Outside, the facade was designed to be simple yet warm and open, embracing passers-by with the sense of cosiness and wholesomeness to be found inside the shop.

WHERE **1-5-10 Kamimeguro, Meguro-ku, Tokyo, Japan**
OPENING **September 2011**
CLIENT **Mikasa Sangyo**
DESIGNER **Ito Masaru Design Project/SEI (p.546)**
FLOOR AREA **55 m²**
WEBSITE **soaks.jp**

AVERAGE PRICE OF MAIN COURSE *JPY 1100–1600*
TYPE OF KITCHEN *Pasta, doughnuts and meals using dried vegetable powder*
OPENING HOURS *10.30–23.00*
CAPACITY *26 seats*

A transparent approach links
the restaurant interior with
the outside greenery.

Plants invade the interior too, bringing the garden indoors.

The space conveys the ideas of 'natural' and 'organic'

A stripped-down approach reflects the back-to-basics ethos of the eatery.

The simple, wooden interior – including all the floors, furniture and fittings – promises authentic, honest food.

Rows of hanging and ceiling lights give the casual space a clear sense of structure.

SOUTH OF HOUSTON
Pubblik

A tiled entrance way sets the tone.

Asked by New York fans Jaimy and Dylan Schmitt to design a SoHo-inspired restaurant in The Hague, design office Pubblik came up with a concept for a loft-style, open plan interior with an easy-going atmosphere. A feature wall is stripped back to expose the original brickwork and combined with oak timber flooring, painted beams and metro tiles. Vintage blue carpets, a velour banquette and visuals of New York help to give the bar area a homely feel.

In the middle of the long narrow building, Pubblik introduced a small patio to bring extra daylight into the space and to act as an entrance to the open kitchen. In this area, the wall art tells the history of the SoHo neighbourhood, where artists once worked on huge paintings in cavernous warehouses. At the back of the space there is a large garden and an extension of the restaurant with the second bar.

The specialty of the house is dry aged meat which is displayed in glass-fronted fridges next to the kitchen. Two large tables invite you to linger there and watch the cooks at work. Throughout the venue, glass cabinets display beer, wine and typical New York items, such as a pair of worn All Stars, a used metro ticket and a map of lower Manhattan. Lyrics from the song *New York, New York*, immortalised by Frank Sinatra, are found on one wall. Simple bistro furniture adds a touch of international style.

Pubblik was also assigned to design the entire graphic identity of the restaurant and shaped every detail including the menu, napkins and even the soap dispenser.

WHERE **Lange Houtstraat 3, The Hague, the Netherlands**
OPENING **December 2012**
CLIENT **Jaimy and Dylan Schmitt**
DESIGNER **Pubblik (p.549)**
FLOOR AREA **255 m²**
WEBSITE **southofhouston.nl**

AVERAGE PRICE OF MAIN COURSE **EUR 21**
TYPE OF KITCHEN **Classic French cuisine**
OPENING HOURS **12.00–22.00**
CAPACITY **120 seats**

Garlanded lights add a festive
touch to a fairly industrial interior.

A map of lower Manhattan illustrates the neighbourhood that inspired the design.

Glass doors at the front of the venue is another intervention that allows light to flood in.

This corner in the dining area has painted wooden panels and a glass-fronted shelving unit.

Original brickwork has been exposed to create a warm backdrop for the bar area.

A relaxed bistro with a New York-style vibe

The vintage rugs and a velour banquette create a cosy ambience.

STADIO
PickTwo Studio

Stadio is a new concept for Bucharest: an Italian-style restaurant combined with a sports pub in its atrium and a Prosecco bar for aperitifs. The location, the ground floor of a business centre, might seem unpromising, but the designers have pulled off a warm, welcoming trio of spaces.

In the restaurant, the food has an American and Italian accent – they do a popular burger here, as well as pizza and pasta – and so does the interior. Vintage 1960s furniture combines in a happy jumble with wall installations featuring Campbell's soup, as well as jars of pasta. The venues name is spelt out in spotlights with a row of retro bowling skittles line up beneath.

The internal courtyard of the building is where homage is paid to the American sports bar. Its centerpiece: a giant 600-kg metallic cylinder suspended in the centre of the space, with screens mounted on it for viewing the current game or event. There's an abundance of detail here, all paraphernalia associated with sport, from bootlaces and trophies to table football and a vintage poster for Steve McQueen's 1971 action film *Le Mans*. It all adds up to a lively and interesting interior.

There's a further shift of gear moving into Proseccheria, the bar devoted not only to Prosecco, but also to music: a DJ table takes the place of the bar and two tall industrial tables add presence to the space. Concrete walls give what the designers call a more 'masculine' look.

Warm wood and diner-style tiles create an Americana atmosphere with an Italian accent.

WHERE **Strada Ion Câmpineanu 11, Bucharest, Romania**
OPENING **September 2013**
CLIENT **Stadio Atrium Bar**
DESIGNER **PickTwo Studio (p.548)**
FLOOR AREA **330 m²**
WEBSITE **stadio.ro**

AVERAGE PRICE OF MAIN COURSE **EUR 10**
TYPE OF KITCHEN **Italian**
OPENING HOURS **9.00–00.00**
CAPACITY **260 seats**

PHOTOS Arthur Tintu

A happy jumble of 1960s furniture and Campbell's soup cans

A raw material palette of concrete, metal and wood is combined with a concoction of retro touches.

The design details in the sports bar demonstrate local artisanal craftsmanship.

STAN & CO.
De Horeca Fabriek

The black-walled space is illuminated with a bespoke light box on the far wall, spelling out the venue's tagline: 'for the good life'.

The client Debuut wanted a new concept restaurant design for a target group aged 25 to 55 years. The new venue had to be innovative, timeless and accessible and use sustainable materials. Ideally, it would become a hotspot not only in Utrecht, but in the Netherlands as a whole. A tall order perhaps – but Rein Rambaldo of De Horeca Fabriek delivered, with an attention-grabbing interior designed for a sophisticated audience.

Within a basically industrial, New York-style space – think raw brick and exposed mechanical elements – Stan & Co. packs in plenty of diversity and many unexpected details. Diners may find themselves seated on a Vitra chair, for example, or on one made from old rubber tires. Materials are very varied and never off-the-shelf: the floor is taken from an old monastery and the tiles fronting the bar are imported from the United States. Lighting comes from Jacco Maris and from the House Doctor. A blackboard-style wall is decorated with chalk scrawls, and the beautiful tiles in the kitchen were found in Marrakech. There's also a vintage corner filled with furniture bought on Ebay.

A fairly strict layout stops this rich mixture of styles looking messy and brings order to the variety of surfaces. The solidity of many elements – including the round sofas, hardwood tables and robust steel cabinets – also helps to ground the space, as does the focal point: the dramatic island bar in the centre of the restaurant, surrounded by (what else?) vintage bar stools.

WHERE **Ganzenmarkt 16 A, Utrecht, the Netherlands**
OPENING **April 2013**
CLIENT **Debuut**
DESIGNER **De Horeca Fabriek (p.543)**
FLOOR AREA **600 m²**
WEBSITE **stan-co.nl**

AVERAGE PRICE OF MAIN COURSE **EUR 18**
TYPE OF KITCHEN **International**
OPENING HOURS **Mon–Thu & Sun 11.00–23.30, Fri 11.00–01.00, Sat 10.00–01.00**
CAPACITY **136 seats**

Raw brick and the choice of lighting gives an industrial feel, while the beautiful turquoise tiles on the back wall add a splash of colour.

An attention-grabbing interior designed for a sophisticated audience

An island bar, lined with vintage bar stools, creates an intimate area in the sizeable space.

SUPERNORMAL CANTEEN
Projects of Imagination

Above the bespoke oak furniture, the 'cherry-eyes' of the logo keep watch over proceedings.

What better way to arrive at a winning design formula for a restaurant than to try it out first? That is exactly what happened with Supernormal Canteen. The design team at Projects of Imagination and owner/chef Andrew McConnell got together and envisioned a 'test kitchen'. This experimental eatery opened as a pop-up precursor to its more permanent sister venue that would subsequently open in the city.

The first version of Supernormal popped-up for just 3 months spanning two shop-fronts that were formerly a steelworks. Given an open design brief, the designers responded with a scheme that embraces every visual touchpoint – from the brand experience and printed matter, to uniforms, furniture and interior. The notion of 'supernormal', influenced every aspect of the design process. The fabric of the existing space was therefore left in its raw (or normal) state and was complemented by a suite of bespoke oak timber benches, tables and stools. These custom-manufactured pieces give structure to the interior, as well as drawing upon Japanese principles in their design.

White-washed brick walls form a neutral but far from boring backdrop for a range of what the designers call 'urban pop culture references', which feature throughout the space as a counterpoint to the restrained furniture. They include vending machines serving small treats, a glowing red neon sign and graphic elements. Most dramatic are the custom lanterns filling the ceiling – all hand-decorated with the Supernomal 'cherry-eyes' logo that the designers created for the brand. Screen-printed clear vinyl tablecloths, reminiscent of vintage picnic placemats, accentuate the canteen theme.

WHERE **53 Gertrude St, Melbourne, Australia**
OPENING **November 2012** (venue has since closed)
CLIENT **Andrew McConnell**
DESIGNER **Projects of Imagination** (p.548)
FLOOR AREA **100 m²**
WEBSITE **supernormal.net.au**

AVERAGE PRICE OF MAIN COURSE *AUD 16*
TYPE OF KITCHEN *Japanese*
OPENING HOURS *Tue–Sat 17.00–00.00*
CAPACITY *60 seats*

The form of the elongated
dining area is mirrored with
the side window, positioned
beneath an exposed steel girder.

SUPERNORMAL

CANTEEN

スーパー・ノーマル

EAT

From outside, the lantern installation and neon lights are an effective beacon.

Urban pop culture references are a counterpoint to the restrained furniture

Storage elements are given the custom treatment.

The graphical arrows bring further attention to the lanterns.

SUSHI ONO
Archiplan Studio

A simple, rounded logo announces the spare but harmonious aesthetic of a Japanese sushi restaurant in Italy.

According to designers Diego Cisi and Stefano Gorni Silvestrini of Archiplan this project, a Japanese restaurant in Brescia, enquires into the expressive qualities of images. For the restaurant space, in other words, they took classically Japanese images, including a tea leaf, incense smoke and a lotus flower, and decontextualised them, playing with scale until the images are no longer recognisable.

Large plywood leaves (they could just as well be petals) on the facade create an impressive geometric pattern that all but masks the motif's organic roots and act as a screen – a very Japanese intervention – partially concealing yet partly revealing the inside of the eatery. Inside, a simple and elegant wooden interior works hard to earn the description: 'zen-like'. The furnishings, all inspired by traditional Japanese furniture, was all produced especially for the interior by the designers. It is very minimal, with low wooden tables and floor cushions in one aspect of the dining area, while simple chairs and tables are also on offer for those who prefer to eat in a more Western-style setting.

In this simple and earthy interior, the bar makes a real impact. A backlit counter and backdrop are printed with the image of a leaf, massively magnified. The reception desk has a similar backlit design, this time an extreme close-up of incense smoke. These glowing features provide a touch of drama and are the main focal points in the restaurant. They also, of course, suggest an illuminated Japanese lantern – yet another cultural reference in an interior which evokes Japan with every detail.

WHERE **Borgo Wuhrer 137, Brescia, Italy**
OPENING **October 2013**
CLIENT **Sushi Ono**
DESIGNER **Archiplan Studio (p.540)**
FLOOR AREA **320 m²**
WEBSITE **sushionobrescia.it**

AVERAGE PRICE OF MAIN COURSE **EUR 18**
TYPE OF KITCHEN **Japanese**
OPENING HOURS **12.00–15.00, 19.00–00.00**
CAPACITY **50 seats**

PHOTOS Martina Mambrin

Bespoke furniture, all produced by the designers especially for the restaurant, evokes traditional Japanese pieces.

The interior space is organised with the help of simple wooden screen partitions

Simple and elegant furniture earns the description 'zen-like'

The counter (left) and reception desk (right) feature backlit images, hugely magnified, of a leaf and incense smoke, respectively.

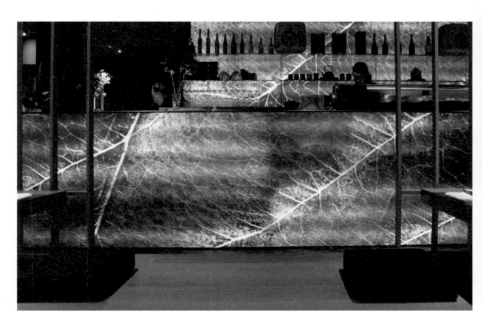

FLOOR PLAN

1 Dining area
2 Waiters' station
3 Bar
4 Kitchen
5 Lavatories

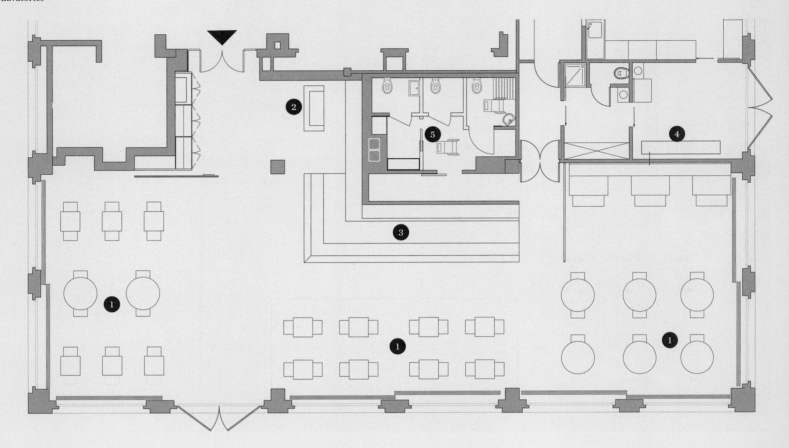

Classically Japanese symbols create an impressive geometric pattern

WINDOW DETAILING

TAYIM
Andrea Lupacchini

The interior layers bleached wood, aluminium and textiles to create fascinatingly patchworked surfaces.

'The idea for the project arose from the desire to create a magical, dynamic, surprising and highly emotional space,' says Andrea Lupacchini about his design for Tayim, a restaurant in Rome serving kosher food. The object was also to convey 'the values of the Jewish cultural tradition'.

Tayim (which means tasty) presents the symbolic and formal aspects related to Kasherut, a set of Jewish dietary laws based on the Torah. The project is an attempt to interpret the 47 laws as architectural elements. Geometries, inclined planes, disjointed forms, cuts, asymmetry and other qualities are not purely formal therefore, but are endowed with meaning. 'The apparent chaos is revealed as regulated by a primeval order,' says Lupacchini.

Giving the room a somewhat ethereal feeling, 80 panels float in the air and, of these, 47 represent the laws of the Torah – their different forms not quite touching the ceiling (as food should not touch the ground or other contaminating objects in the Torah). The materials used are raw, untreated and neutral in colour because the preparation of pure, natural foods is seen as being close to holiness in the sacred text.

Throughout the space, arrow-like pieces of solid wood give a feeling of unstoppable movement. These increase the dynamism of the design and symbolise a three-dimensional Star of David. The designer hopes that the interior will be 'a source of curiosity and that will strongly appeal to a younger, multi-ethnic audience' – not necessarily only a Jewish one.

WHERE **Viale Libia 50, Rome, Italy**
OPENING **December 2013**
CLIENT **Amos 2012**
DESIGNER **Andrea Lupacchini (p.540)**
FLOOR AREA **250 m²**
WEBSITE **tayim.it**

AVERAGE PRICE OF MAIN COURSE **EUR 20**
TYPE OF KITCHEN **Kosher**
OPENING HOURS **11.00–00.00**
CAPACITY **110 seats**

Floating elements that don't quite touch the ceiling represent the Torah injunction to keep food from contacting the ground and other objects.

White flooring and furniture add
to the ethereal, dematerialised effect.

From outside, an interesting and well-lit abstract pattern (representing a sort of exploded Star of David) intrigues passers-by.

Attempting to interpret the 47 laws of the Torah as architectural elements

Untreated materials were chosen to convey the idea of purity behind the dietary conventions of Judaism.

THE JANE

Piet Boon

A divine transformation from chapel to fine-dining destination.

Commissioned by three-star Michelin chef Sergio Herman and chef Nick Bril to help create their 'fine dining meets rock 'n' roll' restaurant vision, Piet Boon transformed the chapel of a former military hospital in Antwerp, Belgium into a high-end contemporary restaurant. The Jane has international allure where experience is key, serving as the authentic host for the ultimate 'divine' fine-dining experience.

The studio of Piet Boon was responsible for the bespoke interior design and styling, staying true to its belief in authenticity during the restoration of the space. An example of such preservation is the chapel's ceiling, which has largely been left untouched with the original peeling plaster and paintwork reminding diners of the history.

Natural, high-quality and rich materials are expressed in the interior in which natural stone, leather and oak wood are used. The original altar gave way to a modern shrine – the kitchen – contained within a glasshouse-like room, built to curve around the chapel's chancel. The glass enclosure is echoed at the other end of the room in the waiters' service station. By enlarging the mezzanine, the Upper Level Bar becomes a second dining experience.

To furnish the grand setting, the team worked with a number of creative partners on commissioned elements. There are a few standout bespoke pieces, most eye-catching the enormous chandelier – created by Beirut-based .PSlab – hanging in the centre of the vast room. The impressive fixture weighs in at 800 kg with over 150 lights splaying out on black metal rods from a central core. Stained glass windows that surround the room were illustrated by Studio Job. The 500 panels that make up the windows include contemporary motifs referencing food and drink.

WHERE **Paradeplein 1, Antwerp, Belgium**
OPENING **March 2014**
CLIENT **Sergio Herman and Nick Bril**
DESIGNER **Piet Boon (p.548)**
FLOOR AREA **403 m²**
WEBSITE **thejaneantwerp.com**

AVERAGE PRICE OF THREE-COURSE MENU **EUR 45**
TYPE OF KITCHEN **Fusion**
OPENING HOURS **12.00–18.00, 19.00–00.00**
CAPACITY **90 seats**

The impressive chandelier
by PSLab, nicknamed the
'Lionfish', contributes to the
sense of awe and wonder within
the former chapel.

To add to the 'rock 'n' roll' experience, a giant neon-lit skull hangs above where the altar once stood.

A former chapel serves as an authentic host for the ultimate 'divine' fine-dining experience

THE PROUD ARCHIVIST

Studio Tilt

The double-height space is treated in a simple way to ensure versatility for a variety of functions.

The Proud Archivist is based around an engaging and versatile concept – a combined gallery, bar, restaurant, cafe and events space, all designed and programmed to echo, emulate and revive the traditions of London's grand coffee houses of the 17th and 18th centuries. Studio Tilt was commissioned to design both the canal-side physical space and furniture plus the branding, way-finding and signage.

The end result creates an immediate impression thanks to the double-height windows and waterfront location. An interlaced larch ceiling runs across the whole space but has different depths and heights, creating both visual cohesion and varied options for programming. A restrained and harmonious material palette provides a simple backdrop to the multitude of events and atmospheres that the space can accommodate, playing with heights, depth of field, visual perspectives, lighting and architectural interventions.

The kitchen is open, allowing for demonstrations and theatrics, while the bar anchors the central space from which visitors can opt to explore either left or right. To the far left, a light wall running the whole width of the space illuminates the gallery and provides a stunning backdrop for art and photography.

A mezzanine level in steel separates the open kitchen from a dining area above, which has views across the canal. Meanwhile gigantic doors, also in steel, define the gallery and event space at the other end of the building. This multipurpose venue successfully caters for everything from a gallery opening for 300, to a sit-down meal for 100.

WHERE **2-10 Hertford Rd, London, United Kingdom**
OPENING **October 2013**
CLIENT **The Proud Archivist**
DESIGNER **Studio Tilt (p.550)**
FLOOR AREA **484 m²**
WEBSITE **theproudarchivist.co.uk**

AVERAGE PRICE OF MAIN COURSE **GBP 15**
TYPE OF KITCHEN **Modern English**
OPENING HOURS **8.00–22.00**
CAPACITY **100 seats**

PHOTOS Jill Tate

The kitchen has maximum openness, allowing for food-related performances.

A restrained and harmonious material palette for a versatile concept

Pale wood furnishings and fittings contrast well with the black metalwork.

The larch ceiling creates interesting patterns that run overhead.

FLOOR PLAN

1   Lobby
2   Bar
3   Restaurant
4   Terrace
5   Kitchen
6   Event space
7   Office
8   Back-of-house
9   Lavatories

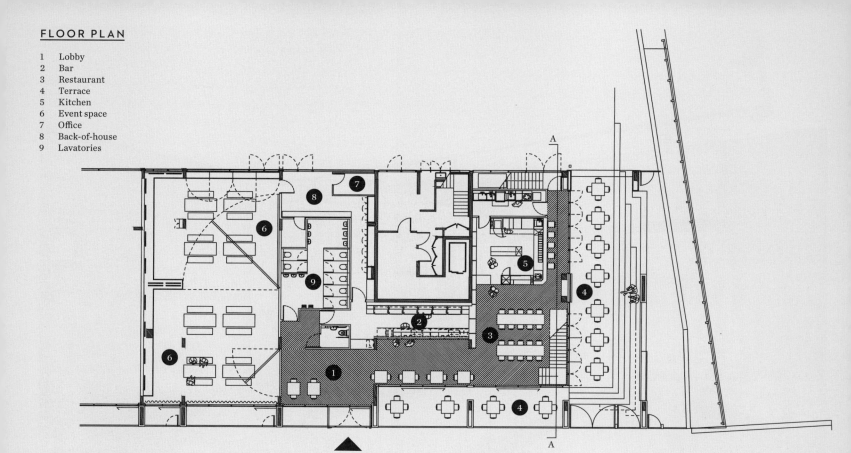

SECTION A

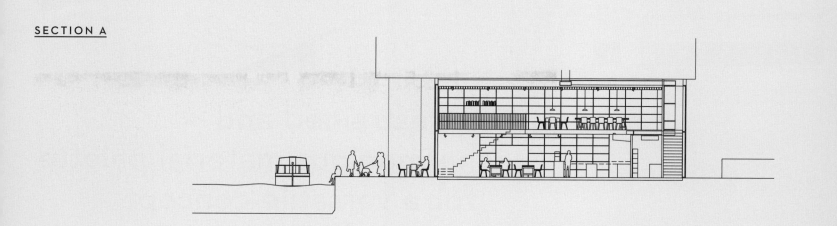

TABLE DRAWING

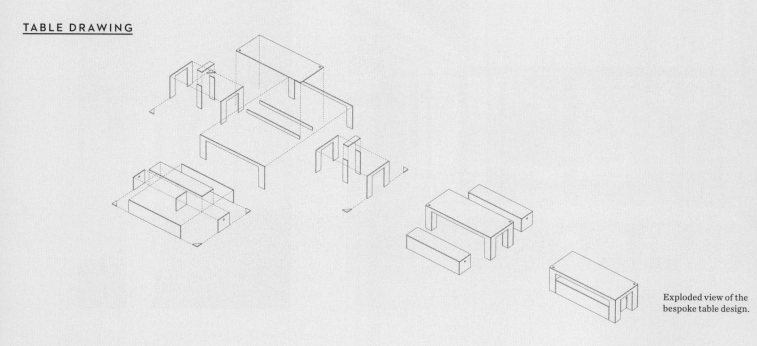

Exploded view of the
bespoke table design.

Architectural interventions play with heights, depth of field and visual perspectives

The mezzanine level was the most decisive intervention.

During the construction phase, much of the height of the space was preserved in order to accommodate large-scale artworks, for example.

THE TOWN MOUSE

AllistarCox Architecture

The back courtyard has a relaxed, cosy vibe.

The tall dining tables are each additionally lit by quaint, retro wall lights.

In the old story, the town mouse embodies worldly sophistication – as does this restaurant which takes its name. Tucked away off a busy city thoroughfare, The Town Mouse inhabits a narrow site on Drummond Street, which has long been a destination for Melbourne foodies. However, all the ghosts of eateries past have been stripped away and an extensive facelift has given new life to the compact space.

Glossy-black tiled walls contrast with the restored original ceiling and give unity to the space, while an appealingly perchable bar next to the dining area brings an almost metropolitan feel to the interior. The design team's objective was a space that appears as though it could have come from any decade. Nostalgic yet hard-to-place typography completes the picture.

In the darkened interior there's a certain twinkle and cheekiness to the detail, from gilded gold leaf on the windows (which is intended to acquire patina with time), to the rather quaint pendant lighting hanging over the raised oak tables. These slightly offbeat touches add an endearing quirkiness to the interior that reflects the food on offer (for example, venison with cocoa). For the regulars perched in this bijou space, their 'local' skirts a line between glamour and comfort, fine dining without being a big deal.

It's all the result of an enduring relationship between AllistarCox Architecture and an ex-pat New Zealand restaurateur, which originated with the celebrated restaurant, The Matterhorn. The partnership looks set to continue with plans to expand upstairs, taking this little celebration of excess long into the future.

WHERE **312 Drummond Street, Melbourne, Australia**
OPENING **February 2013**
CLIENT **The Town Mouse**
DESIGNER **AllistarCox Architecture (p.540)**
FLOOR AREA **220 m²**
WEBSITE **thetownmouse.com.au**

AVERAGE PRICE OF MAIN COURSE **AUD 40**
TYPE OF KITCHEN **Fine dining**
OPENING HOURS **Wed–Thu from 17.00, Fri–Sun from 12.00**
CAPACITY **35 seats (inside), 16 seats (outside), 21 seats (courtyard)**

The contemporary typeface
at the entrance invites guests
to 'come in for good times'.

COME IN for good times

WAKUWAKU
Ippolito Fleitz Group

For WakuWaku, an Asian fast food restaurant and organic food store under one roof, the design office Ippolito Fleitz Group set out to communicate brand values, such as 'organic' and 'sustainable'. Solid and untreated wood panelling was therefore a logical material choice, and it covers virtually the whole interior – walls, fittings, furniture and part of the floor. It also sends a strong message to the street outside, since it is visible through the large, open facade which provides an unrestricted view of the space.

A long, central counter and parallel niches provide seating spots for a variety of customer needs. Different shapes of chair help to break up the seating landscape and hark back to the original WakuWaku outlet – as do the chair legs, dipped in the WakuWaku corporate palette of magenta, a colour which recurs in the shelving panels too. Plenty of plants echo the ecological theme and add a homely touch.

The wood-lined interior creates a warm, neutral backdrop for displaying the colourful products in the WakuWaku range on the abundant rows of shelving. One side wall with floor-to-ceiling shelves integrates both display compartments and glass-fronted refrigerators.

Rough, untreated wood might become boring in itself, but here it makes a superb background for the stencilled lettering and the intricate wall sketches created by Chris Rehberger using taut string – a feature which adds a lot of interest and greatly personalises the space. A collection of wire, hanging lampshades picks up the playful theme. Who says sustainability can't be fun?

At the service point, the shelving and counter are both formed from untreated solid wood, catering to WakuWaku's dual shop and restaurant function.

WHERE **Dammtorstrasse 29–33, Hamburg, Germany**
OPENING **June 2012**
CLIENT **Good Restaurants**
DESIGNER **Ippolito Fleitz Group (p.545)**
FLOOR AREA **145 m²**
WEBSITE **waku-waku.eu**

AVERAGE PRICE OF MAIN COURSE **EUR 8**
TYPE OF KITCHEN **Asian**
OPENING HOURS **Mon–Fri 8.30–22.00, Sat 10.00–21.00, Sun 11.00–19.00**
CAPACITY **58 seats**

Chris Rehberger's creative string doodles on the wall fascinate diners, like an eco-story with images of windmills.

A wood-lined interior echoes the ecological theme

Magenta creates a splash of colour in the decor, including spelling out one of the venue's taglines on the wall: 'good for earth'

WORKSHOP KITCHEN & BAR

Soma Architects

Michael Beckman approached Soma Architects to create a fresh new architectural identity for his new Workshop Kitchen & Bar restaurant in Palm Springs – easier said than done, perhaps, given that the site was the historic El Paseo building, which immediately constrained the design possibilities. However, the designers turned these restrictions to their advantage, with an eventual solution that retains the elegance of the existing space by enhancing its verticality.

The original fabric boasts a beamed roof, so the design team added concrete furniture for immediate contrast. In the central aisle, a long banqueting table acts as a more public dining space, with its long horizontal lines balancing the many verticals of the interior. On either side, rows of monolithic concrete booths provide a more intimate dining setting. In addition, there is a private dining area at the rear of the space and a bar.

The lighting design by Beirut-based .PSLab works wonders with the austere, rather brutalist interior, adding warmth and a cave-like cosiness to the minimalist concrete furniture. In lieu of other decoration, the lighting becomes an important focal point in the interior. The rows of long pendant lamps, hanging from the wooden beams overhead, again emphasise the verticality of the building and the new interior design.

A high-gloss white epoxy floor finish helps to lighten the potentially heavy effect of the architecture, and blends well with the white-painted brick walls. The space holds on to its American origins thanks to the rustic roof with its massive beams, and the cacti placed on the tables.

The bespoke lighting by .PSLab accentuates the height of the space yet softens the bold architectural lines.

WHERE **Palm Springs, United States**
OPENING **October 2012**
CLIENT **Michael Beckman**
DESIGNER **Soma Architects (p.549)**
FLOOR AREA **325 m²**
WEBSITE **workshoppalmsprings.com**

AVERAGE PRICE OF MAIN COURSE **USD 30**
TYPE OF KITCHEN **New American**
OPENING HOURS **17.00–23.00**
CAPACITY **95 seats**

The monolithic bar becomes a magnetic focal point, thanks to lines of light.

Customers can opt for booths, private dining or a spot at the communal table.

The new concrete booths and custom concrete tables make monumental interventions in the cavernous old space with its dramatic beamed roof.

ZONA
Position Collective

Mirrored panels reflect lamps
and illuminated shelves to create
a jewel-like effect.

The project developer Baldaszti Group
called upon Position Collective, and
Ms Heni Kiss, to come up with a design for
the gastronomic concept of Zona. The name
comes from the core idea which utilises
'zones', both in the interior design and in the
food. The challenge for the design team was
to simultaneously combine and separate two
differently functioning areas – casual fine
dining restaurant and wine bar – into a
single space of 102 m².

The interior had to reflect the culinary
concept of the restaurant – based on the
smaller portions that feature in traditional
Hungarian cuisine and the Basque pintxo
kitchen. Mixing the culinary styles of
Hungarian, Mediterranean and Asian
gastronomy results in a unique (and award-
winning) experience, thanks also to the
interior design. The bar is defined by the
hot-rolled steel which was used to cover the
wall, floor and ceiling, the bar counter and
the wine storage shelves, creating a darkly
glamorous effect.

In the main restaurant, original features
such as the stunning parquet floor have been
lovingly preserved, creating a grand yet
homely scene. The design team complemented
the original fabric of the space with wooden
chairs, tables and barstools by Wild Spirit,
Magis and Tom Dixon.

Opposite the dining area, the wall
surface is covered along its full width with
mirrored panels. Mounted at a certain angle,
this surface corrects the inclination angle of
the rear wall and at the same time reflects
the beautiful panorama of Pest (one half of
Budapest, which was once two cities), with
diners getting a wonderful view of the
Chain Bridge and the Danube. This solution
also gives an optically elongated feeling
to the space.

WHERE **Lanchid Utca 7-9, Budapest, Hungary**
OPENING **September 2012**
CLIENT **Baldaszti Group**
DESIGNER **Positon Collective (p.548)**
FLOOR AREA **102 m²**
WEBSITE **zonabudapest.com**

AVERAGE PRICE OF MAIN COURSE **EUR 20**
TYPE OF KITCHEN **Hungarian, Mediterranean, Asian**
OPENING HOURS **Tue-Wed 12.00-00.00,**
Thu-Fri 12.00-01.00, Sat 13.00-01.00;
Kitchen: 12.00-15.00, 18.00-22.30
CAPACITY **45 seats**

The restaurant's lighting installation features 80 hanging lamps, created in a Hungarian lamp factory 40 years ago and mounted by a master artisan.

The core concept utilises zones, both in the interior design and food

The flooring clearly defines the zones: dark tiling in the wine bar versus the restaurant's beautiful parquet tiles.

26%

feature a swimming pool or spa

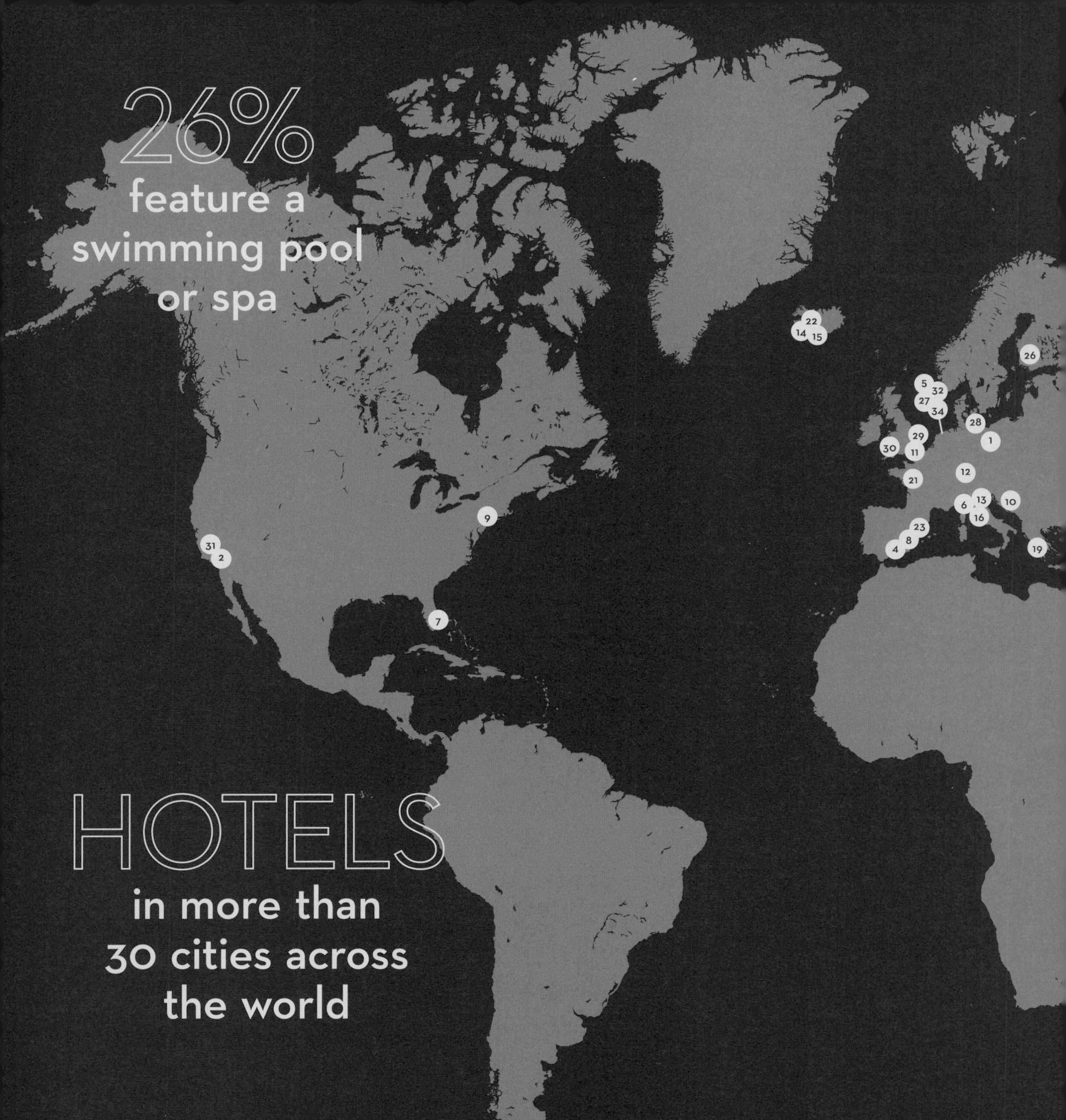

HOTELS

in more than 30 cities across the world

1 **25Hours Hotel Bikini Berlin → p.374**
Berlin, Germany

2 **Ace Hotel → p.380**
Los Angeles, United States

3 **Adelphi Hotel → p.386**
Melbourne, Australia

4 **Ambassador Hotel → p.392**
Benidorm, Spain

5 **Andaz Amsterdam → p.396**
Amsterdam, the Netherlands

6 **Barcelo Milan → p.404**
Milan, Italy

7 **Blanc Kara Hotel → p.406**
Miami, United States

8 **Caro Hotel → p.412**
Valencia, Spain

9 **citizenM Hotel New York Times Square → p.418**
New York, United States

10 **Emanuel Hostel → p.424**
Split, Croatia

11 **Generator Hostel → p.428**
London, United Kingdom

12 **Hotel Ritter Durbach → p.432**
Durbach, Germany

13 **Hotel Valentinerhof → p.434**
Siusi allo Sciliar, Italy

14 **Icelandair Hotel Reykjavik Marina → p.436**
Reykjavik, Iceland

15 **Ion Luxury Adventure Hotel → p.444**
Selfoss, Iceland

16 **La Bandita Townhouse Hotel → p.448**
Tuscany, Italy

17 **Long Beach Hotel → p.452**
Belle Mare, Mauritius

18 **Macalister Mansion → p.456**
Penang, Malaysia

19 **New Hotel → p.462**
Athens, Greece

20 **Nui. Hostel → p.468**
Tokyo, Japan

21 **Okko Hotel → p.472**
Nantes, France

22 **Reykjavik Lights Hotel → p.476**
Reykjavik, Iceland

23 **Room Mate Pau → p.480**
Barcelona, Spain

24 **Ruco Guesthouse → p.486**
Yamaguchi, Japan

25 **Sala Rattanakosin → p.488**
Bangkok, Thailand

26 **Scandic Hotel Paasi → p.494**
Helsinki, Finland

27 **Sir Albert Hotel Baranowitz → p.498**
Amsterdam, the Netherlands

28 **Superbude → p.504**
Hamburg, Germany

29 **The Ampersand Hotel → p.510**
London, United Kingdom

SLEEP

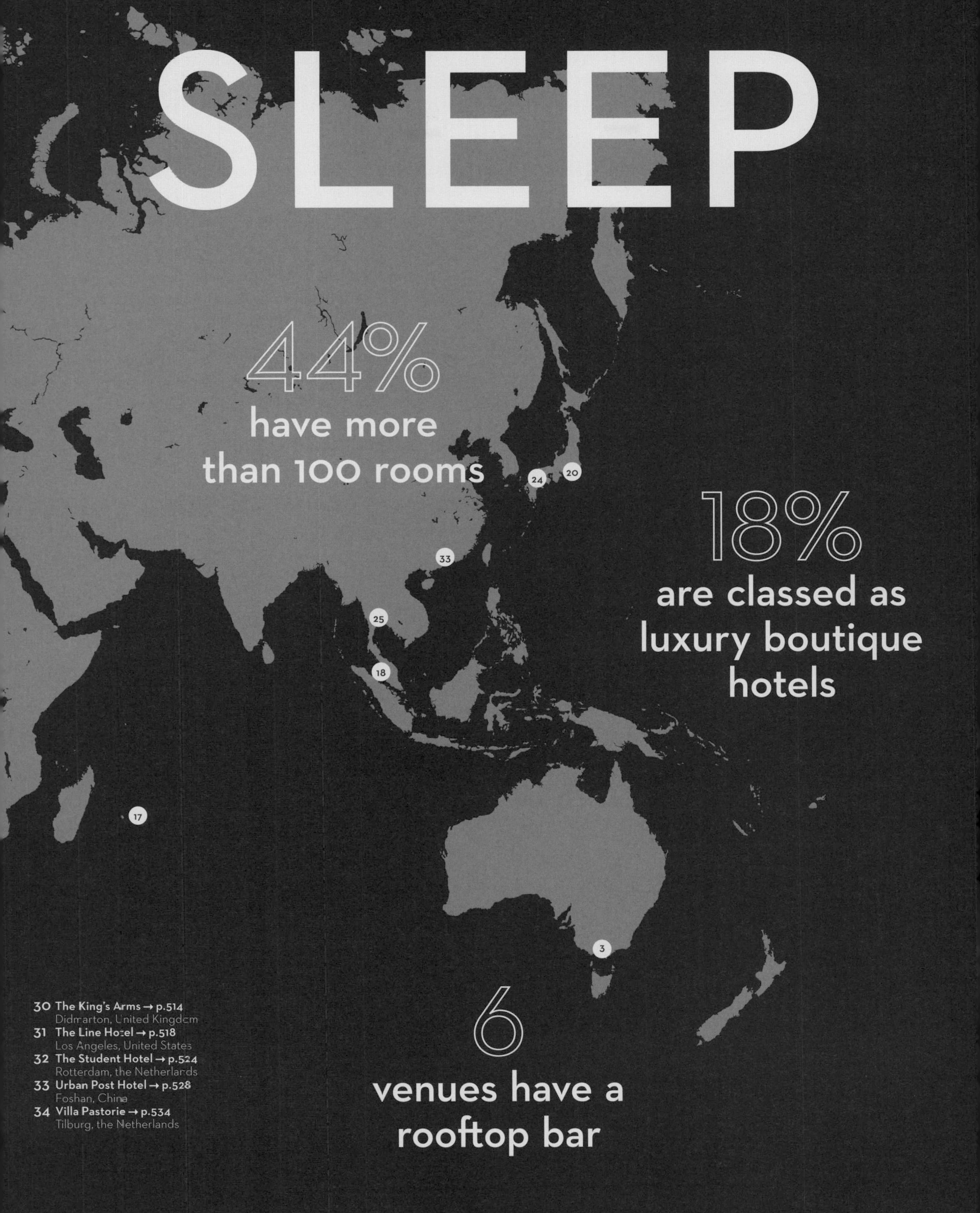

44%
have more than 100 rooms

18%
are classed as luxury boutique hotels

6
venues have a rooftop bar

30 **The King's Arms → p.514**
Didmarton, United Kingdom
31 **The Line Hotel → p.518**
Los Angeles, United States
32 **The Student Hotel → p.524**
Rotterdam, the Netherlands
33 **Urban Post Hotel → p.528**
Foshan, China
34 **Villa Pastorie → p.534**
Tilburg, the Netherlands

25HOURS HOTEL BIKINI BERLIN

Studio Aisslinger

The corridors have an industrial air, lit by the neon room numbers.

Two key factors helped to establish the identity of this new Berlin hotel, positioned within a unique building – constructed in the 1950s by architects Paul Schwebes and Hans Schoszberger: the so-called Bikini House – and twinned with its unique location (next to the zoo). With its 149 rooms, the 25hours Hotel Bikini Berlin is part of an emerging contemporary complex on the border between the vibrant city and the expansive Tiergarten park.

The location and the architecture inspired the interior design by Studio Aisslinger. The designers came up with a holistic design concept straddling nature and culture that had an 'urban jungle' theme, bearing in mind the hotel's proximity to the zoo – more than half of the 149 rooms look out over the ape house and elephant enclosure. These have a warmer design scheme featuring natural materials and colours. The other rooms have a stunning view of West Berlin landmarks. These rooms have a somewhat rougher, more urban feel, inspired by Berlin's edgier, creative side.

Breaking from the norm, the ground floor foyer starts with a surprising twist: there is no reception to be seen. Instead, the space's most striking feature is its incredibly high ceiling where guests are greeted by a gallery-like space, with the entrance flanked by two pillars adorned with original graffiti. It is on the third floor that the hotel's reclaimed-tiled-reception can be found, along with a loft-like living room (aka a buzzing lounge), hammocks and hanging chairs, kiosk, in-house bakery, worklabs and numerous cosy corners. Perched above everything else, the tenth storey is a lively social hub with a restaurant – in a greenhouse made from parts of old hothouses – as well as the bar and rooftop terrace.

WHERE **Budapester Str. 40, Berlin, Germany**
OPENING **January 2014**
CLIENT **25hours Hotel Company**
DESIGNER **Studio Aisslinger (p.550)**
FLOOR AREA **10,000 m²**
WEBSITE **25hours-hotels.com**

NO. OF STARS *n/a*
NO. OF ROOMS **149**
AMENITIES *Living room with lounge, work corners, kiosk, in-house bakery, DJ corner, event space, restaurant, bar, rooftop terrace*

The reception desk on the third floor has reclaimed turquoise tiles from the Alexanderplatz subway station.

The aroma of fresh bread makes it tempting to take a seat and relax near the in-house bakery.

TENTH FLOOR

1 Reception
2 Hammock corner
3 Bakery
4 Worklab zone
5 Office
6 Lounge
7 DJ corner
8 Conference suite/meeting rooms
9 Monkey Bar
10 Neni Restaurant
11 Microfarm
12 Rooftop terrace
13 Lavatories

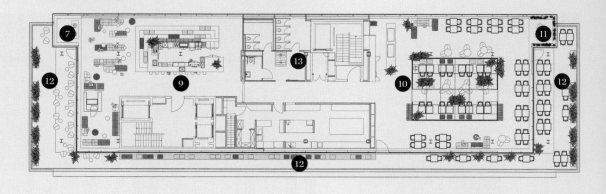

THIRD FLOOR

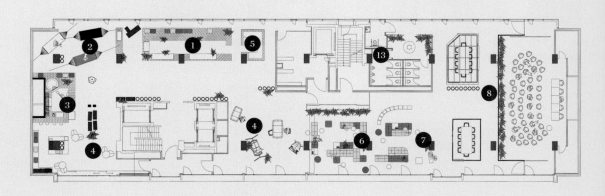

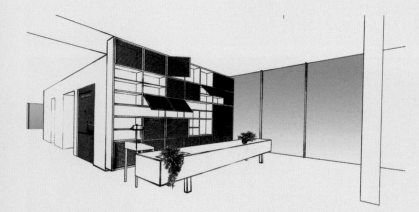

Sketch of the breakfast buffet
in the Neni Restaurant.

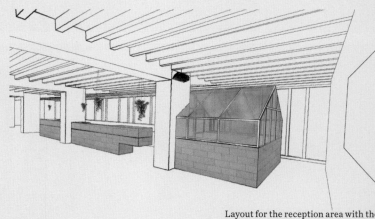

Layout for the reception area with the
back office located in the greenhouse.

Stepped seating areas recur in the
hotel, here in the Monkey Bar.

The Woodfire Bakery is located in the
lobby, near the reception area.

The Neni Restaurant has a jungle-inspired setting with abundant greenery and great city views.

Microgarden by Infarm, located in the restaurant, has a recycled print work lampshade and edible plants.

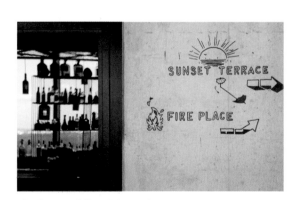

The characterful hand-drawn signage appears throughout the hotel and is by illustrator Yoshi Sislay.

Stepped seating in the Monkey Bar, complete with tree-trunk tables and ethnic cushions.

The holistic design concept straddling nature and culture

Quirky touches include the copper-sheet wall and cheeky phrases printed on the pillows.

This room comes replete with binoculars to get a good view of the urban vista.

There is a tropical air, thanks to its greenery and climbing plants, in the Bikini Island Lounge.

The 'jungle style' rooms have a hammock where guests can gaze out over the zoo.

ACE HOTEL DOWNTOWN LA

Atelier Ace and Commune Design

In an under-loved, under-used part of downtown Los Angeles, the new Ace Hotel is a keyed-up reconsideration of the historic United Artists building and theatre, originally commissioned in the 1920s by the film studio's cofounder Mary Pickford. Atelier Ace, the creative group behind the project, collaborated with Commune Design from initial space layouts, concept narratives and shared mood boards, through to artist curation and graphic design. All the creative stages of the project were intertwined, dynamic and natural.

The constraints of retrofitting such a historic building to create the perfect layout for the hotel turned out to be an excellent source of creativity. For Ace Hotel Downtown LA, a challenge was the square format of the guest rooms. The design team's focus was to give a feeling of space, of fluid circulation around the room and providing essential furniture pieces.

The result? An interior of cool concrete layered with materiality and warm references. The rooms convey the feeling of a California artist's studio space – airy and raw, yet refined with a sense of texture.

Most of the furnishings, custom lighting and finishes were designed, made or found in California or Mexico, with contributions by local artists, artisans and craftsmen. The designers also completed a dramatic restoration of the ornately decorated grand theatre – whose lobby alone is 214 m² with 11-m-high ceilings – within its new infrastructure, with refurbished original seats, custom carpet and an art deco-inspired ticket booth that doubles as a newsstand.

The gothic architecture of the 1920s building inspired the design direction of the hotel's interior.

WHERE **926 South Broadway, Los Angeles, United States**
OPENING **January 2014**
CLIENT **Ace Hotels**
DESIGNERS **Atelier Ace (p.540), Commune Design (p.542)**
FLOOR AREA **10,000 m²**
WEBSITE **acehotel.com**

NO. OF STARS **4**
NO. OF ROOMS **182 rooms, 16 suites**
AMENITIES **Rooftop pool and bar, theatre, restaurant, communal spaces**

The lobby carves out an impressive double-height space with book-lined walls giving it a clubby library vibe.

Cool concrete in the industrial-style bar receives a touch of warmth thanks to wood panelling, shelves and stools.

Embracing a mash-up of architectural styles, from Tudor to Renaissance to Normandy

The interior is akin to a collection of architectural and design references piled on top of one another.

A sharp monochrome palette makes for a defined dining space, replete with original art deco detailing.

The rooftop was transformed into an indoor/outdoor lounge and pool inspired by Frank Lloyd Wright's Ennis House.

Rooms are furnished in LA's quintessential mid-century modern style.

The vast theatre has sweeping design features combined with the minutest of delicate details.

ADELPHI HOTEL

Hachem

The 'engage your senses' dessert theme bares
fruit in the Om Nom restaurant.

When it first opened in 1992, the Adelphi
Hotel immediately captured the public's
imagination. An innovative example of a
boutique hotel, it combined stark,
contemporary design with sensational
features, such as its famous ninth-floor
swimming pool overhanging the bustling
street below. However, a period of decline
followed its initial success, and by 2013
the Adelphi had lost its status and its glamour.
Enter the hotel's new owners, Dion Chandler,
Ozzie Kheir and Simon Ongarato, determined
to turn things around.

Hachem was commissioned to undertake
the project design and revitalise the brand.
The designers came up with a concept based
on the tagline 'engage your senses' and the
theme of desserts. 'The idea was to create an
environment and visual identity that stirs and
delights each of the senses, and to initiate an
irresistible talking point – the Adelphi, now
the world's premier dessert hotel,' explains
principal Fady Hachem.

The result is a visual and experiential
feast – sophisticated and richly detailed, with
more than a touch of the whimsy and magic
of a Willy Wonka wonderland. The focal
point is Om Nom, the decadently dessert-
themed restaurant, but the references to
exquisite treats, sensations and indulgence
occur throughout the building: sumptuous
lounges feature plush armchairs and
graphic carpeting, while a dark and glassy
ceiling spans the lobby like an expanse of
shimmering melted chocolate. Eclectic
furnishings present an array of texture,
pattern, colour and shape, yet the final
outcome avoids becoming overly ornate or
saccharine thanks to the counterbalancing
effect of neutral walls and bedding of
modernist simplicity, and of expanses of
space and greenery.

WHERE **187 Flinders Lane, Melbourne, Australia**
OPENING **November 2013**
CLIENT **Iconic Hotels Group**
DESIGNER **Hachem (p.545)**
FLOOR AREA **3000 m²**
WEBSITE **adelphi.com.au**

NO. OF STARS **5**
NO. OF ROOMS **34**
AMENITIES **Pool deck and function area, restaurant,
dessert bar, cocktail bar, conference room**

The decor in the restaurant is as decadent as its food, with designer F-A-B chairs by Färg & Blanche.

Art adds to the visual feast in the hotel's lobby.

A sensory delight awaits guests at the magical reception desk, like something straight out of a fairy tale.

Home comforts: the Adelphi Hotel's rooms get a stylish yet practical makeover.

The hotel's visual identity stirs and delights each of the senses

A graphic bathroom treatment makes a serious splash.

The big beds are all about the
Adelphi keyword: indulgence.

The rooms have a sweet
theme too, from carpets
patterned like cakes to
'liquorice allsort' stools.

AMBASSADOR HOTEL

Oscar Vidal Studio

The concept was akin to a riverbed with stones eroded by water and wood bleached by the sun.

The Ambassador Hotel in Benidorm is located in the bustling 'English area' of the seaside city. Built 30 years ago, the hotel had suffered some partial refurbishings, resulting in a mishmash of styles and no distinctive design. Oscar Vidal Studio was called in to give a fresh and bright look to the tired hotel, particularly to the hotel lobby and wellness centre.

At the entrance, the design team placed the reception desk in a more visible and prominent position, moving the other functions (tour operator desk, waiting areas, internet points, etc.) to the sides. Traffic flow was previously a problem in the hotel, so the fluid concept of a river was introduced.

The natural theme resulted in the use of soft, organic shapes, with pools of light sunk into the ceiling echoing the curved forms. The resulting lobby space becomes cosy and almost cave-like with its organically shaped pillars and a playfully subdued use of light which changes, at the flick of a switch, from cool and cosy to mysterious and magical. Stone pillars and benches complete the effect.

The wellness centre continues the lobby concept, with extra elements referencing Mediterranean water culture. A totally white and continuous space is designed to look as though it was 'formed by water', says Oscar Vidal Quist, while mosaic tiles look back to an ancient bathing culture. To create a magical and fun atmosphere, the lighting system, which can be dimmed, floods the space with changing colours.

WHERE **C/ Gerona 39, Benidorm, Spain**
OPENING **May 2013**
CLIENT **Ambassador Hotel**
DESIGNER **Oscar Vidal Studio (p.548)**
FLOOR AREA **11,200 m²**
WEBSITE **hotelesbenidorm.com**

NO. OF STARS **3**
NO. OF ROOMS **398**
AMENITIES *Two pools, wellness centre, restaurant, two bars, parking*

Organic forms flow from natural materials

To add colour and dynamism to the space, RGB lights were recessed into the droplet-like shapes in the ceiling.

A fresh modernity was imbued at the entrance to the wellness centre, with white wood lattice to sieve the light.

Illumination was a special feature, as if reflecting the light of the Mediterranean.

The space accommodates pools, jacuzzis and saunas, harking back to an ancient bathing culture.

Elements reference Mediterranean water culture

White mosaic tiles were used to envelop the entire space.

Coloured lighting was used to create a relaxing ambience.

ANDAZ AMSTERDAM
Marcel Wanders studio

PHOTOS Marcel Wanders

The graffiti artwork by Van Iwaarden overlooks the magical garden where chef Julien Piguet grows his culinary herbs and spices.

In 2012, Hyatt Hotels Corporation opened its first location in the Netherlands: in the cultural heart of Amsterdam, right on the canals and inside a historic building – a former public library – Amsterdam-based Marcel Wanders was commissioned to design the interior. The brief called for the hotel to be given a truly Dutch look.

The concept behind the design is a modern take on Dutch history. Throughout the hotel, Wanders played with various sources of inspiration, integrating the heritage of the hotel surroundings (including the Golden Age, Dutch Delft blue, tulips and the colour orange), the knowledge of the books once housed in the grand former library, and the connecting polarities. The latter refers to the city of Amsterdam as a cultural-melting pot, representing two individual, non-related elements that are stitched together to form a new logical whole.

Guests experience personal style, comfort and sophistication in the hotel's 122 guest rooms, all of which have either canal or garden views. Each has an open plan layout that allows for maximum space and natural light, with specially designed chairs, mirrors and closets.

The social heart of the hotel is located on the ground floor, where the restaurant, bar, lounge and library are seamlessly intertwined. Each space is distinct on its own and together create a vibrant, exciting and open space. The restaurant is also accessible to non-guests of the hotel. Its open kitchen has a striking blue mosaic back wall which also forms the backdrop of the chef's table.

WHERE **Prinsengracht 587, Amsterdam, the Netherlands**
WHEN **October 2012**
CLIENT **Hyatt Hotels Corporation**
DESIGNER **Marcel Wanders studio (p.547)**
FLOOR AREA **7476 m²**
WEBSITE **hyatt.com**

NO. OF STARS **5**
NO. OF ROOMS **117 rooms, 5 suites**
AMENITIES *Restaurant, lounge, bar, meeting facilities, library, fitness centre, pool, spa, guest bicycles*

The lavishly-proportioned
Bell Lamps in the lobby create
an awe-inducing interior.

The Bluespoon restaurant, as elsewhere in the hotel, features custom-designed furnishings, with every piece telling a story.

The mural in this open space features a pixellated image taken from a historical Dutch still-life painting.

The concept behind the design is a modern take on Dutch history

Traditional Delftware pieces and Wanders' own designs applied on carpets and lamps fill this dining area.

The blue-and-white ornamental plasterwork in the meeting studio are characteristic of the traditional canal houses of wealthy traders in the Golden Age.

FLOOR PLAN

1   Entrance hallway
2   Lounge
3   Meeting studio
4   Bluespoon restaurant
5   Private dining
6   Bluespoon bar
7   Observatory

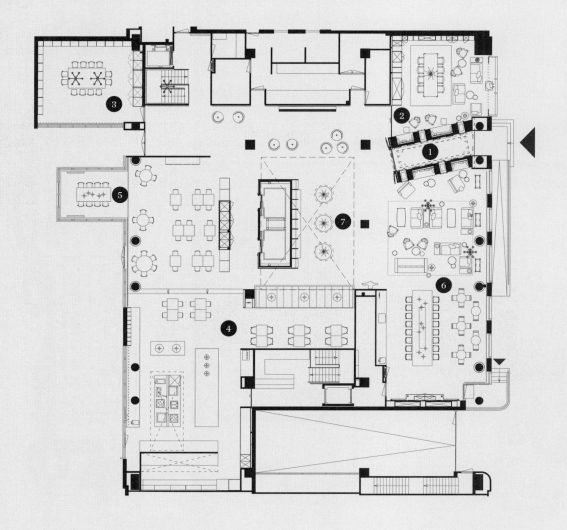

PRESIDENTIAL SUITE

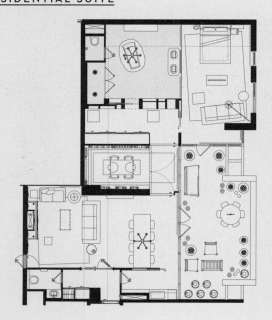

Individual elements are stitched together to form a new logical whole

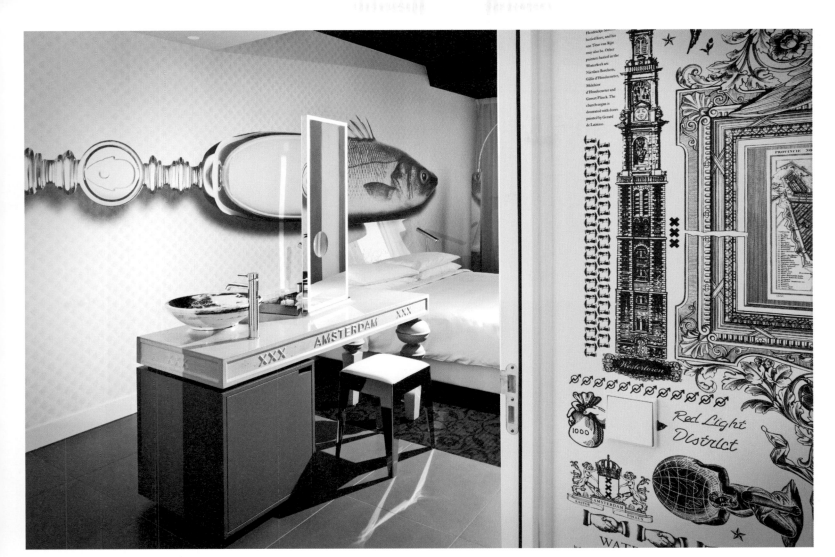

This guest room has unique wall-
coverings and decorations featuring
typical Amsterdam elements.

Most of the furniture is designed by Wanders
himself, such as the One Minute Lampshade on
the New Antique table.

The oversized yellow armchair was
specially designed for the hotel.

Guests are pampered in
the spa area with sauna
and treatment rooms.

BARCELO MILAN

Simone Micheli

Curvy, colourful armchairs dot the lofty lobby of the hotel, where sculptural features and light installations resemble an art gallery.

The Barcelo Milan, previously known as the B4 Milano, is intended as an entirely new take on the business hotel. Designer Simone Micheli has therefore shaped a surprisingly hybrid space: the lobby for example is not only a welcome area, but also a gallery for shopping, relaxation and play, hosting virtual stores and reading areas. It is also connected to the restaurant and cafe, and all the spaces flow into each other.

The forms and colours used are even more radical departures from the usual business hotel formula. What Micheli calls 'phytomorphic sculptures' constitute the entire structural and functional apparatus of the ground floor: columns, reception desk, bar counter and other elements form a Dali-esque landscape of fluid, glossy, colourful forms. Bright greens and reds contrast with the Luserna stone floor that stretches, uninterrupted, over the whole area. Sculptural armchairs, upholstered in a lime-green fabric, are dotted the entire entrance hall and lobby, creating relaxing islands. Huge chandeliers descend from the ceiling, futuristic compositions of globular bright balls, are hung at different heights and fill up the double-height void.

Elsewhere in the hotel, a more subdued approach predominates, with the rooms wrapped in sleek, honey-toned wood, combined with soft lilac shades. Rounded, organic elements highlight the spa and bedroom facilities. The atmosphere in the dining areas is relaxing, with wallpaper of an infinite forest becoming a relaxing kaleidoscope. Space dividers of real birch branches and tree trunks that go from floor to ceiling, tie in with the natural stone flooring adding to the more serene, harmonious ambience.

WHERE **Via Stephenson 55, Milan, Italy**
OPENING **February 2012**
CLIENT **Barcelo Hotels & Resorts**
DESIGNER **Simone Micheli (p.549)**
FLOOR AREA **15,000 m²**
WEBSITE **barcelo.com**

NO. OF STARS **4**
NO. OF ROOMS **280**
AMENITIES **Conferencing facilities, two restaurants, spa/wellness centre, bar**

Oversized printed pictures by Maurizio Marcato are teamed with a simulated infinite birch forest in one dining area.

Exuberance returns in the second-floor spa: a vibrant yet organic space dotted with fluid yellow forms dubbed as 'macro sea anemones'.

A Dali-esque landscape of fluid, glossy, colourful forms

BLANC KARA HOTEL
DFC

Blanc Kara occupies one of Miami's famous
art deco buildings, fringed with palm trees.

DFC, the agency behind the Blanc Kara
Hotel in Miami, was approached by a private
investor wanting to implement a brand new
chain of 'hotels that make a difference'. The
design office came up with a concept it calls:
Art de Vivre à la Française. Centred around
the idea creating a nest in the international
market, to unite tranquillity and culture and
make it appeal to global art lovers.

The resulting hotel occupies a low-rise
building in an ideal South Beach bustling
location – close to the beach, luxury shopping
and Miami's famous night life – yet DFC
set out to make it an island of serenity. An
exclusive number of guest studios offers
luxurious space (each one is an expansive
37 m²), plus all the comforts of home.

The design is restful, with white
predominating, although fresh, vibrant
colours pop out – a refreshing change from
Miami's 1930s pastel palette – keeping it all
from being too cool or bland. Furnishings are
clean and contemporary. Only the outside of
the building, painted in the palest yellow and
fringed by palm trees, pays homage to the
famous local art deco architecture.

DFC approached the project holistically,
designing the hotel's branding from the
graphic deco-inspired logo to its soundtrack,
by French band Nouvelle Vague (an album
sold in specific concept stores worldwide,
including Colette in Paris, Pream in Tokyo
and 10corsocomo in Milan), and even the
development of an original magazine – all to
ensure that the first Blanc Kara is the start of
something big.

WHERE **205 Collins Avenue, Miami, United States**
OPENING **September 2013**
CLIENT **Blanc Kara**
DESIGNER **DFC (p.544)**
FLOOR AREA **1200 m²**
WEBSITE **blanckara.com**

NO. OF STARS **3**
NO. OF ROOMS **25**
AMENITIES **Rooftop terrace, 24-hour front desk, gift shop**

PHOTOS: Drew Hadley

Large prints add a feel good factor and adorn the walls throughout, from the lobby to the corridors.

Furnishings are kept resolutely simple and contemporary, avoiding a retro look.

Jazzy hues (top left) and warm wood furnishings (top right) avoid the pastel clichés of Miami deco interiors.

White predominates, with pops of fresh, bright colour

Amidst the bursts of colour, white predominates in various textures including the fluffy chairs.

Huge white sofas create an atmosphere of pure relaxation.

Low-key bedrooms add to
the 'oasis of rest' concept.

With geometric flooring and
huge black-and-white prints,
corridors are a graphic treat.

The hotel's guest stationery gets a unique look.

The same graphic style adorns various other items of hotel merchandise.

A hotel CD creates an all-encompassing experience.

The interior concept unites tranquillity and culture

Even scooters, available to guests, get the graphic lettering treatment.

Toiletries too echo the same consistent style.

CARO HOTEL
Francesc Rifé Studio

The neoclassical facade is painted stucco and has natural limestone moulding.

The lobby walls are adorned with gothic tiles from the 15th century that were found on-site.

In 2005, a major renovation project began to transform the centuries old Palace of the Marquis of Caro in Valencia. Francesc Rifé, the interior designer, worked closely with the owners in the preservation of this significant, listed building. The subsequent integration of newly uncovered elements forced a constant rethink at every corner; layouts were altered, spaces were reconverted and impossibly contorted within a vulnerable structure to give, 7 years later, the first historical monument-hotel in Valencia.

Guests are able to locate and identify the different architectural features within the hotel, including the noteworthy 12th-century Almohad city wall standing 15-m high, which runs lengthwise down the centre of the building. The ash-toned monumental facade contrasts with a bright, open interior, in light colours where the design team sought to create the perfect balance of ancient and modern.

The lobby serves as a connection between the reception area, which is built into the original brick wall like a light box, and the 19th-century staircase. This is a focal point for generating spaces and leads towards the first floor rooms and the library. To complement the existing structural elements, neutral materials were selected, such as glossy resin floors in very light colours, arabescazo marble for the bar counter and furniture that contrasts with other designer pieces.

The complexity of the spaces means that each guest room is unique, with the items of historical value conditioning the distribution and morphology of each room. Accommodating both contemporary or historic styling, key rooms feature ceilings with exquisite plasterwork and restored frescos. Mink-hued concrete floors and walls contrast with the earthy colours of the stone walls.

WHERE **Almirante 14, Valencia, Spain**
OPENING **March 2012**
CLIENT **Regia Urbanitas**
DESIGNER **Francesc Rifé Studio (p.544)**
FLOOR AREA **2000 m²**
WEBSITE **carohotel.com**

NO. OF STARS **5**
NO. OF ROOMS **26**
AMENITIES **Restaurant, bar, library, pool**

PHOTOS Fernando Alda

In the Meta Bar, historical artefacts are hung suspended over the marble countertop.

At the foot of the main staircase, the oldest mosaic in the city (1st century BC) was uncovered during the renovation.

The rooms have a neutral palette, with lacquered wood furniture accentuated by warm and understated lighting.

Guest rooms feature ceilings with exquisite plasterwork and restored frescos

The modern concept harmonises with the 12th century preserved wall.

A preserved fresco from the 19th century refers to the family origins of the Marquis of Caro.

Beneath the glass-floored landing, the vibrant green freeze-dried moss is eye-catching.

A two-level space is considerately created within the watchtower, possibly the oldest room in the palace.

The historical hotel is rich in textures, with intricately carved wood contrasting with exposed brick.

Creating the perfect balance of ancient and modern

CITIZENM HOTEL TIMES SQUARE

concrete

Less is more for citizenM, attracting global nomads with its small yet luxurious guest rooms.

Amsterdam-based hotel chain citizenM, which aims to bring affordable luxury to all mobile citizens, is reaching for the sky with its American debut: a 19-floor high-rise located in New York's bustling heart, Times Square. Designed by concrete, the new citizenM hotel consists of 230 of its signature guest rooms, stacked on top of a vibrant 'living room' plaza – a double-height space which combines the NYC-vibe with a home-away-from-home feel.

Within this lobby plaza, the living room is a social hub – open to both guests, locals and passers-by – with seating options suitable for work or play plus the canteenM and a Mendo bookstore. A floor-to-ceiling cabinet is full of inspirational material – from books to art, and items relating to New York. At the plaza's heart is a striking centrepiece: an artwork by Julian Opie.

The Cloud Bar is the crowning feature, a small sky-high bar and terrace, designed to be a 'pocket park' on the roof. A tree trunk bar, picnic tables, plant-filled cabinets, fireplace, hanging lanterns and other cosy, outdoorsy trimmings make it just the spot to take in the bustling vista and enjoy the sunset – replete with binoculars to get a good close-up of the cityscape below.

The citizenM concept is to offer 'more for less' by cutting out all hidden costs and removing all unnecessary items. Each room therefore measures just 14 m², but the idea is that a comfy, wall-to-wall bed and a rain shower provide all the luxury you're likely to need during a city or business trip. Guests can also personalise their rooms, by choosing a piece of art for the digital art frame and selecting the colour of the lights.

WHERE **218 West 50ᵗʰ Street, New York, United States**
OPENING **April 2014**
CLIENT **citizenM**
DESIGNER **concrete (p.542)**
FLOOR AREA **7740 m²**
WEBSITE **citizenm.com**

NO. OF STARS **n/a**
NO. OF ROOMS **230**
AMENITIES **Gym, canteenM, rooftop bar**

The welcoming lobby has a home-away-from-home vibe, stacked full of ornaments and books.

The 'living room' plaza forms the sociable heart of the hotel, which is open to locals as well as guests.

Purveyor of affordable luxury reaches for the sky in the bustling heart of New York

High-rise location in the heart of New York.

The position of the building is determined by a 6-m-deep garden in the rear. As a result, an entrance plaza is created at the front.

The daylight lines dictate the top of the volume and the set-back floors.

By introducing a double-height, transparent lower level, the urban life continues into the building and is connected with the garden in the rear.

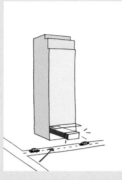

To attract people coming from Broadway, an additional volume is placed in the open first floor, extending to the street and housing a cafe.

A public programme is placed on top. The rooftop bar and a large terrace is placed under the bulkhead, providing a 360-degree view in a 'pocket park' type of environment.

Window frames are 'pushed' out of the main volume to express each individual room.

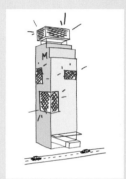

Large bespoke works of art on the facade and in the interior express the cultural identity of citizenM.

GROUND FLOOR

1	Check-in area	9	Terrace
2	Living room plaza	10	Luggage room
3	Cabinet wall	11	Lounge seating area
4	Iconic sofa	12	Low seating area
5	Cafe & bookstore	13	Cabinet wall with fireplace
6	Bar	14	Picnic table
7	citizenM canteen	15	High tables
8	Kitchen service point	16	Binoculars

TOP FLOOR

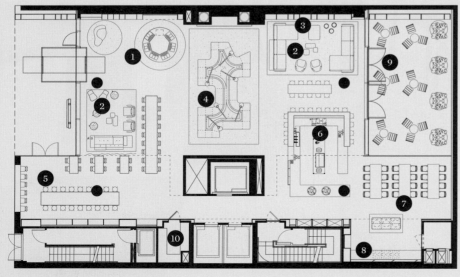

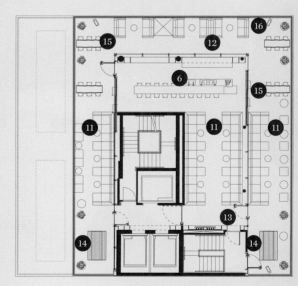

The bar is open to the city, underlining the venue's ambition to be a New York hub.

Rooms have huge beds and come fully equipped for guests' comfort.

Each room has a walk-in rain shower to heighten the luxurious feeling.

EMANUEL HOSTEL

Atom Design

Retro furnishings and colour blocking
lends character to a hostel in a converted
1930s building.

Proving that hostel accommodation doesn't
need to be down at heel, Emanuel owners
Mila and Toni Radan worked with Lana Vitas
Gruić of Atom Design to convert a disused
1930s apartment block with a great location:
'From the beginning, it was our desire to
create a comfortable, functional and modern
space that has the spirit of Split,' they say.

Positioned close to the city's port and
the historic Diocletian's Palace, Gruić has
created a contemporary design in which
15 beds are divided between two rooms. The
sleeping space is accessed from the lobby, and
the interior was carefully arranged so as to
preserve a feeling of space throughout. Bunk
beds were an obvious choice to maximise the
amount of accommodation available and by
housing them in blocks, Atom Design achieves
an architectural effect – not to mention
maximum privacy for guests. In one room,
the bed blocks are brightly coloured, while
in the other room Gruić opted for an all-white
palette. In both cases, the effect is fresh
and modern.

The lobby features branding also
designed by Gruić, the hotel logo in white set
crisply against a large photographic print
of Split. Similar prints are found in the two
dorms. In all cases, the images were chosen
because they present a fresh view of the city,
rather than the usual tourist clichés.

Furnishings have a retro look, evoking
the 1950s and 1960s, but are also designed to
suggest the local streets – so there are painted
patio chairs and a barrel serves as a table.
Chairs, desks and shelves allow guests to
not only sleep, but also socialise or eat in
the hostel.

WHERE **L N Tolstoja 20, Split, Croatia**
OPENING **June 2013**
CLIENT **Mila and Antonio Radan**
DESIGNER **Atom Design (p.541)**
FLOOR AREA **90 m²**
WEBSITE **n/a**

NO. OF STARS **n/a**
NO. OF ROOMS **2**
AMENITIES **Lobby, lounge, kitchen, bar**

The lobby features Emanuel's graphic signature, also created by Atom Design.

One room features stacked beds built into colourful boxes which extend from the wall.

Images of Split enliven the interior with an urban, street feel – heightened by 'street' items such as a painted barrel doubling as a table.

Spaces to sit and work add a homely feeling.

Unexpected details and wall 'doodles'
keep the atmosphere light.

Bed blocks offer guests maximum privacy and create a sculptural design

The second room features
space-saving bunk beds in
blocks, this time all in white.

GENERATOR HOSTEL

DesignAgency

A cheerful welcome awaits hostel-goers at the reception in the lobby.

London became the first of the Generator brand locations when its flagship hostel opened back in 1995. After almost 20 years, it was time to give the flagship a revamp. The new concept by Toronto-based DesignAgency emanates Generator's young, vibrant style whilst hammering home the local theme.

The interior was refurbished to express the dynamism of London's bustling streets. The team worked in partnership with local creatives – architects Orbit and art collective Acrylicize – to play with bold graphics, rich patterns and British cultural icons.

The reception area, decked out in reclaimed wood and brick, serves as the entry to all the areas of the hostel. Guests are greeted by a laser cut 'hello', a saluting British bobby, and a glowing smiley face atop a monolithic, metallic reception desk. A custom-design train station information board buzzes on the back wall with the excitement of the early, halcyon days of travel.

From here, the vibrancy continues in the Vivienne Westwood-inspired, tartan-clad cafe and the canary-yellow chill-out room. With its zig-zagging forms and its colourful striped upholstery, this zone can also be used for screenings thanks to its tiered seating. Eclectic aspects throughout see diverse areas for groups large or small to eat, drink and hang out – such as the row of wooden pods connecting the cafe with the bar, where intimate 'rooms' are created within an informal streetscape.

The entire interior has an energy and a touch of class, with designer furnishings in numerous nooks and crannies from the likes of Tom Dixon and Moooi. The rooms, decorated with bold graphics, are simple yet functional, encouraging guests to spend time in the social areas.

WHERE **37 Tavistock Place, London, United Kingdom**
OPENING **March 2014**
CLIENT **Generator/Patron Capital**
DESIGNER **DesignAgency (p.543)**
FLOOR AREA **6000 m²**
WEBSITE **generatorhostels.com**

NO. OF STARS **n/a**
NO. OF ROOMS **212**
AMENITIES **Restaurant, bar, lounge, screening room, games area, kitchen**

PHOTOS Nikolas Koenig

The chill-out zone is decked with designer details: cork stools from Vitra and Tacchini Spin ottomans.

In the dorm rooms, boldly coloured graphics wrap the walls and ceiling.

Runway floor markings lead guest towards the bar, with Castor reclaimed fire extinguisher lights above.

The design emanates Generator's young, vibrant style whilst hammering home the local theme

With a contemporary-styled pub aesthetic, guests can gather the around Goodwives and Warrior's hand-painted piano.

HOTEL RITTER DURBACH

Joi-Design

Deep olive, berry and golden hues are illuminated by contemporary lights, creating a relaxing ambience.

Dating back to 1656, the Hotel Ritter Durbach in Southern Germany's Black Forest is one of Europe's oldest hotels, nestling in an idyllic wine region between the German Baden-Wurttemberg and the Alsace in France. In 2007, the Ritter family acquired it and charged Joi-Design with creating a four-star, superior scheme. This proved so successful that the interior architects were called back to realise an extension and second restoration of the historic building which opened in 2013.

Joi-Design's challenge was to update the hotel without damaging its soul. The solution bridges traditional and modern by adapting typical emblems of Germanic culture with 21st century twists, palettes and materials. So a raspberry wall in the reception (reflecting the forest and its fruits) is hung with a line of traditional cuckoo clocks labelled to display times around the globe and finished in cool white to create a contemporary energy.

The restaurant Wilder Ritter received a refined makeover befitting its Michelin star class, thanks to a vibrant play on baroque style. Scrolled tone-on-tone ebony wallcovering and rich timber panelling are emboldened by splashes of crimson velvet in the upholstered chairs and twinkling crystal chandeliers. On the walls, curated collections of vintage silver dining utensils are displayed in a modern way, becoming art installations.

The spa has doubled in size, with a Kräuterkammer (herb chamber) in soothing shades of lavender and honey reminiscent of Pinot Noir and Riesling grapes. By uniting contemporary and natural inspirations, Joi-Design celebrates the hotel's provenance while keeping it relevant for today's guests.

WHERE **Tal 1, Durbach, Germany**
OPENING **November 2013**
CLIENT **Hotel Ritter Durbach**
DESIGNER **Joi-Design (p.546)**
FLOOR AREA **7000 m²**
WEBSITE **ritter-durbach.de**

NO. OF STARS *4*
NO. OF ROOMS *80 rooms, 7 suites*
AMENITIES *Fine-dining restaurant, traditional Baden restaurant, wine bistro, bar, wellness centre and spa, eight conference rooms*

Tucked under the eaves, this two-storey suite blends a rich mix of local timber veneers with vivid bursts of colour to create an especially cosy feel.

In the reception, a raspberry-tinted wall displays a row of white cuckoo clocks as a contemporary twist on a traditional local motif.

One of Europe's oldest hotels gains a new lease of life

A flickering fireplace warms guests as they unwind in side-by-side chaise lounges or on extended sofas.

HOTEL VALENTINERHOF

noa*

Inspired by natural rock and Alpine spring water, this installation was created by craftsmen as a metaphor for the South Tyrolean soul.

Hotel Valentinerhof is located near the well-known Seiser Alm in the Italian Dolomites, at around 1200 m above sea level. The design and architecture studio noa* was commissioned to develop the establishment, with the addition of a new wellness area and lobby, bar and restaurant and 14 spacious suites, increasing the hotel's size by 1100 m².

The aim of the design concept was to reinforce the impressive Alpine scenery. The panorama with its mountain silhouettes remains the main focal point of the new intervention. Natural wood and stone elements constitute the primary material palette, with water a major theme in the wellness area. Forms are inspired by local building traditions, with the extension's irregular wooden framework interacting dynamically with the landscape.

The suites are characterised by almost square floor plans. Full-height windows allow natural daylight to flood in, illuminating every corner of the rooms and the bathrooms. The beds are positioned facing the valley: on waking, every guest can enjoy the view, almost as if sleeping outdoors. The spa too takes full advantage of the Alpine setting, with an infinity pool, sunbeds and even windows in the sauna making the mountains all but inescapable.

Furniture and lighting, interior design, architecture and landscaping were conceived holistically, with a focus on tradition and local craftsmanship. Throughout, the designers used only traditional materials such as natural stone cladding, wood, glass or linen. The most challenging internal feature was an impressive lighting installation. It was created with a Roman glassblower and a German designer, using water-filled, mouth-blown glass beads, inspired by the local mountainous crags and stone.

WHERE **San Valentino 10, Siusi allo Sciliar, Italy**
OPENING **August 2011**
CLIENT **Family Mulser**
DESIGNER **noa* (p.547)**
FLOOR AREA **2000 m²**
WEBSITE **valentinerhof.com**

NO. OF STARS 4
NO. OF ROOMS 40
AMENITIES Pool (indoor, outdoor), wellness area, restaurant, bar, natural pond

Bespoke furniture and lighting, conceived holistically, focuses on tradition and local craftsmanship

The installation in the atrium serves as gateway between the old and new parts of the venue.

Rooms make the most of the wonderful Alpine scenery.

Outside, a system of wooden verticals and horizontals helps to frame the views.

ICELANDAIR HOTEL REYKJAVIK MARINA

THG Architects

Icelandair Hotel Reykjavik Marina is located in the up-and-coming harbour district of downtown Reykjavik, next to the Slippur dry dock – meaning that you can almost touch the sea-going vessels that are being worked on as you walk towards the main entrance of the hotel. The old dock function now coexists alongside an upcoming arty, cultural scene.

The hotel's atmospheric setting inside the repurposed four-storey building lends for a design that ties in with the industrial setting, whilst being conferred with quirky and colourful touches. The bespoke look results from all the furniture being either custom manufactured in Iceland, or collected as vintage and antique pieces from the surrounding area. The graphics used in the hotel hint at the local harbour history, longstanding maritime connections and the area's latest culture of art and crafts.

The ground floor is the public area, with various spaces and seating areas designed to appeal to a local crowd as well as the hotel guests. Here, the hotel is open to the harbour, with a pedestrian street connecting it with the old city. Facilities include Iceland's largest cocktail bar, and a cosy cafe for healthy, energising breakfasts and some might say the best coffee in town. A movie theatre – devoted to showing Icelandic films (with English subtitles) – completes the hotel's engaging public face.

The rooms and suites are also entertaining, and far from uniform: shipping maps and brightly coloured wallpapers are combined with comfy furnishings and an eclectic mix of locally sourced pieces.

In the lobby, and everywhere else in the hotel, furniture is either custom-designed or consists of locally-collected vintage items.

WHERE **Myrargata 2. Reykjavik, Iceland**
OPENING **April 2012**
CLIENT **Icelandair Hotels**
DESIGNER **THG Architects (p.551)**
FLOOR AREA **4100 m²**
WEBSITE **icelandairhotels.com**

NO. OF STARS **4 (equivalent)**
NO. OF ROOMS **106 rooms, 2 suites**
AMENITIES **Meeting rooms, restaurant, bar, gym, cinema**

PHOTOS: Iceland Hotels and Paolo Gisafrancesco

The pavement at the front of the hotel has colourful, directional lines linking to the lobby, bringing the outside in and vice versa.

Seating niches upholstered in local fabrics add a snug touch, aided by a sunny colour palette.

Weathered wood forms a stunning display for the cured meats hanging above the cafe's counter.

Graphics used in the hotel hint at the local harbour history

Graphics including vintage photography celebrate the local maritime heritage of the Slippur dock.

A single (local) fabric covers walls and seating in this corner, creating a deluxe effect in contrast to the rough and ready treatment of the ceiling, covered with old sails.

A life-sized wooden figure adds a friendly character (literally) to the lounge, where the raw fabric of the formerly industrial building is softened by colourful upholstery.

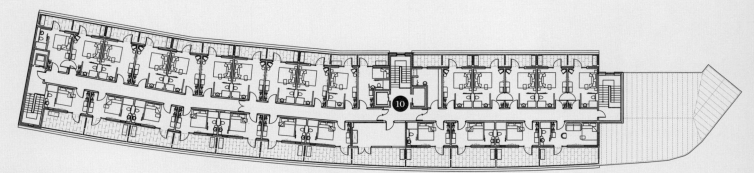

GROUND FLOOR

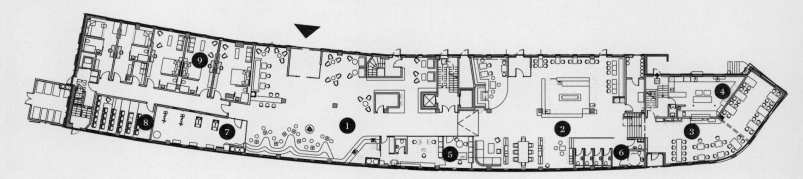

The industrial setting is conferred with quirky and colourful touches

A colourful watercolour conveys the design team's vision for the harbour-based project.

Another fun element is the colourful text boards placed in the rooms, adorned with messages and an informal dialogue with the guests.

All guest rooms have habour-related visuals in the rooms, with some having direct views of sea-going vessels.

ION LUXURY ADVENTURE HOTEL

Minarc

The vision of the Ion Luxury Adventure Hotel is to offer a holistic experience, appealing to the upscale adventurer seeking a more personal, intimate and eco-responsive expression of luxury. The design needed to reflect the natural beauty of the region with clarity and simplicity, in a manner that is environmentally considerate, which is where Minarc came in.

The design team considered how such a built environment could profoundly impact on the natural environment, so utilised an approach where the built and natural aspects could coexist, integrate and even synergise. With respect for nature, the designers incorporated innovative materials, sustainable practices, and the natural features of Iceland into its concept – an understated design that allows the extraordinary landscape to take centre stage.

The Ion Hotel emerges proudly from the moss-covered mountain base with a stark appearance. The extensive use of oversized windows ensures the interior is flooded with natural daylight, reducing the need for artificial lighting, while providing unobstructed views of the natural wonders beyond. In the interior, there is an extensive use of recycled and repurposed materials reflecting the commitment to environmental simplicity – driftwood, lava, recycled rubber and corrugated cardboard are all utilised to create bespoke furnishings such as lamps and tables.

Adding to the overall ambience, throughout there are Icelandic references, with finishing touches inspired by the local surroundings, wildlife, culture and traditions. Fair Trade certified products, such as linens, blankets, towels and bathrobes, are available for guests when local Icelandic items cannot be sourced.

The hotel, projecting out from the moss-covered mountain, is positioned on concrete pillars and was constructed with a panelised building system.

Natural wood predominates in the restaurant's interior.

WHERE **Nesjavellir vid Thingvallavatn, Selfoss, Iceland**
OPENING **February 2013**
CLIENT **Hengill Fasteignir**
DESIGNER **Minarc (p.547)**
FLOOR AREA **2130 m²**
WEBSITE **ioniceland.is**

NO. OF STARS **4**
NO. OF ROOMS **46**
AMENITIES **Lounge, restaurant, bar, spa, outdoor geothermal pool**

PHOTOS Art Gray and Torfi Agnarsson

The guest rooms are a mix of raw surfaces and luxurious fabrics.

Icelandic imagery features highly throughout the hotel.

An understated design that allows the extraordinary landscape to take centre stage

The blue seating is like a sparkling water pool, as a reminder that the hotel draws its heat from surrounding geothermal hot springs.

The design team's approach was to
create a hotel experience as dramatic
and otherworldly as the natural
Icelandic surroundings.

LA BANDITA TOWNHOUSE HOTEL

Ab Rogers Design and DA.studio

Every room has in-built furnishings and fittings, with metallic finishes and bursts of colour.

In his previous life, New York-raised John Voigtmann was a record company executive. Then he discovered a new passion – breathing life back into abandoned buildings in the Italian countryside. In an idyllic Tuscan town, Voigtmann and his partner discovered one such destination, a former convent. They commissioned Ab Rogers Design to renovate the Renaissance-era palazzo – where nuns lived for over 500 years – into a relaxing and nurturing 12-room luxury boutique hotel tucked inside the town's historic centre.

The London-based design team collaborated closely with an Italian architecture practice – DA.studio in Florence – to considerably revitalise the interior. Having previously created a small hotel in an old farmhouse for the client in 2007, Ab Rogers was invited once again to lead the creation of the concept for this new hotel. The brief called for a boutique experience, deeply immersed in the beautiful historic town, that would offer fresh contemporary design and high-end service. Comments Rogers, 'At the heart of our practice is a desire to innovate, while learning from the best that history has to offer, particularly the energetic optimism of the 1960s.'

The team respectfully restored the original features of the listed building by exposing the existing structure, whilst introducing contemporary objects and interventions to offer both surprise and comfort. The design both inspires and animates guests through its vibrant use of colour in the bespoke fittings, with a simple material palette that sees geometric, metallic furnishings mixed with the natural feeling of leather and white-washed wood. The team successfully created an overwhelmingly tactile space, with an innovative approach to layout in the guest rooms creating a clear distinction between old and new.

WHERE **111 Corso Rossellino, Pienza, Italy**
OPENING **April 2013**
CLIENT **John Voigtmann and Ondine Cohane**
DESIGNERS **Ab Rogers Design (p.540), DA.studio (p.543)**
FLOOR AREA **950 m²**
WEBSITE **labanditatownhouse.com**

NO. OF STARS **n/a**
NO. OF ROOMS **12**
AMENITIES **Library, restaurant, spa, walled garden**

Bespoke furniture has been positioned in all the guest rooms.

The building is in an idyllic Tuscan town that began life as a model Renaissance city in the 1500s.

An overwhelmingly tactile space, creating a clear distinction between old and new

Stone walls and exposed beams sit happily alongside bespoke cabinets and modern four-poster beds.

GROUND FLOOR

1   Reception
2   Dining area
3   Library
4   Kitchen
5   Spa
6   Lavatories

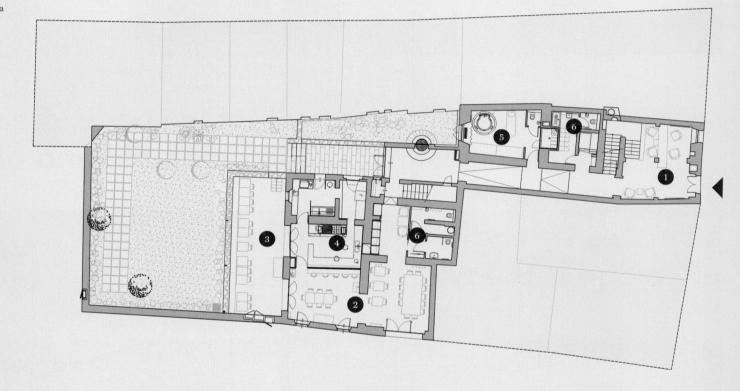

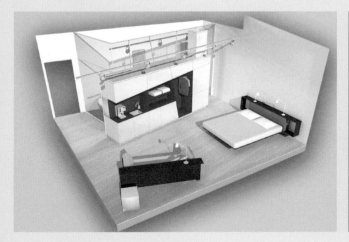

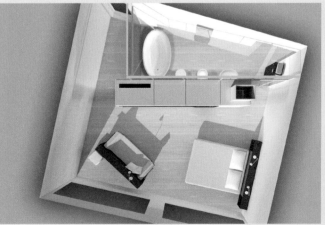

At the centre of each room, a dividing unit separates the bedroom from the bathroom and includes all the services.

A traditional service strategy would have a strong impact on the existing building envelope. The contemporary comfort standards and building regulations require the installation of services that have never been installed before in the building.

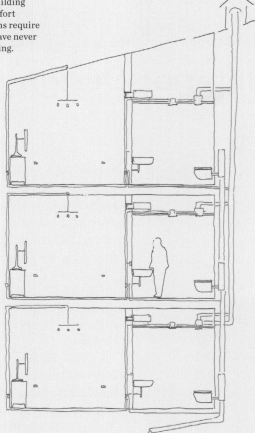

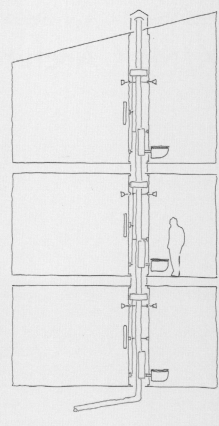

The utilised strategy respects the existing building fabric and at the same time supplies the necessary comfort and services required by the brief and the regulations.

The design both inspires and animates through its vibrant use of colour in the bespoke fittings

The positioning of the central unit (including the wardrobe) liberates the space and creates a clear distinction between old and new.

LONG BEACH HOTEL

K/M2K Architecture and Interior Design

Wooden slatted screens filter light into the dining area.

How do you compete with an amazing location? You don't, if you're the Long Beach Hotel Resort and Spa. Situated on a 59-acre site on the east coast of Mauritius, on the longest and widest stretch of beach on the island, the resort occupies a stunning site. The interior design team worked closely with the architects and landscape designers from the start of the project, wisely creating an understated complex that allows the setting to shine.

The brief was to 'create a hotel that is different from any other in Mauritius', with a guest experience both truly Mauritian and embracing the magnificent location. The result is a contemporary and restrained architecture and interior design that work together to frame and accentuate the beauty of the place. The design incorporates textures, colours and shapes found on the site as a starting point, allowing the interiors to become an extension of the tropical gardens and endless beach.

The tone-on-tone selection of materials and colours is layered with patterns and textures, resulting in a rich, sophisticated and elegant palette to all the spaces. Individual spaces are accentuated with a spectacular level of detail, creating unique environments within a cohesive collection.

The beach theme is subtly embraced; custom chandeliers with glass pendants are reminiscent of worn beach glass, while white-washed wood speaks of the driftwood along the shore. The overall atmosphere is modern and sophisticated, while remaining warm and inviting, living up to the resort's ambition of being a highly sought-after island destination.

WHERE **Coastal Road, Belle Mare, Mauritius**
OPENING **April 2011**
CLIENT **Sun Resorts**
DESIGNER **K/M2K Architecture and Interior Design (p.546)**
TOTAL **26,541 m²**
WEBSITE **longbeachmauritius.com**

NO. OF STARS **5**
NO. OF ROOMS **255**
AMENITIES *Eight food and beverage outlets, multi-function room, spa, sport and fitness centre, night club and bar, clubs for kids and teenagers*

A cool but sparkling palette and pebble forms bring touches of the beach into the lobby.

A rich, sophisticated and elegant palette accentuates all the stunning spaces

Wood is shaped to form stunning custom chandeliers in this timber-clad dining area.

All the 255 rooms have a sea view: colours and details are kept low-key so as not to detract from it.

Unique environments are created within a cohesive collection

A 1960s-inspired backlit wood-panelled wall gives a warm ambience to this cocktail bar.

Verandas act as extensions of the tropical gardens.

Detailing is layered with pattern and texture, with the ceiling decorated with shutters used in local style architecture.

MACALISTER MANSION
Ministry of Design

Designed and branded as a lifestyle-oriented 'residence', Macalister Mansion consists of eight guest rooms, two restaurants and two lounges, plus a poolside bar. Ministry of Design took on the task of turning a 100-year-old mansion in Penang into a quirky and sophisticated lifestyle destination where guests are treated to a series of experiences similar to the hospitality offered by an actual home. Each room is enjoyed as part of the overall experience but branded as a distinct space, all of which might typically be found in a English country mansion – dining room, den, bar, living room, cellar.

Major infrastructural work was required to restore and adapt the mansion for hospitality use. The heritage features have been carefully adapted and key details combined with a playful contemporary design, striking a balance between a nostalgia for the past and a forward-looking modernity.

The mansion's stately dimensions mean that all eight guest rooms are generously sized, ranging from 45 to 60 m² in size and featuring 3.5-m-high ceilings. Each is designed to be unique, featuring exclusive furniture pieces, carpets and artworks selected for each room's proportions, layout and lighting. Outside the entrance to each room is a bespoke acrylic mirror. These mirrors incorporate the room number and the traditional 'Do not disturb' and 'Please make room' signs appear on them as backlit LED text.

The public areas meanwhile have equal mixtures of fantasy and fun, with original art greeting guests in the hotel's driveway. Original elements in the interior like a galvanized spiral staircase leading to a viewing tower, a balcony overlooking the pool and wooden trusses are retained and celebrated, but brought firmly into the 21st century.

The surreal reception area has a reflective desk that seems to hover in the plain white space.

This room opens onto the gardens and is designed as a modern take on the classic conservatory.

WHERE **George Town, Penang, Malaysia**
OPENING **November 2012**
CLIENT **TheMacalister Berhad**
DESIGNER **Ministry of Design (p.547)**
FLOOR AREA **1700 m²**
WEBSITE **macalistermansion.com**

NO. OF STARS **5**
NO. OF ROOMS **8**
AMENITIES **Pool, fitness centre, restaurants, bars, lounges**

PHOTOS Edward Hendricks

The fairy-tale-like pastel animals and central white tree add a touch of whimsicality to the Dining Room.

This guest room features a specially-commissioned love sonnet, scribed on the wall above the bed.

One room has a separate study area with a textile artwork by Grace Tan called the *Tartan Cube*.

Playful contemporary design strikes a balance between nostalgia and forward-looking modernity

Reflected in the mirror of this bathroom, an artwork by Indonesian artist Albert Yonathan can be seen above the bed.

Many rooms highlight unique features, such as the old truss beams from the original colonial building.

The Den is the hotel's whisky bar, with the dark, rich and polished decor reflecting the character of the Scottish spirit.

NEW HOTEL
Estudio Campana

The New Taste restaurant with its 'Favela columns' is stamped with the unmistakable signature of the Campana brothers.

In the penthouse suite, the design takes a on a much quieter and restful dimension.

Adding the finishing touch to its already impressive New Hotel in Athens, Estudio Campana has unveiled a spectacular rooftop Art Lounge on the seventh floor of the 1950s landmark building, which was originally designed by Iasonas Rizos. The new lounge is the crowning glory of the hotel, which not only features stunning interiors by the Campana brothers but also exceptional pieces from the contemporary art collection of owner and collector Dakis Joannou.

Part library, part gallery and part panoramic viewing terrace, the wood-lined lounge – which serves food and cocktails – has some 2000 books on art and architecture, which guests can borrow for the duration of their stay. Artworks by Maurizio Cattelan and Pierpaolo Ferrari also feature prominently (it is the Art Lounge after all), although it has to be said that it's the incredible view of the Acropolis that really steals the show.

Back on the ground floor, the Campana brothers have also reworked the organic restaurant, New Taste. The interior is now a lavish interpretation of the designers' iconic Favela chair. 'Favela' columns are covered with pieces of recycled wood and furniture from the old hotel interior in place here before. The beautiful and dynamic result is both a tribute to the past, and an evocation of the favelas of Brazil. The columns also give a warm, natural and woody feeling to the space, evoking a forest.

Another new addition to the hotel is an elegant 70-m² penthouse suite, equipped with bespoke features and fittings and drop-dead gorgeous views.

WHERE **16, Filellinon Str., Syntagma sq., Athens, Greece**
OPENING **July 2011 (completion 2013)**
CLIENT **Yes! Hotels**
DESIGNER **Estudio Campana (p.544)**
FLOOR AREA **3674 m²**
WEBSITE **yeshotels.gr**

NO. OF STARS **4**
NO. OF ROOMS **79**
AMENITIES *New Taste restaurant, bar, meeting spaces, New Sense gym and wellness club, rooftop Art Lounge*

A dynamic display of lamps lends some extra arty energy to the already intriguing space.

The new lounge is the crowning glory of the hotel

The seventh-floor Art Lounge is designed by the Campana brothers, in conjunction with architectural students from the University of Thessaly, and features an art collection by Italian art aficionado Maurizio Cattelan and Pierpaolo Ferrari.

Facetted, metallic forms add interest to marble-lined bathrooms.

The penthouse suite comes complete with its own dining area, with custom furnishings.

NUI. HOSTEL

Tadafumi Azuno

A delicate, glass frontage opens up the former warehouse and makes it welcoming to visitors in the hostel's ground-floor cafe.

Creating Nui. Hostel in Tokyo meant converting a six-floor former-warehouse building in Tokyo. The ground floor forms a cafe, bar and lounge, with the dormitories and private rooms arranged on the five floors above. For the lower level sociable space, which is open to the general public as well as guests, carpenters and artisans from all over Japan were brought together to discuss the design possibilities with the owner and designer Tadafumi Azuno.

The resulting design, unusually for a low-budget hostel, uses carefully constructed furniture and architectural details. For the hostel's bar and lounge, the craftsmen implanted a sturdy, Japanese oak tree as an eye-catching feature. The 10-m bar counter is made of oak, Amur cork-tree and Japanese ash, with a bespoke bench made of layered veneer, both of which were designed by Azuno. Other elements – door handles, table legs and hinges – were made especially for the venue by an artisanal metalworker. A friend who runs a vintage store in Nagoya hand-picked other furnishings for the interior of the public areas.

'I divided the space loosely into four areas – for sitting, standing, circulating and relaxing,' says Azuno. 'It's up to the guests to choose where to spend their time. This way they're not tied to a particular table – or companion – for the entire evening.'

Across the remaining five floors above, the various dormitory and private rooms have a plain, monastic character and share the emphasis on natural materials. 'By using natural materials and handicrafts to configure most of the space, we aimed to create a story, and a business that would be loved by many,' says Azuno.

WHERE **2-14-13 Kuramae, Tokyo, Japan**
OPENING **September 2012**
CLIENT **Backpackers Japan**
DESIGNER **Tadafumi Azuno (p.550)**
FLOOR AREA **960 m²**
WEBSITE **backpackersjapan.co.jp**

NO. OF STARS **n/a**
NO. OF ROOMS **8 dormitories, 18 twin**
AMENITIES **Cafe, bar, kitchen, lounge**

Solid timber is used both as a functional material and – in its original tree trunk form – as a decorative feature.

Craftsmen, carpenters and artisans constructed the architectural details

At night, lighting adds a warm glow to the organic materials.

In addition to handcrafted natural wood, the interior features vintage furniture as well as classical items, including a grand piano.

OKKO HOTELS NANTES CHATEAU

Studio Norguet Design

Okko Hotels is a collaborative project and human adventure built around an encounter between the founder Olivier Devys and the designer Patrick Norguet. Out of a desire to upend the traditional hospitality model was born the idea of a four star hotel in the heart of the city, where the guests can move around independently and where hospitality becomes the top priority. Breathing life into this unique hotel chain was Patrick Norguet, who was invited to conjure up the 'spirit of Okko' and create a unique identity combining aesthetics and comfort.

Patrick Norguet said of his task, 'Combining the advantages of chain hotels and those of independent hotels, designing functional and appropriately sized rooms, while offering luxury at an affordable rate were the challenges that inspired me.' The idea behind the urban concept was to design a simple and timeless product.

The guest rooms have been designed identically on the basis of two harmonising tones: one clear, Riva; the other darker, Black Out. Decidedly contemporary in design, space is optimised to have a warm and homely feel with a functional desk space. Elegance and sobriety adorn every room, equipped with a high-end bed and all the latest technologies, including a Nespresso machine and iPhone docking station.

The Club is a vast space where design and conviviality meet and where patrons can enjoy special moments freely and at all times, created by Patrick Norguet to be the heart of the hotel. Guests can relax here in an elegant and contemporary place that brings together several services, including a lobby, dining room, business zone and a fitness centre with a room gym and sauna.

Ease, functionality and speed sum up the effectiveness of the check-in process at Okko.

WHERE **15 bis rue de Strasbourg, Nantes, France**
OPENING **January 2014**
CLIENT **Olivier Devys**
DESIGNER **Studio Norguet Design (p.550)**
FLOOR AREA **2700 m²**
WEBSITE **okkohotels.com**

NO. OF STARS 4
NO. OF ROOMS 80
AMENITIES Club, restaurant, bar, lounge, fitness centre, business zone

The Club is a welcoming space with its contemporary furniture, textured surfaces and luxurious upholstery.

Pale concrete and wood-lined walls envelop the ground-floor social hub of the hotel.

Patrick Norguet designed each room to be a contemporary and comfortable space.

There is perfect harmony between the calming yet contrasting hues of the interior.

Elegance and sobriety adorn every room

The 18 m² guest rooms are compact yet well-equipped with all the essentials.

Colourful, modern furnishings stand out against the pale grey background.

The bathroom offers a walk-in shower for guests to enjoy relaxing moments.

REYKJAVIK LIGHTS HOTEL

Haf Studio

The mysterious and mystical qualities of Icelandic light – seen here beautifully illuminating the windows of the facade – inspired the designers of this concept hotel.

Visitors to the Reykjavik Lights Hotel quickly see the light – namely, the unique and ever-changing natural light that characterises the mystical atmosphere of Iceland. This hotel offers a series of experiences based on Icelandic light, and Icelandic culture's relationship with it.

The concept, interior and visual design was realised by Hafsteinn Júlíusson and Karitas Sveinsdóttir of Haf Studio, working in collaboration with architects Tark to reconfigure the layout of the hotel. A key element in the concept is a unique visual calendar based on Icelandic daylight and inspired by the ancient Icelandic calendar that is called *Rímtafla*. The calendar is divided into 12 parts and distributed through the 12 corridors of the hotel. Every corridor represents one month of the year, and each room is linked to a specific day in the ancient Icelandic calendar.

Rímtafla roughly translates as 'rhythmic tablet' which conjures up images of ancient scripts. Such an idea is also evoked by the graphic illustration that decorates the walls throughout – a visual identity developed in collaboration with graphic designer Sveinn Þorri Davíðsson. The typography is inspired by old Icelandic runes and is a font called Grindavík (which also happens to be a town on the southwestern coast of Iceland).

The hotel creates a serene effect, thanks to all the clear, calming hues of the colour scheme which reflect Icelandic light. In fact, light in all its natural forms is celebrated. Star constellations decorate the lobby, and a large lamp hangs like a moon in the bar.

WHERE **Sudurlandsbraut 12, Reykjavik, Iceland**
OPENING **June 2013**
CLIENT **Kea Hotels**
DESIGNER **Haf Studio (p.545)**
FLOOR AREA **3000 m²**
WEBSITE **keahotels.is**

NO. OF STARS **3 (equivalent)**
NO. OF ROOMS **105**
AMENITIES **Bar, lounge, restaurant, meeting rooms**

Behind the reception desk there is a sole focus on the wall art devoted to the Icelandic calendar.

Graphic detailing is inspired by the ancient Icelandic calendar *Rímtafla*

The typography used throughout the interior was inspired by old Icelandic runes.

The wayfinding signs associate different groups of rooms with different seasons and their light effects.

Over the bar, a large illuminated globe is suspended like a celestial full moon.

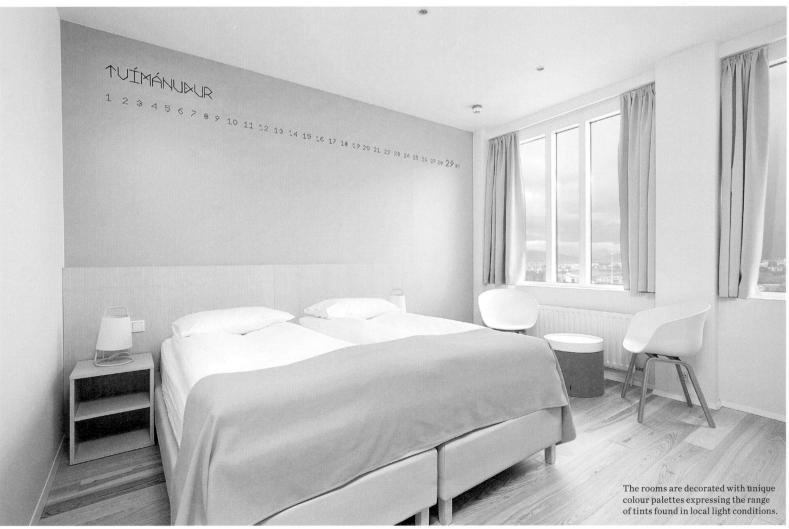

The rooms are decorated with unique colour palettes expressing the range of tints found in local light conditions.

Artworks in the rooms link to local traditions and seasonal experiences, including the Northern Lights and midnight sun.

The sky at night was a further inspiration, with star constellations decorating the walls of the lobby.

Calming hues which reflect Icelandic light create a serene effect

ROOM MATE PAU

Teresa Sapey Estudio de Arquitectura

The bar extends into an outdoor terrace,
adorned with head-shaped stools.

This is a hotel with real personality – that of Pau, a charming, perfectionist chef and owner of a famous restaurant. This fictional character's passion for food (and Barcelona) was the basic concept for the design of this hotel, Room Mate Pau, by Teresa Sapey.

In a series of funky and fresh graphics and furnishings, Pau appears throughout the highly differentiated spaces of the hotel. Most dramatic of all is his incarnation in the hotel lobby – where his back appears as a giant graphic covering the wall and lift doors. He's wearing a houndstooth jacket, which matches the carpet. His head, however, is only a squiggle – leaving room for the visitor's imagination.

From the entrance, stairs lead up to the lounge and cafe/bar, which opens onto a large terrace dotted with furniture – in the form of human heads. These are multi-functional pieces (Adán, designed by Sapey herself for Vondom), which function as stools, side tables and planters. In the atrium and corridors, guests might feel like they are being watched, thanks to large portholes containing different-coloured eyes peering out of them.

In the guest rooms, the evasive Pau appears once again – or rather, stencilled images of his hands do. Corian room dividers are punched full of holes like Swiss cheese, a motif that recurs in the breakfast bar. The lobby space meanwhile, is refreshingly low-key – with black and white modular furnishings and a stacked wood reception desk. The relatively monochrome palette used throughout the hotel is enlivened by brightly striped carpets in the corridors, intended so as to help guests navigate their way. A perfect place to find yourself in an unknown city.

WHERE **7 Fontanella Street, Barcelona, Spain**
OPENING **September 2012**
CLIENT **Room Mate Hotels**
DESIGNER **Teresa Sapey Estudio de Arquitectura (p.551)**
FLOOR AREA **12,000 m²**
WEBSITE **pau.room-matehotels.com**

NO. OF STARS **3**
NO. OF ROOMS **66**
AMENITIES **Restaurant, cafe, bar, terrace**

PHOTOS: Jose Irun

The quirky design of
the lobby represents the
character of Pau – a fictional
chef and restaurant owner.

GROUND FLOOR

1 Lobby
2 Reception
3 Pau mural/elevators
4 Stairs up to restaurant, terrace and rooms

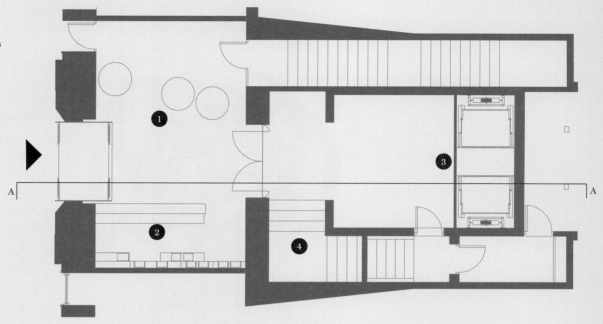

UPPER FLOOR

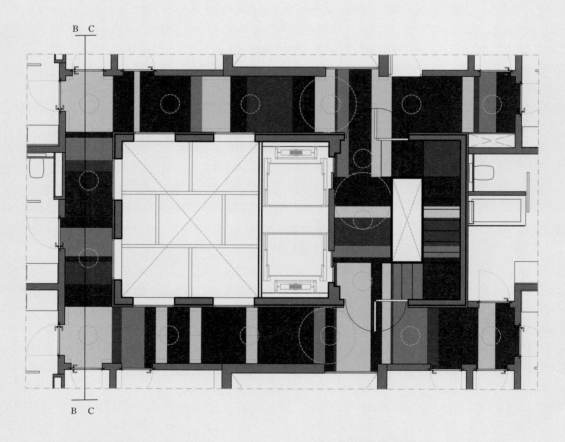

SECTION B

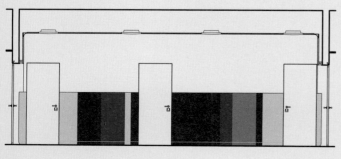

SECTION C

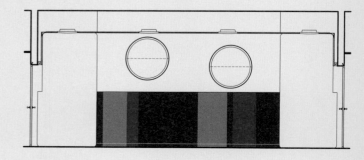

Guest rooms are fresh and playful, thanks to a palette of lemon and white and Corian elements punched with portholes of various dimensions.

Room dividers are punched full of holes like Swiss cheese

The breakfast bar, in shades of olive green, repeats the circle motif.

The eyes have it – large photographic prints underline the eyeball theme.

Porthole windows filled with huge coloured irises spy on guests and draw attention to the voyeuristic aspect of hotels.

The eyes have it – large photographic prints underline the eyeball theme.

LOBBY SECTION A

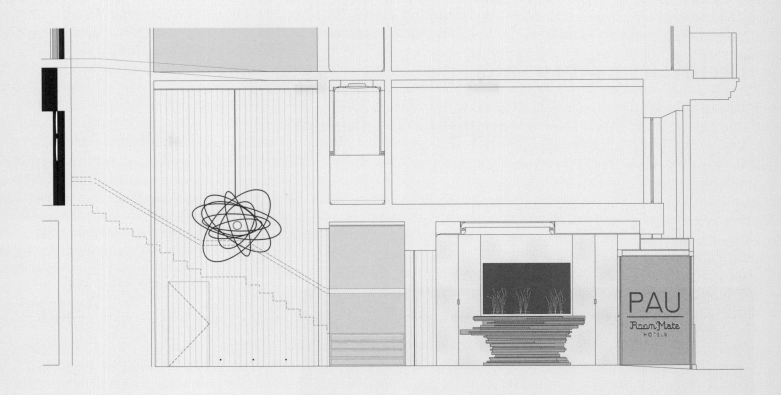

Drawings reveal the hotel scheme – and the designer's debt to surrealism.

CONCEPT VISUAL

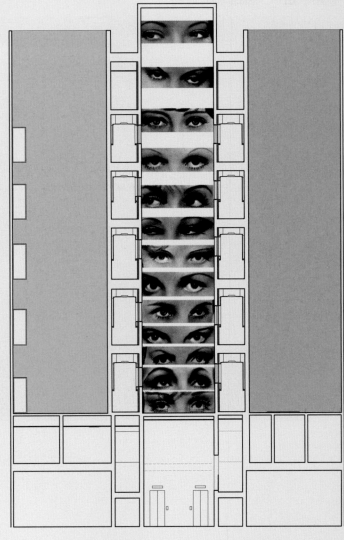

RUCO GUESTHOUSE

Tadafumi Azuno

'I want to cheer up Hagi city, that's why I wanted to open a guesthouse.' This what designer Tadafumi Azuno was told by his client, when he was commissioned to design the project. 'He thought that Hagi needed a different way of promoting tourism,' adds Azuno, explaining that the guesthouse's name – Ruco – comes from the Chinese characters for 'flow' and 'interact'. So the aim of the guesthouse was to connect people's lives – both locals and visitors.

To make that connection, the guesthouse is thoroughly rooted in the locality. It was constructed using local timber and other materials, including recycled old doors, with local artists, carpenters and craftsman doing all the work. 'We didn't use any special materials, only ones that are commonly found in the area,' says the designer. 'And everything here is the result of the labour of local people. So when people come here from, say, Tokyo, they will interact with those local elements.'

The ground-floor cafe and first-floor lounge have a rustic and comfortable atmosphere, and the spaces can be used for hosting local events and exhibitions. 'I wanted people in Hagi to know that making a fascinating space is possible with local materials, and I hope they are proud of Ruco,' says Azuno. 'Having lived in Hagi for 4 months and joined in with all the construction, I think the result is a design rooted in the area which has a high level of quality comparable to the big city.'

The first-floor lounge combines a recycled, old pine floor with walls of burnished blue plaster.

WHERE **92 Karahimachi, Hagi, Yamaguchi, Japan**
OPENING **October 2013**
CLIENT **Naohiro Shiomitsu**
DESIGNER **Tadafumi Azuno (p.550)**
FLOOR AREA **189 m²**
WEBSITE **guesthouse-ruco.com**

NO. OF STARS **n/a**
NO. OF ROOMS **2 dormitories, 1 private room**
AMENITIES **Cafe, bar, lounge, gallery**

The lower level is versatile enough to be used for a variety of events, and gains a literally earthy touch thanks to its traditional dirt floor.

The space showcases local carpentry skills, with Japanese cedar as the principal material.

SALA RATTANAKOSIN

Onion

The boutique hotel's riverside location affords guests glorious views of Wat Arun, the 'Temple of Dawn'.

For Sala Rattanakosin, the design studio Onion was commissioned to realise a luxurious boutique hotel with views of some of central Bangkok's most prized landmarks. Located in an old market neighbourhood of the city, the designers renovated seven 'shop houses' to create a hotel that truly makes the most of the spectacular views of the Chao Phraya, Temple of Dawn and Wat Po. Framing these views was a central concern of the designers, so that guests can get the 'wow factor' throughout the hotel.

On arrival, therefore, a first glance of the Temple of Dawn is revealed after the right turn at the end of the reception area. Laminated glass partitions, coated with black and golden films, mirror the temple too (an effect repeated in the lavatories next to the restaurant, in which the laminated glass is designed to reflect only the upper half of the monument). Upstairs, each guest room has its dramatic view maximised by the unfussy window treatments. Then, naturally, guests are treated to the best viewing point from the rooftop bar.

Onion paid much attention to the original architectural elements and materials of the building's exterior – for example, the original sets of folding doors remain at the entrance. Within the interior, a more playful approach to these original elements was taken. For instance, the plaster surface of the restaurant wall was flaked-off to reveal the original brick. At the same time, Onion opted for new materials to invent Sala Rattakosin's modern image, namely the dark-gold laminated glass, black-and-white ceramic tiles and aluminum panels. Sala Rattanakosin thus combines ancient with modern.

WHERE **39 Soi Ta Tien, Bangkok, Thailand**
OPENING **April 2013**
CLIENT **Sala Resorts & Spa's**
DESIGNER **Onion (p.548)**
FLOOR AREA **1500 m²**
WEBSITE **salarattanakosin.com**

NO. OF STARS *4 (equivalent)*
NO. OF ROOMS **17**
AMENITIES *Restaurant, lounge, terrace, indoor bar, rooftop bar*

PHOTOS **Wison Tungthunya**

Inside, the designers used many salvaged details from the seven original structures, with ancient brickwork adding texture, history and warmth to the new interior.

Located in an old market neighbourhood of Bangkok, the hotel occupies a vibrant area with the entrance preserving the original 'shop house' exterior and folding doors.

In the reception area, reflective metal panels in combination with a geometric lighting installation suggest the meeting of modernity with local history.

Solid but simple new interventions, like the iron beams, window frames and staircase, contrast beautifully with the aged original fabric of the building.

Luxurious yet low-key guest rooms are constructed so as not to detract from the stunning vistas of Wat Arun.

Monochrome combinations allow the hotel's context to shine, with laminated glass allowing intriguing reflections of the ancient temple.

A linear touch of black enlivens a simple white corridor.

Framing the spectacular views was a central concern of the designers

SCANDIC HOTEL PAASI

Stylt Trampoli

In the lobby, Ribbon bar stools by Cappellini strike the right note against the stained zig-zag bar and rainbow walls.

In the Siltasaari area, just a 5-minute tram ride from Helsinki city centre, Stylt Trampoli was asked to design a contemporary interior for the Scandic Hotel Paasi. The design team dug deep into the past for inspiration, investigating Siltasaari's history and discovering that it was once the location of a 2000-seat circus, opened in 1885. The opening parade featured 110 artists, 62 horses and a grand orchestra. 'Among the countless performers over the years were Manuel Veltra and his six lions on bicycles, and animal trainer Henrik Henrikssen who wrestled with 15 polar bears,' says Erik Nissen Johansen, Stylt's creative director.

The magnetic appeal of such a colourful episode proved irresistible for Stylt, and the hotel lobby was designed as a modern take on the three rings and big top of the circus, full of colour and contrast. The walls are panelled with wood and leather in harlequin patterns and with lamellae in vibrant colours which also extend across the ceiling. Furnishings in fabrics from Romo, Designers Guild and others add to the fun. Next to the lobby and bar, the drawing room offers a quieter space, with a warm and cosy ambience. A huge bookshelf filled with objects, photos and books tells the story of the area in a decorative celebration of local history – evoking a vivid sense of place.

In the guest rooms, the circus theme continues, with details such as top-hat shaped Wooster lamps by Jake Phipps and striped wallpaper evoking the big top. A chain hotel is thus given a truly local flavour, as well as its own individual character.

PHOTOS Erik Nissen Johansen

WHERE **Paasivuorenkatu 5b, Helsinki, Finland**
OPENING **August 2012**
CLIENT **Scandic Hotels**
DESIGNER **Stylt Trampoli (p.550)**
FLOOR AREA **7765 m²**
WEBSITE **scandichotels.com**

NO. OF STARS **4**
NO. OF ROOMS **170**
AMENITIES **Four restaurants, sauna, gym, free bike rental**

Moooi's Dear Ingo lamp makes a strong statement above a folksy patchwork of upholstery fabrics from Designers Guild, Romo and others.

A multi-coloured, ribbed ceiling is the perfect finishing touch in a spectacular lobby space.

The Drawing Room features a custom 'story shelf' – a wall-to-wall space for local memories.

A colourful episode in history inspired the hotel's circus concept, full of colour and contrast

Custom wallpapers illustrate the hotel concept, based on a colourful local history.

Local characters are immortalised too.

Guest rooms feature a variety of custom wallpapers, with clashing patterns in the mix of furnishings creating a unique effect.

Even the quieter rooms have splashes of bright colour and striped patterns reminiscent of the circuses of the past.

SCANDIC HOTEL PAASI   STYLT TRAMPOLI

SIR ALBERT HOTEL
Baranowitz Kronenberg Architecture

The concept for the Sir Albert Hotel in Amsterdam was 'the ideal residence of an aristocrat' – in the modern sense of a cosmopolitan, free spirit who feels at ease anywhere in the world. Entering the hotel is like arriving at a (rather grand) home.

At Sir Albert, guests are welcomed not by a reception but by a cosy study, checking-in around a big oval table and having breakfast at Izakaya, a restaurant with a 'feels like home' atmosphere. For the design team, this project represented a challenge: to think 'out of the hotel box'. The monumental building, a former diamond factory, remains connected to lively city life, particularly on the ground floor, which houses both the study/lobby and the restaurant – independent but connected spaces, both willing to create a relationship with the world outside. The design concept of raising the floor here creates a visual interaction between inside and outside.

On the upper levels, large windows face towards the street providing each room not only with bright daylight, but also another connection to the lively street atmosphere. The interiors are a mix of detailed furnishings and artworks which convey the idea of being in the residence of a globetrotter: pieces of furniture from Italian manufacturers like Maxalto, Moroso and Ceccotti meet limited edition pieces from different designers. Each and every item might have been picked up by Sir Albert during his travels around the world.

Sir Albert occupies a former diamond-cutting factory on the edge of the fashionable – but still slightly gritty – Amsterdam area known as De Pijp.

WHERE **Albert Cuypstraat 2, Amsterdam, the Netherlands**
OPENING **May 2013**
CLIENT **Grand City**
DESIGNER **Baranowitz Kronenberg Architecture (p.541)**
FLOOR AREA **6200 m²**
WEBSITE **siralberthotel.com**

NO. OF STARS 4
NO. OF ROOMS 98
AMENITIES Restaurant, lounge, bar

The hotel lobby combines furniture by the
likes of Ceccoti, Nika Zupanc and Max Alto,
with quirky design details like the humorous
hippo heads by Dor Karmon.

'A curving, metallic bar is the sociable heart of the drinking and dining space.

In the dining area, a floor of Indian black limestone contrasts with white walls and earthy materials – wood, metal and leather – for a simple, chic effect.

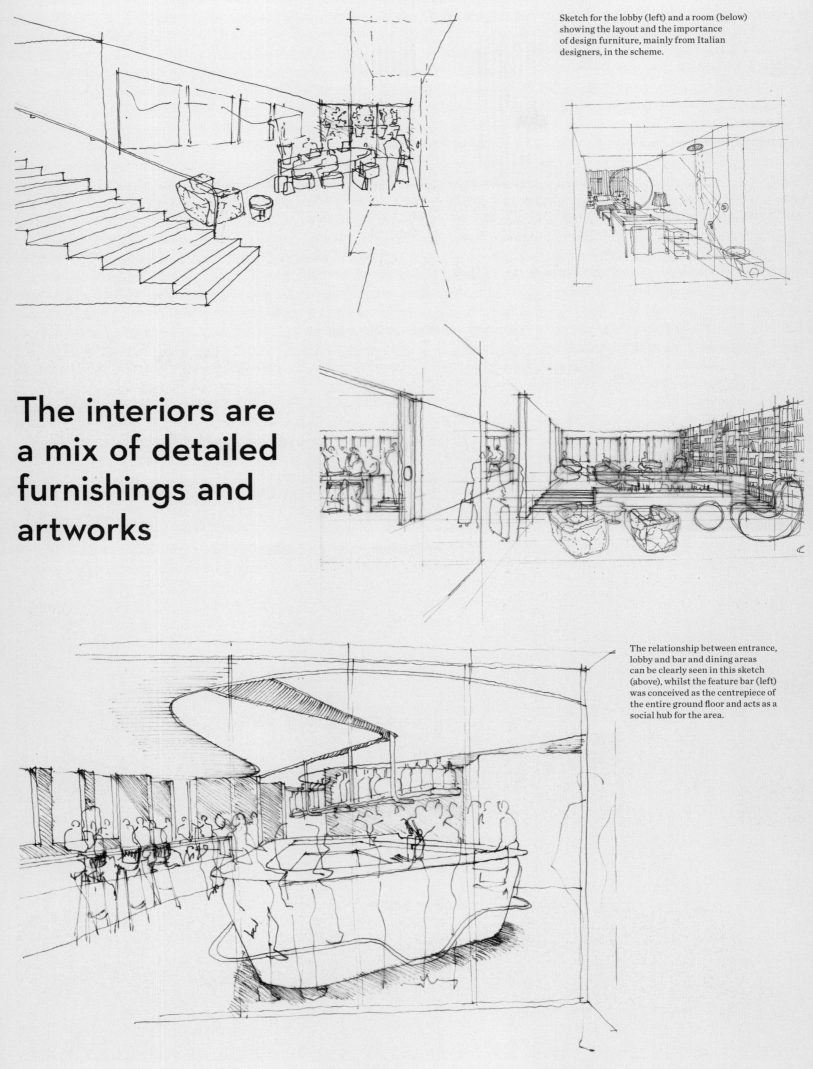

Sketch for the lobby (left) and a room (below) showing the layout and the importance of design furniture, mainly from Italian designers, in the scheme.

The interiors are a mix of detailed furnishings and artworks

The relationship between entrance, lobby and bar and dining areas can be clearly seen in this sketch (above), whilst the feature bar (left) was conceived as the centrepiece of the entire ground floor and acts as a social hub for the area.

FLOOR PLAN

1 Welcoming desk/reception
2 Izakaya restaurant
3 Bar
4 Wine fridges
5 Open kitchen
6 The study
7 Ground floor rooms
8 Back office

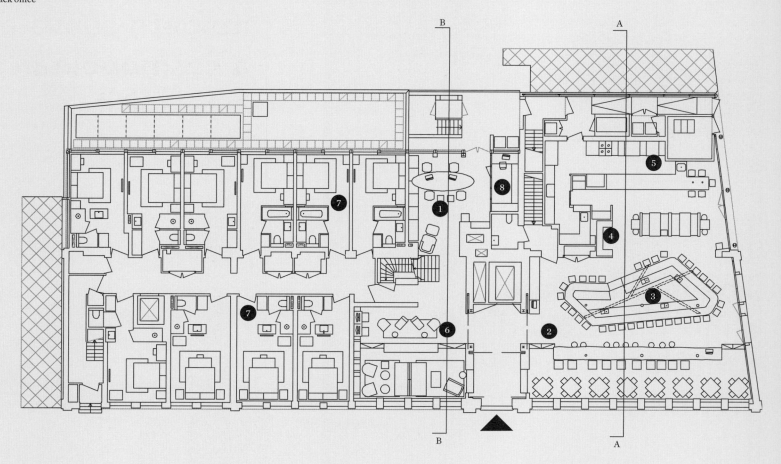

SECTION A

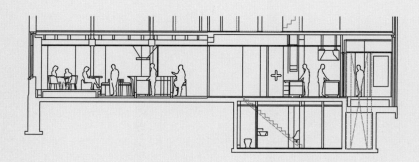

SECTION B

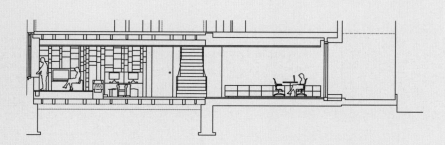

A guest bathroom reveals a distinctly Asian influence.

The ideal residence of an aristocrat – in the modern sense of a cosmopolitan, free spirit

The bright guest rooms were all designed to take advantage of the building's numerous windows and views over the city.

SUPERBUDE

Dreimeta

Custom-designed wallpaper based on old
newspapers, and plungers acting as coat pegs,
add fun and fantasy to the guest bedrooms.

Located in the heart of hip Hamburg district
Schanze, in design terms Superbude is
somewhere between a hostel and a hotel – and
surprisingly unconventional for both. The
listed building that forms this venue, once a
Deutsche Post switching centre, offers guests
super-stylish hostel accommodation, with all
the trimmings of a technically equipped hotel
– in actual fact, 'bude' is a local, colloquial
word used for a home.

Public areas are cheerful – thanks to
the sunshine yellow used as a spot colour
throughout – and functional. For instance, the
zone that serves as a breakfast area, doubles-
up as a central meeting point for guests.
An almost 50-m-long multifunctional wall
made of yellow concrete formwork panels
with rope patterns burnt into its surface gives
the ground floor a distinctive character.
The rope theme references Hamburg's
maritime history. All necessary functions
have been incorporated into this wall – from
refrigerators to the internet station, the guest
safes, benches, and so on. The kitchen, buffet,
bar and tables are made of red silkscreen
panels, while the countertop was faced with
sheet copper.

Each room has its own bathroom and
comes with stackable beds, designed by Rolf
Heide to maximise their capacity. Double
rooms can be switched to accommodate more
people at a moment's notice. Yellow formwork
panels and scaffolding tubes were also used
for the guest room furniture, and orange-
coloured safety nets serve as bedheads.
Plungers make quirky coat hooks and beer
crates are stools, while details like ceiling
lights, coat hangers and toilet paper holders
were specially designed.

WHERE **Juliusstrasse 1–7, Hamburg, Germany**
OPENING **February 2012**
CLIENT **Fortune Hotels**
DESIGNER **Dreimeta (p.544)**
FLOOR AREA **2867 m²**
WEBSITE **superbude.de**

NO. OF STARS **2/3 (equivalent)**
NO. OF ROOMS **90**
AMENITIES **Bar, lounge, restaurant, rock-star suite
(offering a stage and technical equipment)**

PHOTOS Steve Herud

Custom-made light fittings over the counter complement the material palette.

One-off furnishings in the guest rooms are made from scaffolding tubes and yellow formwork panels.

Wheel barrows used as chairs stand in front of a 50-m-long wall, clad with yellow concrete formwork panels, which incorporates all the functional elements of the ground floor.

Orange safety nets fastened to scaffolding poles make eye-catching headboards for the beds, while side tables are fashioned from old cable reels.

The looping rope pattern that recurs throughout the hotel is burned into the wall panels.

A former workshop sink enjoys a second life as a drinking-water dispenser.

A rope theme references Hamburg's maritime history

The Kitchen Club is the hotel's meeting point and breakfast area, equipped with a microwave and ovens for use by guests.

A magazine rack constructed from scaffolding doubles as a screen, adding extra colour and cosiness to the boho-looking lounge space.

THE AMPERSAND HOTEL

Dexter Moren Associates

Allegro Assai, a pendant lamp designed by Atelier Oi for Foscarini, hovers above a bespoke perforated brass staircase.

Built in 1888, The Ampersand Hotel is one of London's original Victorian boutique hotels. For its refurbishment, the client wanted to focus less on five-star luxury and more on providing a great guest experience for the right price. The design team at Dexter Moren Associates were therefore called in to create a classic and cosy environment, to steer away from fads, and to provide a modern theme appropriate to the heritage of the building.

Drawing on South Kensington's many and varied neighbourhood attractions, the design tells a story of connections between Victorian history and the museums of the local area. Key themes of botany, geology, astronomy, ornithology and music were intricately incorporated into the bespoke guest rooms and public areas, and offset with contemporary furnishings and themed artwork.

Key internal spaces were replanned to maximise the flow and function of the hotel. The back-of-house area was repositioned to open up the reception lobby space. The central staircase was brought down one level to connect guests to Apero (the restaurant and bar), as well as the library and games room. By repositioning first floor guest rooms, the design team enabled a separate entrance to the restaurant, which was crucial in helping to drive revenue from passing trade.

Grandeur was restored to The Ampersand Hotel by blending luxury with quirky and contemporary design details. Highlights including a bespoke 18-m-high Ingo Maurer goose-feather chandelier in the lobby, a cabinet of curiosities which spans the double-height arrival space of Apero, and a sculptural piece featuring salvaged architectural details taken from site during refurbishment.

WHERE **10 Harrington Road, London, United Kingdom**
OPENING **August 2012**
CLIENT **The Ampersand Hotel**
DESIGNER **Dexter Moren Associates (p.544)**
FLOOR AREA **526 m²**
WEBSITE **ampersandhotel.com**

NO. OF STARS *Luxury boutique*
NO. OF ROOMS **111**
AMENITIES *The Drawing Rooms (coffee lounge and patisserie), Apero (restaurant and bar), The Wine Room (breakout lounge), games room, meeting room, gym*

The lobby's 18-m-high goose-feather chandelier by Ingo Maurer takes a starring role.

Bespoke seating elements from Casa Zeta cluster beneath Tom Dixon pendant lights.

THE AMPERSAND HOTEL   DEXTER MOREN ASSOCIATES

The basement games room is a fresh modern take on a classic idea.

The restaurant Apero has a cosy cave-like bar.

The spectacular double-height arrival space of Apero.

A blend of luxury and quirky detail

There are 111 guest rooms, including five suites, featuring furnishings from B&B Italia and updated touches of Victoriana.

Bathrooms use the classic black and white tiles of the Victorian era, but in a contemporary, colour-block style.

THE KING'S ARMS

Raw Design

Built in 1652 as a coaching inn, The King's Arms was originally owned by the noble Beaufort family. It held a position of great significance in the local community, with a grand hall where wealthy and noble travellers would dine, but which also doubled-up as the local court room where the fate of local criminals was decided.

Raw Design was asked to create a modern country inn, with a short timescale of only 4 months. The team stripped back years of unsuccessful redecoration and conversion to revive the historic fabric of the building, giving it a contemporary twist.

The main lounge was flagged with a stone floor reminiscent of the original, and the restaurant was timbered with blackened ash. A new stove was installed in the bricked up fireplace in the restaurant. The bar area was reworked with antique timber, brick tiles and LED lighting giving a functional yet historic feel. All the furniture was selected from salvaged and up-cycled items. Prints of the surrounding area were similarly sourced. The dining area has large digital print murals to reflect the horse trials at Badminton and new deep-buttoned leather seating breaks up the space, creating cosy corners and intimate yet functional dining areas.

On the first floor, the old grand dining room was brought back into play with dark panels on the walls, large crystal chandeliers and digital artwork of classic historic paintings. Similar paintings can be found in each of the bedrooms.

Digital prints of historic artworks, like this one in the guest dining room, feature throughout this update of an old coaching inn.

WHERE **The Street, Didmarton, United Kingdom**
OPENING **January 2013**
CLIENT **Cirrus Inns**
DESIGNER **Raw Design (p.549)**
FLOOR AREA **874 m²**
WEBSITE **kingsarmsdidmarton.co.uk**

NO. OF STARS *n/a*
NO. OF ROOMS *11*
AMENITIES *Dining area, bar, lounge, historic jail*

PHOTOS: Jake Eastham

A change of scale has the effect of bringing neo-classical paintings right up to date in the guest bedrooms.

A playful combination of recycled antique, retro and modern furnishings and fixtures ensures that each room has plenty of character.

The renovations allow the original building to shine, adding an intelligent mix of old and improvised new furnishings.

A hint of irony hovers around the new interventions, helping to give the historic hotel a contemporary edge.

Large, evocative murals add drama to the rooms, which are painted in deep heritage tones.

The refurbished dining area continues the classical equine theme, reflecting the horse trials at nearby Badminton.

Blackboard walls and smoked ash floors complete the dining space.

The interior was reworked to give a functional yet historic feel

THE LINE HOTEL
Knibb Design

Artworks envelope the reception desk in innovative and compelling new ways.

The Line Hotel, located in a mid-century building in Los Angeles' Koreatown, is a hospitality destination with a collaborative philosophy. Working on everything from the design products available in the boutique to the food offerings, the two main collaborators were Sean Knibb (interior, exterior and landscape designer) and Roy Choi (chef).

Working with the original interior – created by Daniel, Mann, Johnson + Mendenhall in 1964 – as somewhat of a blank canvas, the Knibb Design team has restored and fully renovated the hotel, re-imagining public spaces and guest rooms. Without a doubt, the project showcases the Knibb team's passion for celebrating the undervalued in the urban environment.

The Line lobby is a calm haven of blue – mohair sofas, geometric booths and stained-wood panelling – all combining to create contemporary contours, which continue in the bar with its impressive, sculptural form. With tee-shirts used for ceiling treatments and wildflowers as wall covering, the hotel elevates the quotidian in rich, innovative and compelling new ways.

Raw concrete is a material theme that runs throughout, softened with colourful patterns in the carpets and upholstery. In the guest rooms, floor-to-ceiling windows offer up 'wow'-inducing views across the city. King-size bed are the order of the day, as are the home-away-from-home comforts. Decked out with Latin American textiles, prints and a cacophony of curiosa – nick-knacks mixed with designer pieces – and topped off with furniture from the Knibb studio, the experience at this cultural outpost is bound to evoke powerful human responses.

WHERE **3515 Wilshire Blvd, Los Angeles, United States**
OPENING **January 2014**
CLIENT **Sydell Group**
DESIGNER **Knibb Design (p.546)**
FLOOR AREA **27,426 m²**
WEBSITE **thelinehotel.com**

NO. OF STARS *4*
NO. OF ROOMS *388*
AMENITIES *Restaurants (Pot, Commissary, Feliz), bars (Lobby Bar, Speek), cafe, boutique, newsstand, bakery, meeting rooms, fitness centre, pool*

PHOTOS Cykora and Art Gray

Socialable seating areas have been carved out in the lobby.

A calm haven of blue all combining to create contemporary contours

Commissary restaurant is set in a greenhouse with a focus on fruit and vegetables.

Roy Choi's Pot restaurant calls upon a multitude of senses: vision, touch, sound, smell and taste.

Patterns and textures await guests at every turn, both underfoot and overhead.

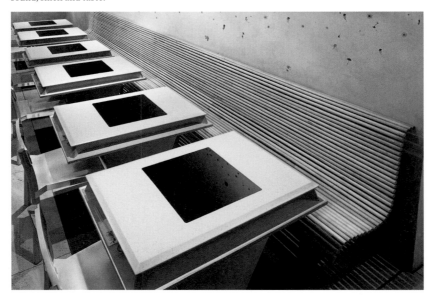

The bar's geometric form has been sculpted from natural wood panels, washed with a blue hue.

The rooms have an appealing rawness, with touches of glamour in the gold-painted frames and pipework.

The guest room interiors borrow from the cultural, natural and designed lexicon of Los Angeles itself.

Knibb Design has created a space where guests can get to know the city and feel at home.

THE STUDENT HOTEL

...,staat creative agency

Quirky signage and vibrant
colours form the signature of
this hotel concept for students.

A new hospitality destination – The Student
Hotel – came into being at the start of
the academic year in the autumn of 2012.
This new concept in the world of student
accommodation, that owner Charlie
MacGregor best calls 'boutique hotel meets
student housing', has since also been rolled
out in three more cities. Dutch creative agency
...,staat was brought on board at the outset
to shape the brand – interior design and
architectural elements, as well as signage and
all the accompanying materials.

The challenge lay in creating the comfort
of a home-away-from-home for students whilst
instilling the air of a hotel. Working around a
three-pillar mantra of 'comfort, convenience
and community', the team conjured up state-
of-the-art living with contemporary design.
Whilst the bedrooms are modern and fully
furnished rooms with large shared kitchens,
it is the 'public' spaces – with their quirky
signage and bright colours – that lend to the
fun, social and inspiring environment.

A layered approach reveals itself across
the ground floor. Furniture forms the first
layer, showcasing an energetic mix of new,
vintage and modern design furnishings.
Supporting the bold and inspirational identity,
the second layer is graphic – club-scene and
street-art murals, old illustrations from study
books, graphic blow-ups and unexpected
colourful statements can be found contrasting
boldly with the coarse concrete framework of
the building. Finally, the third layer consists
of enlarged quotes directly placed on the
tiles, posted in a bespoke type and signage
specifically developed for the concept.

A giant neon lightning bolt, light-flooded
communal areas and quirky talking points;
every element in The Student Hotel is where
the needs of a 21st-century student as well as
the design-savvy traveller may meet.

WHERE **Oostzeedijk 182, Rotterdam, the Netherlands**
OPENING **September 2012**
CLIENT **Charlie MacGregor**
DESIGNER **...,staat creative agency (p.540)**
FLOOR AREA **11,300 m²**
WEBSITE **thestudenthotel.com**

NO. OF STARS **n/a**
NO. OF ROOMS **252**
AMENITIES **Lounges, restaurant, bar, study rooms,
library, games room, gym**

An abundance of stylish but fun ground-floor public spaces gives the hotel its sociable, streetwise identity.

Well-chosen graphics combine with comfortable furnishings to create a relaxed environment where students love to lounge.

The shared kitchen and cafe space carves a new role for a nicely stripped-back interior.

Bold and inspirational identity contrasts with the coarse concrete framework of the building

Bold statements are a theme in the hotel.

Students can socialise even when doing their washing.

IT'S ABOUT THAT TIME

A witty touch awaits students climbing the stairs to their bedrooms.

URBAN POST HOTEL

A00 Architecture

An angular staircase creates interesting geometric forms at the entrance.

Following discussions between the client (Jazon Sze, director of AJ Mason Group) and the designer (A00), a brief came about that included numerous concepts central to the idea of this new boutique hotel – historical locations, storytelling, vintage 20th-century explorations and a strong sense of locality. The new hotel chain's name was selected to be Urban Post, as Sacha Silva from A00 explains, 'The word 'post' plays on both a place to station yourself and get rest, and the whole concept of travelling that is associated with mail.'

As this is to be the first of a series of such boutique hotels, A00 was able to experiment with each room, 'looking to create something very particular and unique to each of them'. With just four guest rooms, it was decided to give each one its own identity, so that repeated stays would result in a new experience each time. No wonder Silva calls the project 'a designer's dream'.

Guests experience a small-scale hotel that feels like a home, with four floors united by a central staircase which is the main element – full of light, it is purposefully muted and roughly textured. It contrasts with the general warmth that pervades the rest of the hotel thanks to the generous use of oak. 'We knew we wanted a less refined look, and this comes through with the rougher finishes – the rough-cut stonework, reclaimed woods – which we left as natural as possible, and the raw concrete walls,' says Silva. Nevertheless, there is still plenty of luxury in the details and amenities.

WHERE **37 Donghua Villa, The Lingnan Tiandi, Foshan, China**
OPENING **May 2014**
CLIENT **AJ Mason Group**
DESIGNER **A00 Architecture (p.540)**
FLOOR AREA **440 m²**
WEBSITE **urbanposthotel.com**

NO. OF STARS **n/a**
NO. OF ROOMS **4**
AMENITIES **In-house kitchen, meeting room, bar-lounge**

PHOTOS A00 Architecture

Raw concrete combines with natural wood to create a richly textured space.

On climbing up the illuminated stairwell, guests find themselves in the dining area.

The colourful, illuminated feature wall makes an eye-catching statement in the hotel's communal zone.

The bathroom walls are finished with stone tiles.

Blocks of recycled wood create different levels.

Perimeter lighting creates a quiet ambience in the guest rooms.

Rougher finishes combine with luxurious details

Custom shelving adds a homely element and acts as a room divider.

Textured surfaces contrast with smooth ones, with elongated forms positioned parallel in the kitchen.

A certain rough edge survives thanks to materials.

VILLA PASTORIE

Beers|Brickworks

Old detailing, used in a fresh way, includes recycled parquet, ceiling coving, a veneered table and furnishings re-upholstered in four different shades of velour.

Villa Pastorie is an old vicarage in Tilburg harbour in the Netherlands, which was converted into a unique hospitality concept according to the motto adopted by owners Michel and Hanneke Deneef: 'Home is not a place... it's a feeling'.

Beers|Brickworks is the design office charged with giving form to the 'feeling' of home in this boutique residence. 'There is a lot to discover in Villa Pastorie,' says Nicole van Beers. 'The interior design is based on past, present and future.'

The space is filled with an eclectic mix of old chairs, modern wall-coverings and specially designed furnishings. The hotel's guest rooms represent the past, with each room having a unique look. In one, the walls are covered with pages from books, and a bath is central in the room. In another, a large embroidered piece is the backdrop to the bed.

On the ground floor, there is a restaurant and a bar. The dining room represents the present, and guests dine at one long table – making chance encounters inevitable and adding a touch of adventure to the experience.

The bar is the design team's take on the future with its experimental and playful use of materials. The bar is covered in leather and salvaged tiles. The walls are enlivened by what the designers call 'a colour wave' and the table in front of the bar is made from a door panel coated in pink epoxy resin. The finishing touch in this space making a vibrant statement overhead is a chandelier of cutlery dipped in neon pink.

WHERE **Hoevensweg 2, Tilburg, the Netherlands**
OPENING **November 2013**
CLIENT **Michel and Hanneke Deneef**
DESIGNER **Beers|Brickworks (p.541)**
FLOOR AREA **300 m²**
WEBSITE **villapastorie.nl**

NO. OF STARS **n/a**
NO. OF ROOMS **4**
AMENITIES **Restaurant, bar, meeting room, garden**

PHOTOS Rene van der Hulst

A key feature in the bar is the chandelier made from knives, forks and spoons.

This guest room has a blue theme with boating paraphernalia used in the decoration.

In the blue-hued dining space, there is a glass feature in one wall made of wine bottles.

A design based on past, present and future

Walls are covered with pages from old books.

An antique bath occupies pride of place.

The 'Bath and Book' room has a red colour theme throughout.

DESIGNER
PROFILES

...,staat creative agency
De Ruyterkade 143
1011 AC Amsterdam
the Netherlands
+31 20 572 1388
contact@staat.com
staat.com

p.524

Amsterdam-based ...,staat is an international creative agency that was established in 2000. A mix of 29 people – strategists, art directors, copywriters, visual artists, designers, digital thinkers, architects, producers and project managers – deliver fully-integrated branding concepts. Knowing no limits and working to turn the everyday into the iconic, the agency works on strategy, design, branding, architecture, PR, advertising and everything in between.

acre
Zeil 127
60313 Frankfurt am Main
Germany
+49 69 2475 2120
info@activconsult.com
activconsult.com

p.262

Founded in 2001, acre – activ consult real estate – is a marketing agency that turns real estate into marketable brands. Whether a restaurant, hotel, office high-rise, shopping mall or a new urban quarter being developed, the property and its potential are always the focus of attention. The team specialises in communication and design and has in-depth expertise in providing consulting and marketing services for mixed-use buildings, with a particular focus on the commercial, hospitality and lifestyle sectors. Pictured is chief executive Elisabeth Kammermeier (right) and art director Sandra Breidbach (left).

Archiplan Studio
Via Chiassi 71
46100 Mantua
Italy
+39 0376 324525
info@archiplanstudio.com
archiplanstudio.com

p.344

Archiplan Studio was founded in 1997 by Diego Cisi and Stefano Gorni Silvestrini. The two architectural designers, who both graduated from Venice, carry out continuous research aimed at providing design solutions for the different needs of contemporary living. Over the years, the studio has completed public, private, residential and commercial architectural projects, as well as landscape design and interior design.

A00 Architecture
135 Guang Yuan Lu, 2nd Floor
200030 Shanghai
China
+86 21 5465 3616
mail@azerozero.com
azerozero.com

p.248, 528

A00 Architecture is a Shanghai-based practice led by Montreal-born architects, Sacha Silva and Raefer Wallis. Founded in 2004, A00 quickly developed a niche creating highly personalised modern interiors in Shanghai's historic district, featuring restaurants and the conversion/reuse of many industrial warehouses, including the award-winning URBN hotel. A00 is internationally-recognised for pioneering solutions that combine ecological, social and economic sustainability, including GIGA – the first online database to focus on green building materials for the China market.

AllistarCox Architecture
193 Victoria Street, Level 1
Wellington 6011
New Zealand
+64 4 384 9981
allistar@allistarcox.com
allistarcox.com

p.362

AllistarCox Architecture is an award-winning team of creatives known for consistently pushing the boundaries in spatial design. The studio was established in 1997 and has a goal of creating 'novel and pragmatic solutions that celebrate the public rooms we congregate, eat and socialise in'. With a portfolio of projects on a variety of scales across several countries, the firm's work encompasses everything from back room boudoirs to urban streetscapes.

AS Design
8A New Timely Factory Bldg
497 Castle Peak Road
Lai Chi Kok, Kowloon
Hong Kong
+852 2191 6433
info@as-hk.com
as-hk.com

p.312

Award-winning firm AS Design was founded by Four Lau and Sam Sum, with a vision that the ideal design contains 'sense and sensibility'. Their ideal is 'the perfect combination of practicality and aesthetics, creating the possibility of a wider range of design and artistic pieces'. The strength of the design studio lies in renewing brand identities, as well as interior design for retail, hospitality, commercial and residential spaces.

Ab Rogers Design
22 Parkside
London SW19 5NA
United Kingdom
+44 208 94 47088
info@abrogers.com
abrogers.com

p.448

Ab Rogers Design is a studio that looks for extraordinary experiences in ordinary objects and environments. With a portfolio that cuts across the cultural, hospitality, retail and work sectors around the world, the team is constantly seeking inspiring design solutions. At the heart of the practice is a desire to innovate, and also a belief in the fruitfulness of collaboration, having worked with a series of talents from the worlds of interactivity, illustration, food, wine, art, film and music since the studio was established in 2004. Ab Rogers heads up the practice and is also the director of interior design at the Royal College of Art in London.

Andrea Lupacchini
Via degli Scipioni 252
00192 Rome
Italy
+39 06 9784 3563
info@lupacchini.it
lupacchini.it

p.350

An architect and designer, Andrea Lupacchini is also a professor at the School of Architecture and Design of the University of Camerino. His work is characterised by strong compositional complexity, aimed at generating emotional and sensory stimuli. His studio's portfolio has embraced such issues such as materials technology, rapid prototyping, ergonomics and eco-design.

Atelier Ace
19 NW 5th Ave
Portland, OR 97209
United States
+1 503-517-9069
acehotel.com/about/
atelierace

p.380

Atelier Ace is an award-winning, in-house creative services firm providing interior, graphic and product design, marketing, PR, development, digital presence and event and cultural engineering for our properties. A hand-selected team of creatives, designers, writers, web developers, marketing and new media innovators make it possible for Ace to express its culture and create an inspiring, cohesive and meaningful experience for guests and fans of Ace at each property and through events, collateral and design.

atelier 522
Fitzenweilerstrasse 1
88677 Markdorf
Germany
+49 7544 9560 522
atelier@atelier522.com
atelier522.com

p.058, 200

Established in 2006 by Philipp Beck, atelier 522 is
a creative agency made up of architects, interior
designers, product designers, graphic designers and
photographers. Working in close cooperation to
turn ideas into reality, the varied personnel create
buildings, retail interiors, products and more. 'The
agency is a place where people bring all of their energy,
knowledge, talent and ideas together in order to design
the things they dream of.'

Baranowitz Kronenberg Architecture
39th Ahad Haam Str
65205 Tel Aviv
Israel
+972 3 5609914
bk@bkarch.co.il
bkarc.com

p.298, 498

Alon Baranowitz and Irene Kronenberg founded
Baranowitz Kronenberg Architecture in 1999.
The studio's portfolio focuses on commercial and
hospitality venues of various scales ranging from
buildings to door handles. The office promotes
multidisciplinary thinking and collaborates with the
creative industries as a modus-operandi wherever it
designs around the globe. The team is made up of a
group of young international, talented architects who
bring their worldly cultural experience to the studio's
creative work activity.

Blocher Blocher Partners
Herdweg 19
70174 Stuttgart
Germany
+49 711 224 82 340
info@blocherblocher.com
blocherblocher.com

p.294

With offices in Stuttgart, Mannheim and New Delhi,
Blocher Blocher Partners was founded in 1989 by
architect Dieter Blocher and interior designer Jutta
Blocher. The firm's core activities are architecture and
interior architecture with a focus on event-oriented
retail concepts. In cooperation with its subsidiaries
Blocher Blocher Shops and Blocher Blocher View, the
company works in brand development, mono brand
concepts, corporate, retail and graphic design, as well
as in communication, public relations, decoration
concepts and visual merchandising.

Atom Design
Vojka Krstulovića 4
21000 Split
Croatia
+385 98 602 326
design@atomgraphicdesign.com
atomgraphicdesign.com

p.424

Lana Vitas Gruić is the owner of the Atom Design
studio, which she founded in 2007. The office
specialises in branding and visual identity design.
Some projects are created individually, but Atom
Design also works with other parties as a team. The
studio has won awards and been widely published.

Barzileye Concept & Design
Renbaanstraat 95
2586 EZ The Hague
the Netherlands
+31 653 134 111
info@barzileye.com
barzileye.com

p.124, 126

Interior designer Angelika Barzilay is the owner and
founder of Barzileye Concept & Design. Established
in 2007, the studio's approach to finding the true
identity of a project entails intensive and extensive
research, delving deep into its cultural, geographical,
historical and literary origins. By collaborating with
highly trained experts and utilising state-of-the-art
technology, she weaves the past into the future for
projects in the realms of interior design for hospitality
projects, private houses and exhibition design.

Brinkworth
4-6 Ellsworth Street
London E2 0AX
United Kingdom
+44 207 613 5341
pr@brinkworth.co.uk
brinkworth.co.uk

p.198, 220

Brinkworth is a London-based design consultancy
working across a range of disciplines including
architecture, interior and brand design. Established in
1990, the company has worked with an extensive range
of clients across various industry sectors, producing
a diverse and international portfolio of work. Clients
include Selfridges, Rapha, Nike and Dinos Chapman.
Photo: Louise Melchior

Autoban
Mesrutiyet Caddesi 99/1
34430 Istanbul
Turkey
+90 212 243 8641
info@autoban212.com
autoban212.com

p.156

Established in 2003 by Seyhan Özdemir and Sefer
Çaglar, Autoban is a design studio developing
architectural and interior projects along with product
designs that engage issues of creativity and knowledge,
realism and imagination, function and culture. In
Autoban's work, every project and product has its
own story, reflecting the culture and social life that
it is designed for, while a unity in the overall design
identity is maintained by the relation between forms
and materials.

Beers|Brickworks
Molenbochtstraat 35
5014 EM Tilburg
the Netherlands
+31 6 1059 9027
nicole@beers-brickworks.nl
beers-brickworks.nl

p.534

In 2008, Nicole van Beers and Kariene van Steenoven
joined forces to found Beers|Brickworks. The
design firm specialises in hospitality design: clubs,
restaurants, hotels and bars. What characterises the
firm's work is a constant search for an ideal balance
between order and chaos, resulting in a
total experience.

brownbag lab.
1-17-16 Kyomachibori
Nishi-ku
5500003 Osaka
Japan
+81 6 6449 1711
info@brownbag.jp
brownbag.jp

p.190, 266

Designer Shingo Abe established his own design
office in Osaka, Japan in 2002. His firm brownbag lab.
offers total design solutions for interiors. The studio's
portfolio includes a range of interior design projects,
mostly in the hospitality category.

Bruzkus Batek
Schwedter Str. 34A
10435 Berlin
Germany
+49 30 440 421 32
office@bruzkusbatek.com
bruzkusbatek.com

p.048

Bruzkus Batek is an architecture, interior and furniture design office with a worldwide client base. Founded by Ester Bruzkus and Patrick Batek in Berlin in 2007, the office has over 20 employees currently working on numerous international projects. The office's design focus is on hotels, offices, shops, restaurants and private housing – particularly in the detailing of high-quality interiors. It has also completed successful exhibition and product design projects, including developing lines of furniture for manufacture and retail.
Photo: Wolfgang Stahr

Cloud-9 interior design
94 Yongjia Rd, # 202
200031 Shanghai
China
+86 13 482 124 129
karin@lovecloud-9.com
lovecloud-9.com

p.136

Karin An Rijlaarsdam founded Cloud-9 interior design in the Netherlands in 2000, but the office has been based in Shanghai since 2005. Cloud-9 has produced designs for restaurants and hotels in China and elsewhere, sustainable showrooms for furniture brand Haworth and recently designed a rug collection for Danskina Kvadrat. The studio develops its own interior products and handmade porcelain lights, collaborating with local craftsmen to explore new ways of using local materials and techniques.

Corvin Cristian Studio
3, Pictor C-Tin Stahi Street
Apt 7, Sector 1
010187 Bucharest
Romania
+40 7 4453 7079
corvincristian.com

p.130

Corvin Cristian is a designer, trained as an architect, who formerly spent a decade as a production designer and art director for movie sets, working on major British and American productions. In between, he designed exhibition pavilions (SAAB, Chrysler Jeep Doge, Mitsubishi), scenography for TV commercials and for corporate events (Orange, Mercedes Benz). From 2008, he has led a team specialised in interior design for hospitality, as well as retail and office spaces (Headvertising Agency, ING Bank).

Buero Wagner
Fabian A Wagner
with Andreas Kreft
Zugspitzstrasse 18
82211 Hersching
Germany
+49 81 522 252
Info@buerowagner.org
buerowagner.eu
studiokreft.eu

p.054

Buero Wagner was founded by Fabian A Wagner in 2012. The studio's recent projects have included a Munich office, a restaurant interior in Shenzhen and the regeneration of a listed industrial building near lake Ammersee. The office portfolio includes planning, architecture and interior design. Andreas Kreft is a Munich-based architect. The portfolio of his office Studio Kreft comprises urban design and residential buildings as well as smaller scale design projects. Wagner and Kreft have collaborated since 2010.
Photo: Niko Schmid-Burgk

Commune Design
650 North Robertson Blvd
Los Angeles, CA 90069
United States
+1 310 855 9080
info@communedesign.com
communedesign.com

p.380

Commune was founded in 2004 as a collective focusing on enhancing life through design. The office states: 'We come from all over the world to share a vision and an aesthetic sensibility in everything we do. Our intent is not to dictate, but to facilitate through unconventional thinking and creative solutions. Our design process is a collaborative effort. Whether the project is a commercial space, a retail environment, a restaurant, a residence, packaging, corporate identity or a website, we approach it holistically.'

Creneau International
Hellebeemden 13
3500 Hasselt
Belgium
+32 11 247 920
info@creneau.com
creneau.com

p.194

Founded in 1989, Creneau International has established a strong reputation as a visionary and trendsetting design office, providing a full service from all-round consultancy to concept development, from logo and packaging design to interior design, and from implementation to franchise follow-up. The office motto *'ihac itur ad astra'* (reach for the stars) expresses Creneau International's lofty ambitions.

Clemens Bachmann
Architekten
Hans-Preissinger Str. 8
81379 Munich
Germany
+49 89 2300 0700
info@cbarchitekten.com
cbarchitekten.com

p.202

Clemens Bachmann Architekten is a multidisciplinary office involved in architecture and design. It was established by architect Clemens Bachmann in Munich, Germany in 2004. The practice has completed a number of large- and small-scale projects and its portfolio includes everything from interior design to planning and architecture.

concrete
Oudezijds Achterburgwal 78a
1012 DR Amsterdam
the Netherlands
+31 20 520 0200
info@concreteamsterdam.nl
concreteamsterdam.nl

p.418

The design studio concrete develops concepts in architecture, interior design, urban development and brand development. It unites people and provides solutions. With a team of 40 multidisciplinary creative, the studio helps businesses and institutions by provoking, confusing and philosophising, whilst making scale models, haute cuisine, burgers and (most of all) shattering dogmas. 'No grand theories or abstract ideas. Just things that work.'
Photo: Ewout Huibers

D/Dock
Nieuwe Spiegelstraat 36
1017 DG Amsterdam
the Netherlands
+31 20 420 1332
info@ddock.com
ddock.com

p.310

D/Dock designs interiors and total concepts for national and international organisations. Going beyond physical and aesthetic aspects alone, the studio adopts a working method in which design, project management and consultancy are the ingredients for innovative business cases built around human requirements. The firm's team also draws on an international network of experts, collaborating with respected professionals in the industry who share a knowledge and passion for what they do, jointly seek solutions that stimulate ambition and education, and contribute to a sustainable future.

d-raw
23o Goodge Place
London W1T 4SN
United Kingdom
+44 207 636 0016
studio@d-raw.com
d-raw.com

p.100

London-based architecture and interior design collective d-raw has a diverse portfolio of bespoke design that covers every creative niche. Experts in branded environments, retail design and renovation, the team has a passion for unusual commissions and an uncompromising understanding of the dialogue necessary to create great design. With its creative home remaining in the heart of London and a satellite team of specialist creative talent stretching across the globe, the company performs on both the local and international level.

De Horeca Fabriek
Laan van Nieuw Oosteinde 131
2274 EE Voorburg
the Netherlands
+31 70 888 0505
info@dehorecafabriek.nl
dehorecafabriek.nl

p.338

De Horeca Fabriek is an interior design company specialising in the hospitality sector. It was founded in 2009 by Rein Rambaldo, who has a lot of hands-on experience in the field, developed by having his own restaurants and bars. Combining experience in hospitality and design is the studio's strength, and already the office has built up a portfolio that includes a number of contemporary bars and restaurant projects across the Netherlands.

DesignPact
Moutstraat 2
3511 XT Utrecht
the Netherlands
+31 646 366 022
info@designpact.net
designpact.net

p.024

Floortje Donia has been an all-round designer and creative entrepreneur since 2004. Taking a light-hearted approach, Donia seeks surprising solutions for all budgets and thus creates special (custom) interior features to match a business identity and help build the brand. Now part of the recently founded collaborative studio DesignPact, her portfolio includes interior design for restaurants, hotels, offices and retail.

DA.studio
Via Bolognese 7
5C139 Florence
Italy
+39 055 552 2526
info@dastudio.it
dastudio.it

p.448

DA.studio is a Florence-based architecture practice that operates internationally. The design practice was founded in 2001 by Arianna Pieri and Ernesto Bartolini and has today a staff of eight architects. The design activities focus on different scale projects, including master-planning, mix-use developments, residential and retail interiors, and historical building restoration. The team has a great passion for challenging briefs to deliver innovative solutions for clients and ultimately to the users.

DesignAgency
845 Adelaide Street West
Toronto, ON M6J 3X1
Canada
+1 416 703 2022
info@thedesignagency.ca
thedesignagency.ca

p.428

The DesignAgency is an award-winning Toronto-based design consultancy. Established in 1998 by partners and long-time friends Allen Chan, Matt Davis and Anwar Mekhayech, the studio unites architectural, interior design, industrial design, branding and digital design expertise. With an international portfolio of projects, the studio's success is rooted in our collaborative and consultative approach. The multidisciplinary team of talented designers craft innovative, custom-designed spaces that help elevate the consumer experience.

Design by Richard Lindvall
Roslagsgatan 27
113 55 Stockholm
Sweden
+46 70 518 5272
info@richardlindvall.com
richardlindvall.com

p.106

Stockholm-based interior design company Design by Richard Lindvall was founded in 2007 by Richard Lindvall, who has 'a passion for everything creative'. Predominantly engaged in making total concepts for interior design, he often incorporates custom furniture into his projects. His work also includes hospitality projects, as well as publications, graphic design and photography.

dan pearlman
Kiefholzstrasse 1
12435 Berlin
Germany
+49 30 5300 0560
office@danpearlman.com
danpearlman.com

p.264

The Berlin-based creative agency dan pearlman takes a unique '360-degree approach' covering everything from strategic positioning and brand development to implementation in brand and leisure environments. The agency says it is 'passionate about creating holistic, sustainable and creative concepts and experiences using strategic processes, innovative methods and a creative, interdisciplinary and intercultural team.'

Designliga
Hans-Preissinger-Strasse 8
Halle A
81379 Munich
Germany
+49 89 624 219 40
hello@designliga.com
designliga.com

p.222

Designliga is a bureau for visual communication and interior design. Founded in Munich in 2001 by product designer Saša Stanojčić and communication designer Andreas Döhring, the office has grown into a team of experienced designers, consultants, interior designers and architects who work in a cross-disciplinary manner to communicate content through design. Getting to the heart of brands, the studio develops inspiring solutions that bring companies and products to life at their spatial, graphic and digital touch-points.

Design Electro Products
Staringlaan 7b
2741 GC Waddinxveen
the Netherlands
+31 182 633 011
info@dep-nederland.nl
dep-nederland.nl

p.006, 042, 210

Entrepreneur Sam Anders Sr founded Design Electro Products (DEP) 25 years ago. The office applies light, vision and sound techniques to specific environments, either for a purely decorative function or to accentuate the function and size of spaces. It has a portfolio of high-profile light-, sound- and video-designs in the hospitality and retail industries, visitor experiences and museum exhibitions.

Dexter Moren Associates
57d Jamestown Road
London NW1 7DB
United Kingdom
+44 207 267 4440
dma@dextermoren.com
dextermoren.com

p.510

Dexter Moren Associates is an award-winning
architecture and interior design practice specialising
in hospitality and hotels. The practice has a design-led
ethos of 'creating places people want to stay' and, over
the last 20 years, has established a reputation as one of
London's leading hotel and leisure architects. Current
projects include Gansevoort Shoreditch, Hilton
London Bankside, Shangri-La at The Shard London,
Jumeirah Dubai, and a new brand concept for
Extreme Hotels.

Dreimeta
Ernst-Reuter-Platz 10
86150 Augsburg
Germany
info@dreimeta.com
dreimeta.com

p.504

Dreimeta was founded in 2003 by Armin Fischer.
The studio's team of creative minds works on both
local and international projects, often in hospitality
areas. Dreimeta's aim is to create spaces with their
own identity and character: Fischer says the office's
approach is to add an emotional appeal to the space
– with interior design that tells tales and touches the
senses. But he stresses that functionality is always
part of the concept, and indeed sometimes leads to
unexpected design solutions.

Francesc Rifé Studio
Escoles Pies 25
08017 Barcelona
Spain
+34 93 414 1288
f@rife-design.com
rife-design.com

p.412

Francesc Rifé founded his interior and industrial
design studio in 1994. Based in Barcelona with a team
of professionals trained in various fields of design,
the studio specialises in commercial and private
projects which encompass spatial order and geometric
proportion with a portfolio covering interior and
industrial landscapes. The studio also has considerable
experience in graphic design projects, photography and
art direction.

DFC
264 avenue Van Volxem
1190 Brussels
Belgium
+32 2 534 50 08
contact@dfc-experience.
com
dfc-experience.com

p.406

DFC is a studio specialised in luxury branding and
retail architecture. An association of Delacroix &
Friant architecture and Coast multidisciplinary
agency, the studio develops premium retail
spaces – bringing branding, interior design and
architecture together to form a unified approach
to retail experience. By bringing the individual
disciplines under one umbrella, DFC's manifesto is
the development of experiences at the cross point of
art, branding and architecture. As a dialogue between
contemporary culture and brands, DFC's purpose is to
fuse brand DNA and customer experience: from visual
representation to architectural icon.

Estudio Campana
São Paulo
Brazil
campanas@campanas.com.br
campanas.com.br

p.462

Founded in 1983 in São Paulo by brothers Fernando
and Humberto Campana, Estudio Campana has a
world-famous portfolio of furniture design, including
intriguing objects such as the Vermelha and Favela
chairs, as well as interior design, architecture,
landscaping, scenography, fashion, artistic
partnerships and more. The work incorporates the idea
of transformation, reinvention and the integration
of craftsmanship in mass production. Giving
preciousness to common materials carries not only the
creativity in the brothers' designs but also their very
Brazilian characteristics – the colours, the mixtures,
the creative chaos.
Photo: Fernando Laszlo

Franken Architekten
Niddastrasse 84
60329 Frankfurt am Main
Germany
+49 69 297 2830
info@franken-architekten.
de
franken-architekten.de

p.262, 282

Founded in 2002, Franken Architekten sees itself as
combining an architectural practice with expertise
in communication through space, whether through a
brand space or permanent building. The office works
on a wide range of concepts and project realisations,
with a portfolio that covers corporate architecture,
office buildings, retail, hotels and restaurants,
urban planning, residential buildings, museums,
exhibitions, trade fair presentations, corporate design,
installations, and themed and branded worlds.

Dittel Architekten
Rotenwaldstrasse 100/1
70197 Stuttgart
Germany
+49 711 4690 6550
info@d-arch.de
d-arch.de

p.030, 320

Founded in 2005 by Frank Dittel, Dittel Architekten
develops distinctive spaces with passion. The
interdisciplinary office's 23 architects, interior
designers and communication designers aspire to
create an intriguing, characteristic and exclusive look
for every brand or company.

Estudio Guto Requena
Rua Oscar Freire 1996, Jardins
05409-011 São Paulo
Brazil
+55 11 2528 1700
contato@gutorequena.com.br
gutorequena.com.br

p.034, 064

Founded in 2010 in São Paulo, Estudio Guto Requena
was formed by architect Guto Requena and five
collaborators. Requena says his office aims at 'the
reflection about memory, digital culture and poetic
narratives in all design scales, investigating the impact
of numeric technologies in the fields of information
and communication on our daily lives, as well as its
deployments regarding projects.'
Photo: Victor Affaro

Galea&Galea Architects
9 Jubilee Esplanade
MGR 1040 Mgarr
Malta
+356 99453100
atelier@go.net.mt

p.250

Set up in 1999, Galea&Galea offers a complete range
of services from architectural, structural and interior
design to project management and design consultancy
for larger projects. The team is managed by Anthony
Galea and partner Monica Audrey Galea, senior
lecturer in design and interior architecture at the
University of Malta. The philosophy of the studio
revolves around a strong conceptual interpretation of
function and aesthetics. With a focus on progressive
residential, commercial and urban intervention
projects, the practice specialises in environmentally
sustainable building adaptations in sensitive contexts.

Genesin Studio
199 Hutt Street, Level 1
Adelaide 5000
Australia
+61 8 8227 1115
info@genesin.com.au
genesin.com.au

p.182, 230, 284

Ryan Genesin established his own interior and architecture studio in 2008. With a wide-ranging breadth of work relative to experience, Genesin Studio prides itself on well-detailed projects across different interior typologies, including retail, residential, commercial and hospitality. The studio's philosophy results in sophisticated residential interiors and innovative and experimental hospitality and retail spaces.

Haf Studio
Bankastræti 6
101 Reykjavik
Iceland
+354 695 8550
info@hafstudio.is
hafstudio.is

p.476

Haf Studio is a multidisciplinary design studio run by designers Karitas Sveinsdóttir and Hafsteinn Júlíusson. The company was founded in Milan, Italy in 2010 and is currently located in downtown Reykjavik. All Haf Studio projects are based on creative and constructive teamwork that involves diverse professionals led by Hafsteinn and Karitas.

Igloo
617-150 St Norbert
Montreal, QC H2X 1G6
Canada
+1 514 933 4456
hello@igloodesign.ca
igloodesign.ca

p.268

Established in 2005 by interior designers Alain Courchesne and Anna Abbruzzo, Igloo is a dynamic firm at the forefront of cutting-edge interior design and branding. Based out of Montreal, the company is internationally-renowned for creating innovative spaces, from hotels, restaurants and retail projects, to residential and condominium design.

Grant Amon Architects
125 Fitzroy Street, Suite 102
Melbourne 3182
Australia
+61 3 9593 9944
info@grantamon.com
grantamon.com

p.082, 088

Grant Amon Architects' involvement in design spans a variety of projects ranging from residential and commercial through to the hospitality industry, with a range of restaurants, hotels, bars and cafes. Based in St Kilda, Australia, since 1993 the practice has been actively pursuing its ongoing interest in spatial manipulation, the crafting of objects and incorporation of local references and histories. It also undertakes larger scale, multi-use projects, including inner urban renewal, coastal and alpine resorts, tourism, landscape and retail projects.

Haldane Martin
176 Sir Lowry Rd, Woodstock
7925 Cape Town
South Africa
+272 1 461 1785
info@haldanemartin.co.za
haldanemartin.co.za

p.150

Haldane Martin graduated with a degree in industrial design in 1992 and started his own design company in Cape Town in 1994. His animated designs, such as the Songololo Sofa and Zulu Mama chair, have become much-loved icons of a new South African design identity. More recently, Haldane Martin's studio has begun to offer interior design consulting. The first large scale commercial project was Truth Coffee's steampunk inspired headquarters in Cape Town.
Photo: Guido Schwarz

Insider Outsider
49/398 La Trobe Street
Melbourne 3000
Australia
+61 4 1213 3156
daveandjames@
insideroutsider.net
insideroutsider.net

p.258

Insider Outsider is an Australian design studio formed in 2011 as a partnership between David Brodziak and Wojtek James Goscinski. The studio has completed residential work in Australia and Asia, restaurants and bars across inner-city Melbourne, lighting and furniture design, and small-scale architectural interventions. Both partners bring to the studio a diverse array of skills and interests, and have come to design via alternative routes, with backgrounds in science, construction, communications and academia between them.

Hachem
Level 2, 2 Drewery Place
Melbourne 3000
Australia
+61 130 734 560
info@hachem.com.au
hachem.com.au

p.092, 226, 386

Hachem is a design studio with architecture, interior and branding at its core. Led by Fady Hachem, the studio is dedicated to creating progressive and cohesive outcomes for clients of all kinds. Projects include contemporary hospitality venues, public buildings and residential developments. Creative and technical skills are utilised in tandem with intuitive research, not only to achieve a responsible practical outcome, but also to make intangible qualities manifest – to create a brand, atmosphere or experience.

Heineken Interior Design
Burgemeester Smeetsweg 1
2382 PH Zoeterwoude
the Netherlands
+31 88 434 3111
heinekeninterieurdesign@
heineken.com
heinekenhoreca.nl

p.006, 210

Heineken Interior Design has existed for more than 50 years, with its head office in Amsterdam, the Netherlands. The studio primarily designs all aspects of commercial hospitality outlets, focusing on conceptual design, routing and layout, as well materialisation.

Ippolito Fleitz Group
Augustenstrasse 87
70197 Stuttgart
Germany
+49 711 993 392 330
info@ifgroup.org
ifgroup.org

p.286, 364

Ippolito Fleitz Group is a multidisciplinary, internationally operating design studio based in Stuttgart. Currently, Ippolito Fleitz Group is a creative unit comprising 37 designers and covering a wide range of design territory, including strategy, architecture, interiors, products, graphics and landscape architecture.

Ito Masaru Design Project/ SEI
101 Daikanyama Tower
1-35-11 Ebisunishi, Shibuya-ku
1500021 Tokyo
Japan
+81 3 5784 3201
sei@itomasaru.com
itomasaru.com

p.272, 326

Masaru Ito was born in Osaka, Japan in 1961 and graduated from Tokyo Zokei University in 1987. He established his own studio, SEI, in 1991, after working in Kawasaki Takao's office. Since then, he has built a reputation as an interior maverick due to his quest for novel ideas and awareness of fashions. is known for his keen sensibility and distinct angle on interior design. His motto is: 'Be a challenger as well as a champion'.

K/M2K Architecture and Interior Design
76 Church Street
8001 Cape Town
South Africa
+27 21 426 4556
info@km2k.co.za
km2k.co.za

p.452

K/M2K Architecture and Interior Design is a creative studio known for its ability to create a sense of place by embracing each project's unique location, having designed hotels in 14 countries across Africa, the Indian Ocean, Europe and the Middle East. The company, founded by Keith Mehner in 2001, specialises in creating spaces that transcend the concept of mere building, requiring insight, inspiration, integrity and an intense desire to exceed expectations. The office team is adept at managing every aspect of a project, from the concept through to the finest interior detailing.

Limtaehee Design Studio
1038 Trapalace
Sunae-dong, Bundang-gu
463-021 Seongnam-si
South Korea
+82 70 8249 5233
taeheelim@naver.com
limtaeheestudio.com

p.302

Lim Tae Hee set up her own design office in Seoul in 2007. The studio specialises in interior design for residential, commercial and office projects, as well as furniture and lighting designs. With all of these, the design team adopts an innovative approach. 'Our main focus is to observe and communicate with society, and impart a new lifestyle to people through our work,' says Lim Tae Hee.

Jens Thoms Ivarsson
Icehotel Jukkasjärvi
Marknadsvägen 63
981 91 Jukkasjärvi
Sweden
+46 980 668 2001
info@icehotel.com
icehotel.com

p.076

Jens Thoms Ivarsson is the director of design at the Icehotel Jukkasjärvi. Having worked with crafts and designs virtually all his life, he came in contact with the hotel for the first time in 2003 and has been involved ever since. He crafts spaces from ice and has designed a number of icebars around the world (from London to Beijing) and has given numerous inspirational TED talks about designing with water.

Kinney Chan & Associates
Chung Nam Building, 11F
1 Lockhart Road, Wanchai
Hong Kong
Hong Kong
+852 2545 1322
info@kca.com.hk
kca.com.hk

p.208

Founded in 1995, Kinney Chan & Associates offers a full spectrum of interior design and project management services across multiple industries, including hospitality, bars and restaurants, residential, commercial and corporate. 'Creativity and originality' is the studio's motto. Its innovative team perceives interior design as not just interior and exterior space planning and material matching, but as a true form of art.

Lotz Interior Design & Styling
Da Costakade 204a
1053 XH Amsterdam
the Netherlands
+31 61 855 6628
info@lotzstyling.nl
lotzstyling.nl

p.008

Charlotte Emmerig has quickly built quite a portfolio since starting her business – Lotz Interior Design & Styling – in 2007. Besides hospitality design, she focuses on residential projects and urban offices in cities like Amsterdam, Ibiza and Barcelona. Characteristically blending innovative ideas with a nostalgic twist, her loves include: 'the natural aging of products; the exciting mix of vintage with modern; antique materials manufactured into contemporary design; glass, concrete, wood and steel; and matching with architecture and its inhabitants'.

Joi-Design
Medienpark Kampnagel
Barmbeker Strasse 6a
22303 Hamburg
Germany
+49 40 6894210
info@joi-design.com
joi-design.com

p.432

Joi-Design was founded in Hamburg in 1984 by Peter Joehnk, who with Corinna Kretschmar-Joehnk has developed the practice into a respected leader in hospitality design. Thirty years of experience endorses their belief that design is the hotelier's best marketing tool. The team's guiding principle is to 'shape atmosphere' by weaving the art, architecture and social inheritance of the location into the interior character of each project. The studio's product design division, Products by Joi-Design, was launched in 2014 and its fifth interior design reference book will be released shortly.

Knibb Design
822 Lincoln Blvd
Venice, CA 90291
United States
+1 310 450 5552
info@knibbdesign.com
knibbdesign.com

p.518

Knibb Design is a full-service design firm specialising in artfully crafting both exterior and interior environments. Founded in 1992 by Sean Knibb, the studio has created everything from private garden sanctuaries to award-winning restaurants, outfitting spaces with custom furnishings and hand-crafted products. The ability to distill the essence of a place is, as Knibb puts it, 'not just about one group of people; it's about the way everyone works together.' The committed in-house team includes architects, industrial designers, interior designers, landscapers, graphic designers and project managers.

Luchetti Krelle
56 Cooper Street
Surry Hills 2010
Australia
+61 2 9699 3425
studio@luchettikrelle.com
luchettikrelle.com

p.050, 122, 234

Luchetti Krelle is an award-winning interior design firm, established by partners Stuart Krelle and Rachel Luchetti in 2008. The studio has a diverse portfolio, with a primary focus on the hospitality sector. As the disciplines of design overlap and limtegrate, Luchetti Krelle offers total-concept solutions, from branding and identity design all the way to customised furniture and fitting design.

Marcel Wanders studio
Westerstraat 187
1015 MA Amsterdam
the Netherlands
+31 20 262 0184
pr@marcelwanders.com
marcelwanders.com

p.396

Marcel Wanders is a prolific product and interior designer and art director, with over 1700+ projects to his name for private clients and premium brands, such as Alessi, Bisazza, KLM, Flos, Swarovski, Puma, amongst scores of others. His mission is to 'create an environment of love, live with passion and make our most exciting dreams come true'. His work excites, provokes and polarises, but never fails to surprise for its ingenuity, daring and singular quest to uplift the human spirit, and entertain.

Ministry of Design
20 Cross Street #03-01
048422 Singapore
Singapore
+65 6222 5780
studio@modonline.com
modonline.com

p.456

Ministry of Design was founded by Colin Seah in 2004. Since then, it has established an international reputation for its lifestyle-inspired design work. Projects range from boutique hotels to master plans and malls. Seah has recently been invited by the Singapore Tourism Board to redefine Singapore as a destination for 2020 and beyond.

noa*
Sernesistrasse 34 via Sernesi
39100 Bozen Bolzano
Italy
+39 0471 188 0941
studio@n-o-a.it
n-o-a.it

p.434

The architecture and design studio noa* (which stands for 'network of architecture') was established by Lukas Rungger and Stefan Rier, who met while working as project architects with Matteo Thun in Milan. Before founding noa* in 2010, they lived and worked in New York, London, Berlin, Milan, Ferrara and Graz. Current projects include a hotel village, a private museum, a wooden look-out tower, a family resort in the Bavarian forest, several luxury hotels and high-end villas in the Italian Alps.

Maurício Arruda arquitetos + designers
Rua Oscar Freire 1996
05409-011 São Paulo
Brazil
+55 11 3159-0396
contato@mauricioarruda.net
mauricioarruda.net

p.034

Architect and designer, Maurício Arruda develops works in architecture, temporary design and product design from his São Paulo-based office. An architecture graduate, with a master's degree in sustainable buildings, the studio has been involved with searching for new perspectives in sustainability for developing nations. His creations are full of colour, identity and 'Brazility', and he is also concerned with social and environmental issues.

Morag Myerscough
London
United Kingdom
+44 207 729 2760
morag@studiomyerscough.co.uk
supergrouplondon.co.uk

p.146

Morag Myerscough's work is characterised by an engaging boldness, creating specific, local responses to each distinct audience that will see and experience the work, using it to create community and build identity. Myerscough makes places from spaces that people like to be in, that stimulate and often make you smile. She creates and curates many different types of work. The eclectic breadth of work covers the conversion of a train to a cafe, The Temple of Agape, a hospital ward and interpreting lots of buildings.

Nordic Bros Design Community
2F 683-46 Hannam-dong Yongsan-gu
140-892 Seoul
South Korea
+82 70 8225 0067
office@nordicbrosdesign.com
nordicbrosdesign.com

p.080, 114

Designer Yong-hwan Shin founded Nordic Bros Design Community in the spring of 2011. Since then, the office has worked on a variety of interior design projects, mainly in residences, offices and hospitality venues. In addition, Shin is also a furniture designer.

Minarc
2324 Michigan Ave
Santa Monica, CA 90404
United States
+1 310 998 8899
info@minarc.com
minarc.com

p.444

Minarc is an award-winning design studio recognised for its modern, innovative and sustainable design solutions. Inspired by the pure, austere beauty of their native Iceland, principals Erla Dögg Ingjaldsdóttir and Tryggvi Thorsteinsson were drawn to Santa Monica, California and the wide-open spaces and rich light that sustain their vision. The studio's portfolio ranges from small-scale renovations to new construction, in residential, commercial and public settings. Each project shares an emphasis on the blurring of distinction between interior and exterior spaces through the exploitation of natural light, creation of outdoor living rooms and artistically framed views of nature.

Nicemakers
Nieuwe Achtergracht 17
1018 XV Amsterdam
the Netherlands
+31 20 354 7228
verynice@nicemakers.com
nicemakers.com

p.324

The creatives behind Nicemakers are Joyce Urbanus and Dax Roll, who started their business in 2011 with a boutique hotel in Amsterdam. Since then, they have added restaurants, private homes and various commercial projects to their portfolio. Hospitality is a main focus. The designers state that they are 'committed to focusing on the client, their goals and location, rather than working within a specific Nicemakers' style. The correct combination of these elements creates a successful and complete concept, in which the client will feel great.'

One Plus Partnership
Unit 1604, Eastern Centre
1065 King's Road
Hong Kong
Hong Kong
+852 2591 9308
admin@onepluspartnership.com
onepluspartnership.com

p.014

One Plus Partnership was formed in 2004 by Ajax Law Ling Kit and Virginia Lung. Based in Hong Kong, the company provides a full range of interior design services from conception to delivery including residential, hospitality, retail, office and cinema projects. A forum for generating cutting-edge ideas, the studio is known for its accomplished and often humorous designs.

Onion
36/1 Soi Ngamduplee
Rama 4 Road, Sathorn
Bangkok 10120
Thailand
+66 2679 8282
info@onion.co.th
onion.co.th

p.260, 488

Onion is a design firm that was founded in 2007 and specialises in both architecture and interior design. Directors Siriyot Chaiamnuay and Arisara Chaktranon preside over the studio, which is based in Bangkok. Onion's works can be seen all over Thailand and include a number of Sala hotel projects: the boutique hotel in mountainous Khao Yai, the resort at Sala Chaweng and the luxurious boutique hotel in central Bangkok.

Pascale Gomes-McNabb Design
85 Chetwynd St
North Melbourne 3051
Australia
+61 4 3821 1117
pascale@
pascalegomesmcnabb.com.au
pascalegomesmcnabb.com.au

p.044, 096, 212

Pascale Gomes-McNabb Design was established in 2010 to create experiential interior architecture: spaces that are visually compelling and memorable, but also comfortable, functional and pragmatic. Founder Pascale has worked as a design consultant in Australia and overseas, having also founded, designed, managed and now owns a number of restaurants, including Cumulus Inc. and Cutler & Co.

Pinkeye
Hessenplein 2
2000 Antwerp
Belgium
+32 3 290 6273
info@pinkeye.be
pinkeye.be

p.162, 180

When Ruud Belmans, Thomas Vanden Abeele and Luc Heylen founded the design studio Pinkeye in the summer of 2006, they had one clear goal in mind: to establish a team of skilled and talented people to work together on a wide range of branding projects. Nowadays, Pinkeye counts over 20 talents in design fields such as (interior) architecture, graphic design and product design. It focuses on creating lasting experiences through retail and hospitality spaces, visual identities and packaging.

OpenAir Studio
7 Narathiwas Soi 10, Sathorn
Bangkok 10120
Thailand
+66 2676 0707
wit@openairstudio.com
openairstudio.com

p.252

OpenAir Studio, founded by Wit Chongwattananukul in 2008, is an interior design firm based in Bangkok which aims to create 'timeless and elegant architectural environments employing high quality materials and fine craftsmanship'. The studio demonstrates an optimal relationship between objects and space, approaching each project considering its own spatial needs, and constructing a sculptural experience through it.

PickTwo Studio
Rosetti Square, No.1
021051 Bucharest, Sector 2
Romania
+40 745 652 843
help@picktwo.ro
picktwo.ro

p.334

PickTwo is a Bucharest-based studio, founded in 2013 by Radu Calin and Sebastian Mindroiu, who say that they are 'mainly dealing with architecture, but we are not afraid to get our hands 'dirty' with graphic design or branding.' The studio's portfolio includes interior design concepts for restaurants, bars, shops and commercial venues. PickTwo draws its spirit from the 'project management triangle', as all projects require a 'two out of three' solution. 'Always given the 'fast, good and cheap' options, you need to … PickTwo.'

Position Collective
Hôtel Nomuri, Sas u. 15/III
1051 Budapest
Hungary
+36 7 0607 8232
info@position-collective.com
position-collective.com

p.370

Position Collective was founded at the start of 2010. The office objective is to perform complex design tasks by making use of the diverse talents of its team. It combines state-of-the-art technical skills with a modern approach to all the applied creative fields (branding, image design, package design, furniture design and interior design). The studio is therefore able to carry out both small orders and complex design tasks.

Oscar Vidal Studio
Peru 64
03803 Alcoy
Spain
+34 62 010 7322
info@oscarvidal.net
oscarvidal.net

p.276, 296, 392

Oscar Vidal Quist graduated in interior design from EASD Alcoi in 2001, after which he worked as a designer before setting up his own studio on the Mediterranean coast. The office works mainly on hospitality projects of which, says the designer, 'I find this branch of interior design much more free and creative than others. You're designing places where people go to have fun, eat, drink. People look for exciting places, they want to be surprised and usually there is competition between businesses. You must always learn from your clients and the way customers behave in these spaces.'

Piet Boon
Skoon 78
1511HV Oostzaan
the Netherlands
+31 20 722 0020
press@pietboon.com
pietboon.com

p.354

Dutch designer and master craftsman Piet Boon founded a multidisciplinary design studio of the same name in 1983. Boon together with Karin Meyn, who joined the company in 1986 as joint business partner, lead an experienced team of highly-skilled professionals. As a multidisciplinary design practice and specialists in total concepts, Piet Boon creates bespoke contemporary architecture, interiors and product designs for high-end international corporate, residential, hospitality and private clients.
Photo: Jeroen Hofman

Projects of Imagination
L1-154 Greville St, Prahran
Melbourne 3181
Australia
+61 3 9533 9991
info@projectsofimagination.co
projectsofimagination.com

p.018, 340

Projects of Imagination (POI) is a multidisciplinary design consultancy active in the areas of conceptual interiors and brand experiences with a core focus on projects defined by strong narratives and collaboration. Established by Dion Hall and Nick Cox in 2007, today POI is an office with an increasingly visible national profile and a client list featuring Australia's leading hospitality operators.

Pubblik
Sassenheimstraat 51
1059 BC Amsterdam
the Netherlands
+31 62 248 5046
info@pubblik.nl
pubblik.nl

p.330

Founded in 2009 and headed by Marjolein Bangma, Pubblik is an Amsterdam-based design firm specialising in hospitality projects. The company's design approach combines contemporary elements with authentic materials, to create a unique venue identity. With over 10 years of experience, the firm offers a full range of services, from concept development to interior design and graphic identity. Dutch projects include De Stationshuiskamer (Rotterdam), The Walter Woodbury Bar (Amsterdam), South of Houston (The Hague), Cafe Schilders (Amsterdam) and Brasserie Bardot (Breda).

Raw Design
118 Hewlett Road
Cheltenham GL52 6AT
United Kingdom
+44 1242 227342
info@matthewrawlinson.co.uk
raw-design.com

p.242, 514

Set up by Matt Rawlinson in 1994, Raw Design is an award-winning creative practice specialising in the design of contemporary social environments. These include cutting-edge bar, restaurant and nightclub design, country inns, country house estates, London townhouses, boutique hotels, high-end domestic interiors, retail spaces and corporate headquarters. Raw Design's highly creative and often quirky style is blended seamlessly with a strong practical approach to design solutions that produces impactful interiors to a wide variety of budgets.

Simone Micheli
Via Aretina 197r
50136 Florence
Italy
+39 055 691 216
simone@simonemicheli.com
simonemicheli.com

p.404

Simone Micheli founded his architectural and design office in 2004, and now has offices in Florence, Milan and Dubai. Micheli works in all areas of architecture and interior design, and his output is typified by a strong identity and unique character. His office has been acclaimed for its work on major projects in the hospitality, residential and public sectors. Micheli has also taught at Polidesign and at the Milan Polytechnic School of Design since 2003.
Photo: Maurizio Marcato

RAD Studio
Suite C level 6
110-114 Kippax St
Surry Hills 2010
Australia
+61 2 9281 9662
info@radstudio.com.au
radstudio.com.au

p.314

Richard Alexander Design was originally founded by Richard Alexander before being renamed as RAD Studio when business partner Quinton Lloyd came on board. The firm is a design and innovation studio centred around creativity, collaboration and best practice implementation. It offers a hands-on design service specialising in creative interiors. Its energetic and dedicated team composed of in-house designers and specialist consultants works collaboratively to deliver innovative design solutions that are sustainable and meet clients' core objectives.

Sanjay Puri Architects
20 Famous Studio Lane
Mahalaxmi
400011 Mumbai
India
+ 91 22 2496 5840 / 44
spstudio@sanjaypuri.in
sanjaypuriarchitects.com

p.022

Sanjay Puri established his own architecture firm in 1992 in Mumbai, India. Sanjay Puri Architects has 72 employees and has designed over 100 projects in 40 Indian cities, as well as projects in Montenegro, Mauritius, Spain and the United Arab Emirates. The firm aims to evolve innovative design solutions that are contextual, contribute to sustainability and create spaces that revolutionise the way they are experienced.

Slade Architecture
77 Chambers St, 5th Floor
New York, NY 10007
United States
+1 212 677 6380
info@sladearch.com
sladearch.com

p.172, 176

Slade Architecture is an award-winning design firm, founded in 2002 by James Slade and Hayes Slade. In collaboration with its clients, the studio designs spaces that merge concept and functionality, favouring an approach that is structured and unique to the situation – creating the design paradigm for the specific context and need. Articulating its clients' needs and interests with simplicity and impact, the studio's portfolio includes commercial, residential and cultural projects, as well as furniture collections.

Rafael de Cárdenas / Architecture at Large
611 Broadway, Suite 627
New York, NY 10012
United States
+1 212 965 8755
enquiry@
architectureatlarge.com
architectureatlarge.com

p.256, 280

Rafael de Cárdenas founded Architecture at Large in 2006 as a small office in Chinatown, New York City. It has since expanded to include a London studio. The practice has a wide-reaching portfolio, with projects in architecture, interiors, temporary spaces and object design. Recent projects have included work for Baccarat, Nike, Ford Models and Nordstrom. The practice states: 'We favour the strategic over the thematic, the cosmopolitan over the typological, and the atmospheric over the static. Ever-focused on the contemporary, we take diligent note of the past while day-dreaming of the future.'

Sarur Arquitectura
Alicama #25
11000 Mexico City
Mexico
+52 55 52022959
info@sarquitectura.com
sarquitectura.com

p.166

Sarur Arquitectura was founded in 2012 by architect Gerardo Sarur. The studio works on high-end hospitality and residential projects guided by the motto: 'true luxury lies within design'. The office pays extra attention to the design of every detail and gives each project equal importance. According to the founder, 'Any single endeavour conveys a level of difficulty that has little to do with budgets or square metres and more to do with creating quality, custom-made experiences.'

Soma Architects
31 West 27th St, Floor 09
New York, NY 10001
United States
+1 212 966 1200
mail@soma.us
soma.us

p.366

Soma Architects is an international office founded by principal Michel Abboud in 2004. The office works closely with clients to understand their needs and desires. Rather than imposing a solution onto a given site, Soma Architects tends to deploy patterns which are seemingly self-organising and grow with the site and its intended and unintended future uses. The office constantly attempts to extend the boundaries of design while incorporating craft, digital technologies and environmental responsibility.

Splinter Society Architecture
1/100 Gertrude St
Fitzroy
Melbourne 3065
Australia
+61 3 9419 4189
info@splintersociety.com
splintersociety.com

p.070

Founded in 2005, Splinter Society Architecture is a Melbourne-based firm with two directors, Chris Stanley and Asha Nicholas, both of whom are practicing architects and teach in the interior design programme at RMIT University, Melbourne. Splinter Society works closely with an engaged, creative client base and group of craft-based makers to produce work primarily in hospitality, commercial fit-out, workplace and residential design. The office continually strives to produce unique, tactile environments for its clients with a diversity of aesthetic and experiential outcomes and the potential for a narrative driven design solution.

Studio Norguet Design
38 rue de Malte
75011 Paris
France
+33 1 4807 2995
info@patricknorguet.com
patricknorguet.com

p.472

Behind the modesty of Patrick Norguet hides a lively spirit driven by the desire for perfection, detail and a thing well done. Since 2002, the designer has etched his name into the world of international design with precision and determination. In addition to striving for accuracy and elegance in his work, Norguet equally appreciates the factories, the workshops, the materials and the workers who make it all possible. He likes to decipher techniques and processes, and has a passion for innovation.
Photo: Alberto Moreu

Tadafumi Azuno
3-22-2 1F Sendagi
Bunkyo-ku
1130022 Tokyo
Japan
+81 80 5602 5437
t.azuno@gmail.com
t-azuno.com

p.468, 486

Still in his 20s, designer Tadafumi Azuno currently works mainly in Japan. The designs that come out of his office specialise mainly in interior design using natural materials and craft techniques, following through all the stages of a project from planning to designing and construction and often working with volunteers (friends, students, etc.), as well as artisans.

Stefano Tordiglione Design
3/F, 37 Staunton St, Soho
Hong Kong
Hong Kong
+852 2840 1100
info@tordiglione.com
stdesign.it

p.120

Stefano Tordiglione Design offers a wide range of architectural and design services which cover retail, hospitality, commercial and residential design as well as product development, project management, graphic design and creative consultancy. Collectively, the team has professional experience from Europe and the United States. Stefano Tordiglione, the Italian creative director and eponymous founder, is a designer and artist. His extensive industry experience was acquired in Italy, New York and London.

Studio Tilt
Unit 202, Mare Street Studios
London E8 3QE
United Kingdom
+44 207 998 3641
info@studiotilt.com
studiotilt.com

p.358

Studio Tilt is an award-winning design and architecture practice with an international reputation as the leaders in co-design. By including users in the design and making of spaces and prototyping scenarios, the unique co-design methodology transforms the way people interact with each other and the environments around them. The studio is focused on helping organisations in the private and public sectors create thoughtful spaces and multi-layered design solutions that respond directly to user needs.

Takenouchi Webb
17 Woking Road
#03–05 Tangier
138696 Singapore
Singapore
+65 64754005
info@takenouchiwebb.com
takenouchiwebb.com

p.084, 134

Established in October 2006, Takenouchi Webb is a partnership between British architect Marc Webb and Japanese interior designer Naoko Takenouchi. The office is an integrated design firm that develops architectural and interior environments, specialising in restaurant, hotel and bar projects. The studio believes in holistic design, developing the architecture, interior and furniture for each project. Its design approach unites an eclectic mix of styles and materials, individually tailored to each project, combined with exact detailing.

Studio Aisslinger
Heidestrasse 46–52
10557 Berlin
Germany
+49 30 315 05 400
studio@aisslinger.de
aisslinger.de

p.374

Based in Berlin, Werner Aisslinger has also had an office in Singapore since 2008. He focuses primarily on product design, and has gained international fame for his LoftCube living units. The designer likes to experiment with new materials spnd technologies and his work can be found in several museum collections. With his team he has dabbled in hotel design, completing the Michelberger Hotel and the 25hours Hotel in Berlin, as well as the Hotel Daniel in Graz.

Stylt Trampoli
Västra Hamngatan 11
411 17 Gothenburg
Sweden
+46 31 708 6800
info@stylt.se
stylt.se

p.110, 214, 494

Stylt Trampoli was founded 20 years ago by Erik Nissen Johansen, a Norwegian artist and visionary. Today, the office creates extraordinary experiences for major chains as well as independent owners, in Scandinavia, Europe and beyond. Says Stylt Trampoli's founder, 'We believe that there is one true reason that anyone returns to a restaurant or hotel: because the experience of it touches their emotions. How do you touch someone's emotions? Tell them a story.'
Photo: Oscar Mattsson

Techne Architects
43 Hardware Lane, Level 2
Melbourne 3000
Australia
+61 3 9600 0222
info@techne.com.au
techne.com.au

p.116

Techne Architects is a medium-sized architecture and interior design practice led by two passionate directors, Nicholas Travers and Justin Northrop. Founded in 2002, Techne's body of work includes hospitality, single residential, multi-residential, commercial, retail, automotive and institutional work. Believing that variety is at the core of architectural design and practice, the firm's projects have a distinctive design and spatial response with its own stylistic character.

Teo Cavallo Architects
7 O'Connell Terrace
Studio 16, Bowen Hills
Brisbane 4006
Australia
+61 7 3257 7828
email@teocavallo.com.au
cavalloarchitecture.com.au

p.060

Teo Cavallo Architects is a multi-disciplinary design practice with a core focus on architectural, interior and urban design. Founded in 2003 by Teo Cavallo, the practice has produced a diverse portfolio of work, including bespoke residential architecture, commercial buildings, and commercial and retail interiors. With a passion for good design, the principle belief is that architecture forms part of our everyday experiences and the architect's role is to enrich and enhance these connections.

THG Architects
Faxafen 9
108 Reykjavik
Iceland
+354 545 1600
thg@thg.is
thg.is

p.436

THG Architects was founded in October 1994 by architect Halldór Guðmundsson. The office specialises in building design, interiors, project planning, management and supervision. Its list of projects is diverse and includes office buildings, shopping centres, hotels, industrial buildings, flats, houses, airports, sporting facilities, and more. THG Architects, with 20 employees who all contribute to the broad skill base within the practice, has offices in Reykjavik, Reykjanesbaer and Copenhagen.

Teresa Sapey Estudio de Arquitectura
7 Ruiz De Alarcon Street
28014 Madrid
Spain
+34 91 745 0876
info@teresasapey.com
teresasapey.com

p.480

Teresa Sapey (born Cuneo, Italy) specialises in beautifying non-spaces, such as underground areas, car parks, roads, tunnels, stations and deserted buildings. Based in Madrid since 1990, she prides herself on 'giving a soul to those highly functional spaces of the urban modern landscape – which, generally, are not considered as aesthetically valid places'. Her studio is characterised by its use of humour, colour and art. Clients have included Madrid's local government, Silken Hotels, Room Mate Hotels and McCann Erickson.

Thilo Reich
Steinstrasse 15
10119 Berlin
Germany
+49 30 98350944
mail@thiloreich.com
thiloreich.com

p.026

Thilo Reich is a Berlin-based architect and interior designer. His studio's work ranges in scale from furniture to urban design, with a focus on architectural craft and detailing, with a strong focus on the characteristics of the site. His professional goal is the creation of innovative spaces that combine modern concepts with personality, cultural awareness and comfort.
Photo: David Paprocki

The Society Inc.
18 Stewart Street, Paddington
Sydney 2021
Australia
+61 2 9331 1592
shop@thesocietyinc.com.au
thesocietyinc.com.au

p.290

Sibella Court travelled the world as an interior stylist before opening The Society Inc. – a haberdashery meets hardware store with lots more intriguing objects – in her native city of Sydney in 2008. Court is an interior stylist and creative director, as well as a product designer with a 110-colour paint range. She works on commercial projects in Australia, as well as New York, where clients have included Bergdorf Goodman, Donna Karan, Bloomingdales and Saks Fifth Avenue.

Woods Bagot
Level 14, 11 Waymouth St
Adelaide 5001
Australia
+61 8 8113 5900
wbadl@woodsbagot.com
woodsbagot.com

p.142, 306

Woods Bagot is a global design and consulting firm, with a team of over 850 people working in 16 studios across Australia, Asia, the Middle East, Europe and North America. The firm's unique 'global studio' philosophy drives knowledge sharing and true collaboration across time zones, producing innovative, inspired and functional design solutions. Underpinning Woods Bagot's knowledge culture is the firm's research arm Public. The studio specialises in: aviation and transport; education, science and health; lifestyle; sport; and workplace.

VENUE ADDRESSES

1NUL8 → p.006
Meent 108
3011 JR Rotterdam
the Netherlands
1NUL8.nl

25hours Hotel Bikini Berlin → p.374
Budapester Str. 40
10787 Berlin
Germany
25hours-hotels.com

Abe Club & Lounge → p.008
Amstelstraat 30
1017 DA Amsterdam
the Netherlands
clubabe.com

Ace Hotel Downtown LA → p.380
926 South Broadway
Los Angeles, CA 90015
United States
acehotel.com

Adelphi Hotel → p.386
187 Flinders Lane
Melbourne 3000
Australia
adelphi.com.au

Aix Arome Cafe → p.014
Baishi Road East, No. 8
Nanshan District
518053 Shenzhen
China
aixcoffee.com

Ambassador Hotel → p.392
C/ Gerona 39
03503 Benidorm
Spain
hotelesbenidorm.com

Andaz Amsterdam → p.396
Prinsengracht 587
1016 HT Amsterdam
The Netherlands
andazamsterdam.com

Apple Daily → p.018
Print Hall, Level 1
125 St Georges Terrace
Perth 6000
Australia
appledailyperth.com

Arcana Tokyo Karato → p.190
JP Tower Kitte 6F
2-7-2 Marunouchi, Chiyoda-ku
100-7006 Tokyo
Japan
arcana.co.jp

Auriga → p.022
Famous Studio Lane, Mahalaxmi
400011 Mumbai
India
auriga.net.in

Bar Brouw → p.024
Ten Katestraat 16
1056 CE Amsterdam
the Netherlands
barbrouw.nl

Bar Marie → p.194
Stationstraat 55
2800 Mechelen
Belgium
barmarie.be

Bar Saint Jean → p.026
Steinstrasse 21
10119 Berlin
Germany
barsaintjean.com

Barcelo Milano → p.404
Via Stephenson 55
20157 Milan
Italy
barcelo.com

Barnyard → p.198
18 Charlotte Street
London W1T 2LZ
United Kingdom
barnyard-london.com

Berufsschulzentrum Friedrichshafen → p.200
Steinbeisstrasse
Friedrichshafen 88046
Germany

Blanc Kara Hotel → p.406
205 Collins Avenue
Miami Beach, FL 33139
United States
blanckara.com

Business Club Allianz Arena → p.202
Werner-Heisenberg-Allee 25
80939 Munich
Germany
allianz-arena.de

Cafe Bord de Mer → p.208
Auberge Discovery Bay
88 Siena Avenue, Discovery Bay
Lantau Island
Hong Kong
aubergediscoverybay.com

Carloft Bar & Lounge → p.030
Liegnitzer Strasse 30
10999 Berlin
Germany

Caro Hotel → p.412
Almirante 14
46003 Valencia
Spain
carohotel.com

Catch By Simonis → p.210
Dr Lelykade 43
2583 CL Scheveningen
the Netherlands
catch-bysimonis.nl

citizenM Hotel Times Square → p.418
218 West 50th Street
New York, NY 10019
United States
citizenm.com

Claude's → p.212
(venue has closed)
10 Oxford St, Woollahra
Sydney 2025
Australia

Club Disco → p.034
Prof. Atílio Inocennti 160
04538 São Paulo
Brazil
clubdisco.com.br

Club NYX → p.042
Reguliersdwarsstraat 42
1017 BM Amsterdam
the Netherlands
clubnyx.nl

Cuckoo's Nest → p.214
Radisson Blue Hotel
Lindholmspiren 4
41756 Gothenburg
Sweden
cuckoosnest.se

Cumulus Up → p.044
45 Flinders Lane
Melbourne 3000
Australia
cumulusinc.com.au/up

Dabbous → p.220
39 Whitfield Street
London W1T 2SF
United Kingdom
dabbous.co.uk

Das Brot. → p.222
Autostadt
Stadtbruecke
38440 Wolfsburg
Germany
autostadt.de

Dean → p.048
Rosenthaler Str. 9
10119 Berlin
Germany
amanogroup.de/eat-drink/dean

Donny's Bar → p.050
7 Market Place
Manly 2095
Australia
donnys.com.au

Ecoville → p.226
1–11 Mazel Drive
Tarneit 3029
Australia

Eden → p.230
Shop 6, Lights Landing Holdfast Shores
Glenelg 5045
Australia
edendiningroom.com

Emanuel Hostel → p.424
L N Tolstoja 20
21000 Split
Croatia

Fat Noodle → p.234
Treasury Casino & Hotel
130 William Street
Brisbane 4000
Australia
treasurybrisbane.com.au

Fleet Street Kitchen → p.242
Summer Row
Birmingham B3 1JH
United Kingdom
fleetstreetkitchen.co.uk

Gamsei → p.054
Buttermelcherstrasse 9
80469 Munich
Germany
gamsei.com

Generator Hostel → p.428
37 Tavistock Place
London WC1H 9SE
United Kingdom
generatorhostels.com

Gessler 1862 → p.058
Friedrichstrasse 53
88045 Friedrichshafen
Germany
gessler1862.de

Green Kitchen → p.248
6 Dongping Lu
200062 Shanghai
China
green-n-safe.com

Honey B Club → p.060
2 Caxton Street
Brisbane 4000
Australia
honeybs.tv

Hot Hot → p.064
Rua Santo Antônio, 570
01314-000 São Paulo
Brazil
hothotsite.com.br

Hotel Ritter Durbach → p.432
Tal 1
77770 Durbach
Germany
ritter-durbach.de

Hotel Valentinerhof → p.434
San Valentino 10
39040 Siusi allo Sciliar
Italy
valentinerhof.com

Howler Bar → p.070
7–11 Dawson St, Brunswick
Melbourne 3056
Australia
h-w-l-r.com

Icehotel Jukkasjärvi → p.076
Marknadsvägen 63
981 91 Jukkasjärvi
Sweden
icehotel.com

Icelandair Hotel Reykjavik Marina → p.436
Myrargata 2
101 Reykjavik
Iceland
icelandairhotels.com

Il-Barri Restaurant → p.250
Church Square
MGR 1040 Mgarr
Malta
il-barri.com.mt

Ion Luxury Adventure Hotel → p.444
Nesjavellir vid Thingvallavatn
801 Selfoss
Iceland
ioniceland.is

Kafe Nordic → p.080
B1, 683-46, Hannam-dong
Yongsan-gu
140-892 Seoul
South Korea

Kaguya → p.252
137-137/1 Thonglor Soi 10
Sukhumvit Road
Bangkok 10110
Thailand

Khokolat Bar → p.082
43 Hardware Lane
Melbourne 3001
Australia
khokolatbar.com.au

Kutsher's Tribeca → p.256
186 Franklin St
New York, NY 10013
United States
kutsherstribeca.com

La Bandita Townhouse Hotel → p.448
111 Corso Rossellino
53026 Pienza
Italy
labanditatownhouse.com

La Svolta Prahran → p.258
3–5 Cecil Place, Prahran
Melbourne 3181
Australia
lasvolta.com.au

Laem Cha-Reon Seafood → p.260
Central Plaza, Ladprao
1691 Phahonyothin Rd
Bangkok 10900
Thailand
laemchareonseafood.com

Laube Liebe Hoffnung → p.262
Pariser Strasse 11
60486 Frankfurt am Main
Germany
laubeliebehoffnung.de

Lieschen Mueller → p.264
Schönhauser Allee 134 A
10437 Berlin
Germany
lieschenmueller-restaurants.com

Long Beach Hotel → p.452
Coastal Road
Belle Mare
Mauritius
longbeachmauritius.com

Loof → p.084
331 North Bridge Rd
188720 Singapore
Singapore
loof.com.sg

Lumière Osaka Karato → p.266
Grand Front Osaka 8F
4-20 Ofuka-cho, Kita-ku
530-0011 Osaka
Japan
k-coeur.com

Macalister Mansion → p.456
228 Macalister Road
10400 George Town, Penang
Malaysia
macalistermansion.com

Mese Verde → p.088
Curtin House, Level 6
252 Swanston Street
Melbourne 3000
Australia
mesaverde.net.au

Mister Steer → p.268
1198 Ste-Catherine Ouest
Montreal, QC H3B 1K1
Canada
mistersteer.com

Mon Bijou → p.092
187 Flinders Lane, Level 10
Melbourne 3000
Australia
monbijou.com.au

Monopole → p.096
71a Macleay St, Potts Point
Sydney 2011
Australia
monopolesydney.com.au

Mr Fogg's → p.100
15 Bruton Lane
London W1J 6JD
United Kingdom
mr-foggs.com

N_1221 Aobadai → p.272
1-22-1 Aobadai, Meguro-ku
153-0042 Tokyo
Japan
n1155.jp

Nazdrowje → p.106
Edövägen 2
132 30 Stockholm
Sweden

New Hotel → p.462
16, Filellinon Str., Syntagma sq.
105 57 Athens
Greece
yeshotels.gr

Nicky's Food & Drinks → p.276
Camp de Morvedre 16
46730 Gandia
Spain
ozonegandia.com

Niko Restaurant → p.280
(venue has closed)
170 Mercer St
New York, NY 10012
United States

Nonna Martha → p.282
Binger Str. 84
55218 Ingelheim
Germany
nonnamartha.de

Nordburger → p.284
168 The Parade Norwood
5067 Adelaide
Australia
nordburger.com.au

not guilty → p.286
Badenerstrasse 29
8005 Zurich
Switzerland
notguilty.ch

Nui. Hostel → p.468
2-14-13 Kuramae, Taito-ku
111-0051 Tokyo
Japan
backpackersjapan.co.jp

Okko Hotels Nantes Chateau → p.472
15 bis rue de Strasbourg
44000 Nantes
France
okkohotels.com

Old Joe's → p.290
135 Elouera Road, Cronulla
Sydney 2230
Australia
oldjoes.com.au

Opus V → p.294
Englehorn, Level 6
O5, 9–12
68161 Mannheim
Germany
restaurant-opus-v.de

Ozone → p.296
Centro Comercial El Planet
Ctra de Moraira
03725 Teulada
Spain
hispabowling.com

Pastel → p.298
27 Sderot Shaul Ha'melech
Museum of Art
6423931 Tel Aviv
Israel
pastel-tlv.com

Pharmarium → p.110
Stortorget 7
111 29 Stockholm
Sweden
pharmarium.se

Pied → p.114
683-47, Hannam-dong
Yongsan-gu
140-892 Seoul
South Korea

Play Pot → p.302
925-23 Bangbae-dong
Seocho-gu
137-843 Seoul
South Korea

Pony Restaurant → p.306
Eagle Street Pier
18/45 Eagle Street
Brisbane 4000
Australia
wponydining.com.au

Prahran Hotel → p.116
82 High Street, Windsor
Melbourne 3181
Australia
prahranhotel.com

Restaurant Vandaag → p.310
Europaboulevard 1
1079 PC Amsterdam
the Netherlands
restaurantvandaag.nl

Reykjavik Lights Hotel → p.476
Sudurlandsbraut 12
108 Reykjavik
Iceland
keahotels.is

Rice Home → p.312
Level 3, Hengbao Plaza
133 Bao Hua Road, Li Wan District
510235 Guangzhou
China

Riley Street Garage → p.314
55 Riley Street
Sydney 2011
Australia
rileystreetgarage.com.au

Room Mate Pau → p.480
7 Fontanella Street
08010 Barcelona
Spain
pau.room-matehotels.com

Ruco Guesthouse → p.486
92 Karahimachi, Hagi
758-0044 Yamaguchi
Japan
guesthouse-ruco.com

Sal Curioso → p.120
Wyndham Street
Hong Kong
Hong Kong

Sala Rattanakosin → p.488
39 Soi Ta Tien, Maharat Road
Bangkok 10200
Thailand
salarattanakosin.com

Sansibar → p.320
Breuninger, Kö-Bogen
40212 Dusseldorf
Germany
sansibarbybreuninger.de

Scandic Hotel Paasi → p.494
Paasivuorenkatu 5b
530 Helsinki
Finland
scandichotels.com

Single Origin Roasters → p.122
60–64 Reservoir Street
Surry Hills 2010
Australia
singleoriginroasters.com.au

Sir Albert Hotel → p.498
Albert Cuypstraat 2
1072 CT Amsterdam
the Netherlands
siralberthotel.com

Sla → p.324
Ceintuurbaan 149
1072 GB Amsterdam
the Netherlands
ilovesla.com

Soaks → p.326
1-5-10 Kamimeguro, Meguro-ku
153-0051 Tokyo
Japan
soaks.jp

South of Houston → p.330
Lange Houtstraat 3
2511 CV The Hague
the Netherlands
southofhouston.nl

Spark → p.124
Hilton Hotel
Zeestraat 35
2518 AA The Hague
the Netherlands
restaurantpearl.com

Stadio → p.334
Strada Ion Câmpineanu 11
Bucharest
Romania
stadio.ro

Stan & Co. → p.338
Ganzenmarkt 16 A
3512 GD Utrecht
the Netherlands
stan-co.nl

Star Alliance Lounge → p.126
Charles De Gaulle Airport
Terminal One
95700 Paris
France
staralliance.com

Studio Hermes → p.130
16 Selari Street
030068 Bucharest
Romania
studiohermes.ro

Superbude → p.504
Juliusstrasse 1–7
22769 Hamburg
Germany
superbude.de

Supernormal Canteen → p.340
(temporary venue)
53 Gertrude St
Melbourne 3065
Australia
supernormal.net.au

Sushi Ono → p.344
Borgo Wuhrer 137
25123 Brescia
Italy
sushionobrescia.it

Tayim → p.350
Viale Libia 50
00199 Rome
Italy
tayim.it

The Ampersand Hotel → p.510
10 Harrington Road
London SW7 3ER
United Kingdom
ampersandhotel.com

The Black Swan → p.134
19 Cecil Street
049704 Singapore
Singapore
theblackswan.com.sg

The Club → p.136
9 Dong Da Qiao Rd
Beijing
China
haworthxfriends.com

The Collins → p.142
233 Victoria Square
Adelaide 5000
Australia
thecollins.com.au

The Jane → p.354
Paradeplein 1
2018 Antwerp
Belgium
thejaneantwerp.com

The King's Arms → p.514
The Street
Didmarton GL9 1DT
United Kingdom
kingsarmsdidmarton.co.uk

The Line Hotel → p.518
3515 Wilshire Blvd
Los Angeles, CA 90010
United States
thelinehotel.com

The Movement Cafe → p.146
(temporary venue)
5 Waller Way
London SE10 8JA
United Kingdom
themovementgreenwich.com

The Proud Archivist → p.358
2–10 Hertford Rd
London N1 5ET
United Kingdom
theproudarchivist.co.uk

The Student Hotel → p.524
Oostzeedijk 182
3063 BM Rotterdam
the Netherlands
thestudenthotel.com

The Town Mouse → p.362
312 Drummond Street, Carlton
Melbourne 3053
Australia
thetownmouse.com.au

Truth Coffee → p.150
36 Buitenkant Street
8000 Cape Town
South Africa
truthcoffee.com

Turkish Airlines CIP Lounge → p.156
Istanbul Atatürk Airport
Yesilköy
34149 Istanbul
Turkey
turkishairlines.com

Urban Post Hotel → p.528
37 Donghua Villa
The Lingnan Tiandi
528000 Foshan
China
urbanposthotel.com

Versuz → p.162
Gouverneur Verwilghensingel 70
3500 Hasselt
Belgium
versuz.be

Vex Cabaret → p.166
Bosques de las Lomas
Mexico City
Mexico

Villa Pastorie → p.534
Hoevensweg 2
5017 AE Tilburg
the Netherlands
villapastorie.nl

Virgin Atlantic Clubhouse → p.172
JFK International Airport
Terminal 4, Queens
New York, NY 11430
United States

Virgin Atlantic Clubhouse → p.176
Newark International Airport
Terminal B
Newark, NJ 07114
United States

WakuWaku → p.364
Dammtorstrasse 29–33
20354 Hamburg
Germany
waku-waku.eu

Wasbar → p.180
Graaf Van Egmontstraat 5
2000 Antwerp
Belgium
wasbar.com

White Rabbit → p.182
(venue has closed)
258a Hindley Street
Adelaide 5000
Australia

Workshop Kitchen & Bar → p.366
800 N Palm Canyon Drive
Palm Springs, CA 92262
United States
workshoppalmsprings.com

Zona → p.370
Lanchid Utca 7–9
1013 Budapest
Hungary
zonabudapest.com

CREDITS

Night Fever 4
Hospitality Design

Publisher
Frame Publishers

Production
Sarah de Boer-Schultz and Carmel McNamara

Authors
Carmel McNamara and Jane Szita

Graphic Design Concept
Mariëlle van Genderen

Graphic Design
Zoe Bar-Pereg

Prepress
Beeldproductie Egbert de Haas

Cover Photography
Victor van Leeuwen

Trade distribution USA and Canada
Consortium Book Sales & Distribution, LLC.
34 Thirteenth Avenue NE, Suite 101,
Minneapolis, MN 55413-1007
United States
T +1 612 746 2600
T +1 800 283 3572 (orders)
F +1 612 746 2606

Trade distribution Benelux
Frame Publishers
Laan der Hesperiden 68
1076 DX Amsterdam
the Netherlands
distribution@frameweb.com
frameweb.com

Trade distribution rest of world
Thames & Hudson Ltd
181A High Holborn
London WC1V 7QX
United Kingdom
T +44 20 7845 5000
F +44 20 7845 5050

ISBN: 978-94-91727-16-0

© 2014 Frame Publishers, Amsterdam, 2014

Whilst every effort has been made to ensure
accuracy, Frame Publishers does not under any
circumstances accept responsibility for errors
or omissions. Any mistakes or inaccuracies will
be corrected in case of subsequent editions upon
notification to the publisher.

The Koninklijke Bibliotheek lists this publication
in the Nederlandse Bibliografie: detailed
bibliographic information is available on the
internet at http://picarta.pica.nl

Printed on acid-free paper produced from
chlorine-free pulp. TCF ∞
Printed in Poland

987654321